the Look & Cook
Air Fryer Bible

ALSO BY BRUCE WEINSTEIN AND MARK SCARBROUGH

the Look & Cook Air Fryer Bible

125 EVERYDAY RECIPES WITH 700+ PHOTOS
TO HELP GET IT RIGHT EVERY TIME

Bruce Weinstein and Mark Scarbrough

Photographs by Eric Medsker

VORACIOUS

LITTLE, BROWN AND COMPANY
New York Boston London

Voracious / Little, Brown and Company
Hachette Book Group
1290 Avenue of the Americas, New York, NY 10104
voraciousbooks.com

First Edition: November 2023

Voracious is an imprint of Little, Brown and Company, a division of Hachette Book Group, Inc. The Voracious name and logo are trademarks of Hachette Book Group, Inc.

The publisher is not responsible for websites (or their content) that are not owned by the publisher.

The Hachette Speakers Bureau provides a wide range of authors for speaking events. To find out more, go to hachettespeakersbureau.com or email hachettespeakers@hbgusa.com.

Little, Brown and Company books may be purchased in bulk for business, educational, or promotional use. For information, please contact your local bookseller or the Hachette Book Group Special Markets Department at special.markets@hbgusa.com.

ISBN 9780316520003
LCCN 2023934482

10 9 8 7 6 5 4 3 2 1

CW

Printed in the United States of America

Contents

Introduction

Our hope is that you'll come to love your air fryer as much as we do ours. You might already have an inkling of how much we love this machine. We've written two previous cookbooks about it. You might even think we've run out of things to say. Hardly! To be blunt, this device not as intuitive as, say, an electric pressure cooker or a microwave. There are lots of tricks to get crisp coatings, tender interiors, and delectable results. So get that air fryer out of its box or out from the cupboard and get ready to find out how to get the best from it. You know, the irresistible crunch. And the healthier ways to make family favorites. And the sheer fun an air fryer brings to meal prep. All in all, this cookbook is a great way to fulfill our hope: 125 simple, straightforward, and original recipes, along with lots of gorgeous, helpful photographs to show you the ins and outs of every dish!

If you've ever wondered what a recipe means when it tells you to "generously coat the fish fillets with nonstick spray" or "gently flip the egg rolls with nonstick-safe tongs," this is the book for you.

If you've ever wished you could decide whether to make a recipe based on exactly what's involved with all the rolling, folding, and/or dredging, this is the book for you.

If you ever wanted to *literally* see what it takes to get to a dish ready for the table, this is the . . . well, welcome!

We photographed these recipes in the same place we tested them: our home kitchen in rural New England. That's our butcher block. Those are our plates. Those are Bruce's hands. (He's six-foot-four, so his fingers make egg rolls look pretty small.) And while we did work with a professional photographer, those photographs show how Bruce makes each dish, no food or prop stylist in sight.

We want you to be able to re-create each dish, exactly as you see it here but in your own home.

These 125 recipes are mostly for lunch or dinner staples, along with a few imaginative concoctions, as well as chapters for snacks and desserts. We've also got a handful of copycats, like those Tex-Mex egg rolls from the Cheesecake Factory (page 50). And we've got quite a few recipes that let you get a full meal out of the machine.

We are probably most excited about those, so permit us to explain. We've written several Instant Pot cookbooks, so we *know* the promise of that machine: You open the lid and see your meal. The air fryer doesn't always give you such a wow-inducing result. You often open the machine and see just your main course. Or maybe your side dish. But we wanted to give you the same experience in the air fryer that we love in the Instant Pot—that of opening the machine and seeing your entire meal. Say, a pork tenderloin and butternut squash dinner (page 178) or a shrimp scampi and green bean supper (page 204). At that point, there's not much more to do than pour something to drink.

We've also included an enormous chart for air-frying the vegetables commonly found in our supermarkets (starting on page 224). Most of these easy methods didn't need the detailed explanation of a full-on recipe but are brought to success by a little finesse (generously or lightly sprayed?), visual cues (brown enough yet?), and even feel (crispy enough?).

Before you head off to the recipes, let's chat about a few important points. We won't cover everything, because almost every recipe in this book includes **Master the Method**, which is a little tip under that header. Read through these to discover the small details that will give you better results every time. Now, let's nail down the basics.

Recipes First, Then Photos

We wish a printed book were more high-tech. We wish the photos were invisible at first, so that you *had to* read the recipe. Only once you'd been red-pilled by the words could you see the photos.

Are we dissing these photos? Not at all! But they capture the steps of these recipes and not the nuances. Yes, you can see a photo of nonstick-safe tongs in Bruce's hand, turning a piece of chicken. But the recipe might indicate that you need to turn the chicken gently because its crust is not fully set and can be chipped off. We can't put a warning like that on a photograph. So recipe, then photos.

Toaster-Oven-Style versus Drawer-Style Machines

There are essentially two types of countertop air fryers: toaster-oven-style and drawer-style (sometimes called basket-style) machines. We tested every recipe in both kinds. We did not write any recipe specifically for one or the other.

That said, there are differences, such as:

1. You often have to cook in batches in toaster-oven-style machines because there's less cooking space.

In many toaster-oven-style models, you slip a cooking tray into the machine, then put an air-frying basket on this tray. That basket gives you the prized air flow around the food for great, crispy crusts. But those baskets can be small. Therefore, you're cooking in batches. To do so, just set the second batch aside at room temperature. There are a couple of exceptions in these recipes. We'll cue you when you should store the coated or marinated items for the second batch in the fridge.

And one note: Even if you can, we do not recommend going without a cooking tray, somehow slipping the basket inside and flying commando in a toaster-oven-style machine. Rendered grease will drip over the heating elements at the bottom of the machine, resulting in the dreaded air-fryer smoke. The cooking tray makes cleanup much easier.

2. Drawer-style machines tend to cook more quickly.

The difference is partly about how air flows. The sides of the drawer are built to channel hot air to the bottom of the machine—which usually has ridges or grooves that direct the air up to the underside of the food and then toward the fan for greater circulation. Drawer-style machines usually have a thicker, metal cooking tray in the basket, rather than the (sometimes flimsy) cooking basket in toaster-oven-style models. Thicker metal = more retained heat against the food sitting on said metal. Therefore, quicker cooking.

In toaster-oven-style machines, the metal cooking tray can block some of the air flow. So you may have to add a minute or two to the cooking time in toaster-oven-style machines, or even subtract a minute or two in a very powerful drawer-style machine. Visual and internal temperature cues, as stated in the recipes, are your keys to determining whether an item is cooked through.

3. Toaster-oven-style machines are often more precise in their temperature readings.

Opening and sliding out the drawer in a drawer-style model does indeed drop the heat more quickly than opening the door of a toaster-oven-style model because you often can slide the cooking tray out without then transferring it to a kitchen towel or a heat-safe work surface.

We've even gone so far as to set oven thermometers inside the machines. Most toaster-oven-style air fryers hold a more even and precise heat than drawer-style machines. The difference may be that most toaster-oven-style machines are made of metal, while drawer-style machines have plastic components that do not retain heat so well.

Learn the quirks of your model. Adjust our recipes based on those quirks. And use visual cues even more than stated timings to know when food is done to your liking.

The Size of Your Air Fryer

We didn't write these recipes with any one size of air fryer in mind. If you want to find a book that calibrates every recipe for every size of machine, check out our first air-frying cookbook: *The Essential Air Fryer Cookbook*.

Instead, as you'll see in the photos in this book, we've used a variety of machine styles and sizes. If you've got a small model, you'll need to cook the fare in batches. And almost every recipe can be scaled up for crowds in larger models or cooked in batches in more standard models for more servings. (We'll tell you when to refrigerate remaining batches as the first ones cook.)

Just keep in mind this basic rule: Never overcrowd. Better to work in more batches than have soggy crusts, right?

The question of the machine's size inevitably brings up the question of the giants in the air-frying world: oven air fryers (that is, a stove with an oven that includes an air-frying setting). The recipes in this book were developed for, tested with, and photographed in *countertop air fryers*. These have a much smaller capacity, so the air currents are more intense and more sustained. Coatings get crunchier faster than they might in many oven models, since those coatings are closer to the heating element and the fan. All that to say, some of these recipes may well work in an oven air fryer, but we can't say for sure because we didn't test any with an oven that includes this setting.

These recipes may also work in countertop convection ovens, specifically the ones that have a dedicated air-frying function. These 5-in-1 and 10-in-1 machines have become increasingly popular, but there's a wide range of capabilities among them, none standardized. If your model has a specific air-frying function, then follow the manufacturer's instructions concerning trays and settings—and these recipes should indeed work. However, if your model has only a convection setting, not a specific air-frying setting, these recipes may not work—for the same reasons that they don't necessarily work with a large oven's air-frying setting. The convection currents are just not intense enough to make a successful dish using the methods and ratios we've developed here.

Timings in the Recipes

Our timings for doneness or other markers are based on the machines we used: several models from several manufacturers. However, timing in an air fryer is a matter of finesse, rather than precision, based on three variables:

1. The specific machine's design.

Some models have more space inside. For example, there may be more "head room" between the food and the fan in some drawer-style models. And many toaster-oven-style machines are quite large. For these, more air has to be heated. Plus, the subsequent air currents travel farther or are not quite so strong. Even a little extra space can mean an extra minute or two to get something done right.

2. The thickness of the coating.

We're admittedly heavy-handed when it comes to the coating on, say, a chicken thigh or a cod fillet. We press and turn and press and turn in the wet and dry ingredients to get a thick coating on each piece. You might work with a little less. Or a little more.

Either way, that coating insulates the food inside. The thicker the coating = the longer the food inside takes to get done.

For larger cuts of various proteins, we often (strongly) suggest that you take the internal temperature with an instant-read meat thermometer. For other items like, say, Cauliflower Patties (page 242), there's no real way to know the final doneness except by touching the outside of a patty to see if it's firm or even breaking one open once it's cooled a bit. What's the worst that can happen? You have to put the patties back in the machine for another minute or two of cooking? That's not so bad when you have the fine crunch of air-fried food to look forward to.

3. The temperature of the ingredients.

We often recommend eggs straight from the fridge. Ours is set at 40°F. Yours might be at 45°F. Believe it or not, these small differences can mean a minute or so difference between our cooking time and yours.

Here's our mantra: Stick to our timings for turning or rearranging items in the machine, but go by visual cues (or the internal temperature of some proteins) for the final results. Let these cues be your final guides, with timing as a mere suggestion.

Spatulas versus Tongs

We have a saying in our house: "Chefs use tongs; people, spatulas." Silly, yes, but mostly true. And a problem in a book about air-frying.

No doubt about it: Tongs work better in many of these recipes. Tongs can get down into the limited space in the machine. They can gently pick up something with a crumb coating rather than spading under it and chipping off some of the crust. And they can keep your fingers away from hot surfaces.

But a spatula has its uses, too. It can lift heavier items. It can balance them more effectively, too.

We call for both tools. You'll see them in the photos. Both must be nonstick-safe. There's a nonstick coating on that cooking surface that can get chipped with standard tools. If it does, you should get a new cooking tray or basket for your machine. (Drawer-style models just need a new cooking tray at the bottom of their drawer, not a whole new drawer.) All manufacturers sell replacements.

But also, nonstick-safe tongs and spatulas have a silicone coating that's gentler on food. Crusts are less likely to break off than they are with metal tongs. Nonstick-safe spatulas are flexible, too, the better to get down into narrow spaces.

And one side point here: As a general rule, foods air-fried in toaster-oven-style machines need to be turned or flipped or rearranged *more frequently* than those in drawer-style machines. In toaster-oven machines, there are often multiple heating elements, top and bottom (rather than just at the top as in drawer-style models). Plus, toaster-oven machines have a cooking tray that's made of shiny metal and reflects the heat more readily than the dark surfaces in drawer-style machines.

All in all, there's just a more consistent heat in a toaster-oven-style machine. So turning food more frequently helps to keep it from burning.

Metric Measurements

We wrote this book with *both* volume and metric weight measurements (e.g., 1½ cups or 375 milliliters milk; ½ cup or 55 grams dried bread crumbs) in the ingredient lists, along with both inches and centimeters as our descriptors for some of those ingredients and both Fahrenheit and Celsius temperatures in the air-frying instructions. Why? For one thing, with the digital age, cookbooks have become an increasingly international commodity. For another, many U.S. home cooks, who used to work exclusively with volume measurements, have now nudged over into

metrics in the kitchen, partly because these people are used to working with metrics in school science labs and partly because they've been buying those international cookbooks! And many Canadian readers of our books have one foot in both worlds!

But note that we've rounded many of the metric conversions up or down to more standard amounts when a few grams or milliliters will make no difference to the recipe. Yes, 1 cup of cored, shredded cabbage may well actually weigh 72 grams. But we rounded that up to 75 grams because, well, it's just easier and that little extra cabbage won't make any difference in the results. We were persnickety when we needed to be—which was almost never.

Don't be put off. The ingredient list may look a little complicated, but go with what you know. Soon, you'll get the hang of the way the ingredients are listed: "4 tablespoons (½ stick) or 60 grams butter," for example. Use whichever measurement you're comfortable with.

Because of that international focus in cookbooks, the names of some ingredients can be a tad confusing: "ground beef" in the U.S. is "beef mince" in the U.K., and "all-purpose flour" in the U.S. is "plain flour" in the U. K. Most of the time, when we felt a fuller explanation of an ingredient was necessary, we wrote more fully about it in the headnote. And a few times, we felt that the name of an ingredient had become common enough that we didn't need to further complicate it—for example, "U.S.-style bacon" is what most U.S. consumers buy and what most people in the U.K. know as "streaky bacon." But the mere notion of U.S.-style bacon has become common enough now that we didn't feel the need to belabor the point.

Look at it this way: You're cooking with people around the globe. What could be more fun than that?

In Conclusion . . .

We hope you can use the recipes and the hundreds of photos in this book to get the best results possible. We want to give you the courage of our convictions about this machine. We think it's one of the best kitchen tools around, so we wanted to offer you a no-hassle way to see exactly what a recipe takes.

If you've got any questions, please look us up on social media. We're @bruceaweinstein and @markscarbrough on Instagram. We've got a Facebook group called "Cooking With Bruce & Mark." And a weekly podcast with the same name, found on almost every platform out there. And a YouTube channel, too, with the same name. (Mark's a tad excited by air fryers, as you'll see.) We'd love to connect with you!

1

SNACKS & NIBBLES

We got into air-frying because of appetizers, snacks, and little bites to enjoy before dinner. Air fryers are especially terrific before parties when you've concentrated your cooking effort elsewhere. They can crisp nibbles in no time, leaving you to tend to your braise or roast. What's more, they're perfect for your next deck or patio party. As the night goes on, you can whip up additional batches as the party lingers into the long light.

Air fryers are also great for last-minute guests, for pop-ins. A friend drops by and you can quickly throw together a bite to go with tea or coffee. What could be more welcoming? These quick nibbles are also great for game day, a midafternoon pick-me-up with friends, or even the midnight munchies.

And if you've got a hungry crowd at your next event, you can pull together a second (or third) batch of many of these nibbles with relatively little fuss or time spent in the kitchen. No wonder we first got into air-frying because of small bites like these. We hope they lead you, too, to bigger things down the road.

Sweet and Salty Party Mix

We've got lots of party mixes in *The Essential Air Fryer Cookbook* and *The Instant Air Fryer Bible* that use boxed cereals. For this book, we wanted to create a mix without quite so many processed ingredients. As a bonus, this version is a little more savory since there is a fair amount of sugar in cereal, even whole-grain cereal. Plus, we wanted a mix that prioritized nuts, for more heft per bite. So here the amazing crunch comes from a mix of pretzel nuggets, nuts, and seeds.

Cooled leftovers can be stored in a sealed container at room temperature for up to 3 days. They can be recrisped in a 350°F or 180°C air fryer for 2 to 3 minutes.

1 cup or 150 grams pretzel nuggets (not twists or rods)

1 cup or 145 grams *raw unsalted shelled* peanuts

½ cup or 75 grams *whole raw unsalted shelled* almonds

½ cup or 35 grams *unsalted shelled* pumpkin seeds or pepitas

1 tablespoon or 15 grams butter, melted

1 tablespoon or 20 grams honey

1 tablespoon or 15 milliliters Worcestershire sauce

1 teaspoon table salt

½ teaspoon mild smoked paprika

½ teaspoon garlic powder

Master the Method

Cooking times in an air fryer are never exact. In this recipe, the pretzels or nuts you use may hold more residual moisture than ours. Always use your eyes and your nose as a key to doneness.

RAISE THE BAR

Add up to ½ teaspoon ground black pepper and/or red pepper flakes with the spices.

1. With the basket in the machine or the tray set at the center level in a toaster-oven-style model, heat an air fryer to 375°F or 190°C on the air fryer setting.

2. Mix the pretzel nuggets, peanuts, almonds, and pumpkin seeds in a large bowl. Ⓐ

3. Stir the melted butter, honey, Worcestershire sauce, salt, smoked paprika, and garlic powder in a medium bowl until well and evenly combined. Because the honey is sticky, a flatware fork is the best tool. Ⓑ

4. Scrape the butter mixture into the pretzel mixture with a wooden spoon or a rubber spatula. Ⓒ

5. Stir and fold repeatedly until well and evenly combined. Dump and scrape the pretzel mixture into the heated machine. (Use a wooden spoon or rubber spatula to get every drop out of the bowl.) Ⓓ

6. Air-fry for 2 minutes, then stir well on the cooking tray or shake the drawer's basket to rearrange all the ingredients. Ⓔ

7. Continue air-frying for 2 more minutes, then toss or shake the ingredients *again*. Go on air-frying for 1 more minute, or until the pepitas have puffed a bit and the mixture is golden brown and fragrant. Pour the contents of the cooking tray or the basket into a serving bowl. Cool for a couple of minutes before serving warm. Ⓕ

Sweet and Spicy Mixed Nuts

This recipe transforms just about any type of toasted nut into a warm, sugary snack or nibble. Although we suggest using a mixture of nuts, you can go "pure" with, say, all raw pecans or walnuts (shelled, of course).

Peanuts (admittedly legumes, not nuts) often have a papery coating, even after shelling. This coating must be removed as it burns quickly. Wrap the shelled but uncooked peanuts in a clean kitchen towel and rub them together to remove as much of the coating as possible. You won't get every speck, but the glued-on bits won't burn as easily.

Hazelnuts have a similar coating that will not come off if they're raw. Unless you can find raw hazelnuts without any papery bits on them, we do not recommend them for this recipe.

3 cups or 350 grams *raw unsalted* shelled mixed nuts, such as walnuts, almonds, cashews, pecans, and/or peanuts

3 tablespoons or 35 grams granulated white sugar

1 tablespoon or 15 milliliters thin red hot sauce (preferably Tabasco sauce)

RAISE THE BAR

Add up to ½ teaspoon ground cumin with the sugar and hot sauce.

To go along with these spiced nuts, try an up (that is, not frozen) margarita. The best is made with an easy formula: equal parts tequila (preferably a silver or white), lime juice (preferably freshly squeezed), and orange liqueur (preferably Cointreau or Triple Sec). Add a pinch of sugar and shake *well* with ice in a cocktail shaker before straining over fresh ice in glasses.

1. With the basket in the machine or the tray set at the center level in a toaster-oven-style model, heat an air fryer to 400°F or 200°C on the air fryer setting.

2. Pour the nuts, sugar, and hot sauce in a medium bowl. **A**

3. Fold or stir well, working to get the sugar to adhere to the nuts with the hot sauce. Pour the nut mixture into the heated machine and spread them into as even a layer as you can. **B**

4. Air-fry for 2 minutes. Shake, toss, and/or rearrange the nuts so that new sections are exposed or turned to face up toward the heat source. **C**

5. Continue air-frying for 2 more minutes, then shake, toss, and/or rearrange the nuts as you did the first time. Go on air-frying 1 or 2 more minutes, *tossing and rearranging the nuts every 30 seconds to keep them from burning,* until golden brown and crunchy. **D**

6. Spread the nuts out on a large lipped baking sheet to cool for at least 15 minutes. You may need to break them apart as the sugar coating will have fused them together in spots. Serve warm or at room temperature. **E**

Bagel Chips

You may never go back to buying bagel chips. With an air fryer, the chips turn out perfectly crunchy and stay whole, not broken to bits in the bag. All the better to hold lots of dip.

We suggest French onion dip as a go-with (and offer a recipe in Raise the Bar). But don't let our choice control your party. Try purchased chipotle hummus, baba ghanoush, or even a 50/50 mix of salsa and sour cream.

3 medium plain bagels

Nonstick spray

1 teaspoon table salt

Master the Method

There's a persistent myth in online groups that you need only the slightest spritz of nonstick spray for air-frying success. Sometimes, sure. But many times, no: You need more. The amount depends on 1) how much fat is naturally in the food (more fat means less added oil), 2) how much residual moisture it has (sometimes more moisture means less oil—but not always), and 3) how crunchy you want it (more oil very often means more crunch—but too much oil can turn anything soggy).

RAISE THE BAR

To make French onion dip for these chips, stir all of the following in a medium bowl until uniform: ¾ cup or 170 grams plain sour cream of any sort, ¼ cup or 60 grams mayonnaise of any sort, 2 tablespoons *minced* fresh chives or the green part of a scallion, 1 tablespoon dehydrated onion flakes, ½ teaspoon granulated white sugar, ¼ teaspoon table salt, and ⅛ teaspoon garlic powder.

1. With the basket in the machine or the tray set at the center level in a toaster-oven-style model, heat an air fryer to 400°F or 200°C on the air fryer setting.

2. Set the bagels flat on a cutting board and slice them vertically into ¼-inch or ½-centimeter thick strips, starting at one side of each bagel and working across it. (When you get to the hole, you'll be making half-length strips until you return to the main part of the bagel.) Ⓐ

3. Spread the slices out and generously coat them *on both sides* with nonstick spray. Ⓑ

4. Turn all of the slices cut side up and sprinkle the salt evenly over them. Ⓒ

5. Pour the bagel slices higgledy-piggledy into the heated machine, creating space between the overlapping slices without compacting them into layers. Air-fry for 3 minutes, then toss and/or rearrange the bagel slices on the cooking tray or in the basket. Ⓓ

6. Continue air-frying for about 4 more minutes, *tossing at least twice*, until golden to dark brown and noticeably crunchy. Tastes do vary. We like ours very browned; others prefer them paler. But remember: no brown = no crunch. Pour the chips onto a wire rack, spread them out, and cool for a few minutes before serving warm or at room temperature. Ⓔ

Salami Chips

Do you like bacon? If so, you'll flip over these simple, crunchy, meaty "chips," made from rounds of salami.

The trick is the type of salami. Don't buy a large, 2- to 3-inch or 5- to 7½-centimeter round soft salami that's best sliced for sandwiches. Instead, buy a dried, hard salami, most often sold in thin "tubes" of meat near the cheese counter.

1 pound or 450 grams small dried salami, about 1½ inches or 4 centimeters in diameter, such as soppressata, fennel sausage, or sweet or spicy Italian sausages

Mustard (deli, yellow, honey, or coarse-grain), for dipping

Master the Method

When cleaning up after air-frying greasy foods, let the cooking tray or basket cool a bit, but wipe it out *before* the grease hardens. Soak the tray or basket, as well as any cooking surfaces, in warm soapy water to remove more gunk. Do not scrub a nonstick coating.

RAISE THE BAR

Swap out the mustard for pesto, tapenade, or chutney of any sort.

1. With the basket in the machine or the tray set at the center level in a toaster-oven-style model, heat an air fryer to 400°F or 200°C on the air fryer setting.

2. If necessary, peel the casing from the sausage. Nick the edge with a paring knife to determine if there is indeed a casing. If so, pull up a little of the casing, then zip it down the tube of sausage to remove it. Slice the salami into ¼-inch or ½-centimeter thick rounds on a cutting board. **A**

3. Dump the salami rounds into the heated machine. Use nonstick-safe tongs to spread them out so that there's space for air flow even where they overlap. Make no more than three layers. Work in batches as necessary. **B**

4. Air-fry for 5 minutes. Use the tongs to toss and/or rearrange the salami rounds. **C**

5. Continue for about 5 more minutes (but maybe just 3 minutes if the salami is super hard), until sizzling with crispy edges. Line the counter with wax paper and set a wire rack on top of it (to catch drips and rendered fat). Pour the salami rounds onto the rack. **D**

6. Cool for at least 10 minutes before serving warm or at room temperature with a bowl of mustard for a dip. **E**

Buttery-Spicy Puff Pastry Twists

A nice alternative to cheesy straws, these crunchy twists are coated with an irresistible combo of butter and sriracha for a spiky flavor that pairs well with a cold beer, shot of bourbon, Old Fashioned, or vodka martini.

The trick is to gently twist the strips of dough without pulling them (and thereby elongating them). If they start to stick to the cutting board as you work with them, use a metal spatula to get them up. They do get stickier as the raw dough gets closer to room temperature, so work quickly to get them in the heated machine.

Any cooled leftovers can be saved in a sealed container at room temperature for up to 2 days. Recrisp them in a single layer in a 350°F or 180°C machine for 1 to 2 minutes.

Half of a 17¼-ounce or 500-gram box of frozen puff pastry (one sheet), *thawed*

4 tablespoons (½ stick) or 60 grams butter, melted and cooled for a few minutes

1 tablespoon or 15 milliliters sriracha

½ teaspoon ground cumin

½ teaspoon granulated white sugar

½ teaspoon table salt

Master the Method

Dripping butter or melting fat can cause even the cleanest air fryer to smoke. A tiny bit of water (no more than ⅛ inch or ¼ centimeter) in the drawer under the cooking plate (in drawer-style machines) or in the cooking tray under the cooking basket (in toaster-oven-style machines) can prevent smoking during *short* cooking times. For cooks over 10 minutes or with exceptionally crunchy breading, the water creates too much steam and you'll lose the crunch.

RAISE THE BAR

Substitute curry powder (of any sort), garam masala, lemon-pepper seasoning blend, or an Italian dried seasoning blend for the cumin.

1. With the basket in the machine or the tray set at the center level in a toaster-oven-style model, heat an air fryer to 400°F or 200°C on the air fryer setting.

2. Unfold the puff pastry sheet and cut into even quarters on a cutting board. Ⓐ

3. Mix the butter, sriracha, cumin, sugar, and salt in a small bowl until the sugar and salt mostly dissolve. Brush this mixture over the tops of the puff pastry quarters. Ⓑ

4. Slice each quarter into four even strips. Ⓒ

5. Separate the strips, pick one up by both ends, and gently twist it two or three times. Set aside and continue twisting the remaining strips. Work quickly but carefully: The pastry will be getting a little fragile. Ⓓ

6. Set the strips in a single layer without touching in the heated machine. Work in batches as necessary. (If you're working in batches, store the unbaked twists in the fridge until you're ready to use them.) Air-fry *undisturbed* for 7 minutes, or until puffed and golden brown. Some may untwist a bit. No worries. Just let them get crunchy. Use nonstick-safe tongs to transfer them all to a wire rack. Cool for at least a few minutes before serving warm or at room temperature. Ⓔ

Crunchy Mozzarella Sticks

Although we've egg-washed and breaded lots of mozzarella sticks in the course of our career, we wanted to create a slightly more sophisticated version of the classic for this book. To that end, we swapped out semi-firm mozzarella for fresh mozz because the fresh melts so much better and ends up so much gooier.

We've also skipped the breaded coating and instead use wonton wrappers. These actually give the sticks an even crunchier coating. What's more, fresh mozzarella won't leak out of them the way it would with a more standard bread crumb coating.

Don't skimp when coating them with spray. They're dry and need a little help getting crisp in the machine.

½ teaspoon dried oregano

½ teaspoon dried thyme

½ teaspoon dried rosemary, crumbled

½ teaspoon onion powder

½ teaspoon garlic powder

½ teaspoon table salt

8 ounces or 225 grams *fresh* mozzarella

32 square wonton wrappers (do not use egg roll or rice paper wrappers), thawed if frozen

Olive oil spray

Master the Method

Never overcrowd an air fryer basket or the cooking rack in a toaster-oven-style machine. The answer to *This looks too crowded—should I do it in batches?* is always "Yes."

RAISE THE BAR

Although warmed, jarred marinara sauce is the natural choice for a dip, consider doctoring that sauce with a splash of balsamic vinegar, some melted butter, and/or red pepper flakes.

1. With the basket in the machine or the tray set at the center level in a toaster-oven-style model, heat an air fryer to 400°F or 200°C on the air fryer setting.

2. Mix the oregano, thyme, rosemary, onion powder, garlic powder, and salt in a small bowl until uniform. Ⓐ

3. Set the fresh mozzarella ball, flatter side down, on your cutting board. Slice the cheese into eight ½-inch or 1¼-centimeter thick rounds. Set the rounds on a cut side and slice each into four rectangle-ish strips. Ⓑ

4. Set a wonton wrapper on a dry cutting board or dry, clean work surface with one corner pointing to you. Sprinkle *lightly* with the oregano mixture. (Remember: There are many to go!) Ⓒ

5. Wet the edges of the wrapper with a clean, wet finger. Set the mozzarella slice as close as possible to that corner while containing the stick completely on the wrapper. Fold that nearest corner over the cheese, then fold the two adjacent corners toward the center. Ⓓ

6. Roll the wrapper away from you to create a log, sealing the cheese inside. Press gently to seal the damp seam without deforming the "log." Set aside and repeat with the remaining cheese sticks and wrappers. Ⓔ

7. Generously coat the wrappers with olive oil spray on all sides. Set them in a single layer without touching in the heated machine. Work in batches as necessary. Air-fry *undisturbed* for 4 minutes, or until the sticks are golden brown in spots. They may ooze a bit but make sure the wrapper looks noticeably crispy at the edges. (They'll get crunchier as they cool for a few minutes.) Use nonstick-safe tongs to transfer the sticks to a wire rack. Cool for a few minutes before serving warm. Ⓕ

Pickle Steak Fries

Do you love fried pickles as much as we do? Then get ready! These are not just fried pickles. They're whole dill pickles, cut into thick juicy strips, then breaded and air-fried so that they're like steak fries, except that they're vinegary, thick pickle fries.

   Why not just use jarred pickle strips (or so-called "sandwich strips")? Because they're too thin. They'll melt in the middle and turn the coating soggy. Better to cut whole pickles into slightly thicker slices so they stay together in the heat.

Three 5- to 6-inch or 13- to 15-centimeter long dill or half-sour pickles

1 cup all-purpose flour or 120 grams plain flour

2 large eggs

1½ cups or 170 grams Italian-seasoned *whole wheat* bread crumbs

Nonstick spray

Master the Method

Once items are on the cooling rack, avoid poking or pricking them for a few minutes, until the crust has a chance to set. You might release internal juices that will turn that crust mushy.

RAISE THE BAR

These pickle fries are great dipped into ranch dressing, a 50/50 mix of mayonnaise and sriracha, or a 75/25 mix of plain yogurt and jalapeño relish or chowchow.

These crunchy pickle "fries" are great when topped with egg salad for more substantial fare. You can buy egg salad at the deli counter or make your own: Peel and chop up 2 hard-cooked large eggs and mix them with 2 tablespoons mayonnaise of any sort, ½ teaspoon Dijon mustard, ½ teaspoon celery salt, and a dash or two of thin red hot sauce, preferably Tabasco sauce.

1. With the basket in the machine or the tray set at the center level in a toaster-oven-style model, heat an air fryer to 400°F or 200°C on the air fryer setting.

2. Cut each pickle lengthwise into ½-inch or 1¼-centimeter thick strips. **A**

3. Pour the flour into a shallow soup plate, small pie plate, or food storage container. Mix the eggs with a whisk or a fork in a second shallow soup plate, small pie plate, or food storage container until uniform, with no bits of white floating in the mix. Finally, spread the bread crumbs in a third shallow soup plate, small pie plate, or food storage container. **B**

4. Set the bowls up in this order: flour, egg, bread crumbs. Dip a pickle slice into the flour and turn it to coat well on all sides. Set it in the egg mixture and turn to coat. Let the excess egg drip off, then set it in the bread crumbs and turn to coat, pressing gently to get an even coating on all sides and along the edges. Repeat with the remaining pickle slices. **C**

5. Generously coat *all sides* of the slices with nonstick spray. **D**

6. Set them in a single layer without touching in the heated machine. Work in batches as necessary. Air-fry for 4 minutes, then flip them over with nonstick-safe tongs. **E**

7. Continue air-frying for 3 more minutes, or until golden brown and crunchy. Use clean tongs to transfer the strips to a fine-mesh wire rack. Cool for a few minutes before serving warm. **F**

Super Simple Blooming Onion

There's nothing like a blooming onion! It's like the perfect cross between crunchy onion rings and soft, luxurious, caramelized onions. Problem is, the traditional, wet batter is no match for the air fryer's winds, which sweep that batter off before it sets. Plus, who wants to deal with the mess of dipping and coating?

Our way takes care of that. We split an onion into eight attached wedges, then give it an egg wash before stuffing it with bread crumbs. Don't overfill it to the point at which it becomes misshapen, but make sure you get plenty of bread crumbs inside. You'll open it up after it's cooked for a while to make sure all of them get crunchy.

1 large, orb-like *sweet* yellow or white onion, preferably a Vidalia onion (avoid onions that seem flattened on one end)

1 large egg, well beaten in a shallow soup plate, small pie plate, or food storage container

⅔ cup or 75 grams Italian-seasoned dried bread crumbs or Italian-seasoned gluten-free dried bread crumbs

Nonstick spray

Master the Method

If you don't want to use an aerosol can of oil, buy small, inexpensive spray bottles at dollar stores and fill these with vegetable oil and olive oil. Keep them at room temperature, and label which is which!

RAISE THE BAR

We love a creamy dip with a crunchy onion. Stir the following in a small bowl until uniform: ¼ cup or 55 grams mayonnaise of any sort, ¼ cup or 55 grams sour cream of any sort, 1 tablespoon ketchup, 1 tablespoon prepared white horseradish, ½ teaspoon table salt, and ⅛ teaspoon cayenne.

1. With the basket in the machine or the tray set at the center level in a toaster-oven-style model, heat an air fryer to 350°F or 180°C on the air fryer setting.

2. Peel the onion and slice off a little of its bottom so that it'll sit flat on a cutting board. Make two cuts to create a "+" sign straight down the onion without cutting through to the bottom. Then make two more cuts, bisecting these original two cuts (or like a second "+" sign turned 45 degrees), thereby slicing it into eight wedges (that don't come apart). Ⓐ

3. *Gently* pry open the onion wedges and even the sections of layered rings to brush the onion inside and out with the beaten egg. Take care not to break the sections apart. Ⓑ

4. Using about two-thirds of the bread crumbs, stuff them inside of the onion without breaking the wedges or layers. Then press the remaining bread crumbs onto the outside of the onion and across its top. (There will be bare spots outside—you're looking for an overall crumbed texture rather than a thick coating.) Ⓒ

5. Generously coat the onion with nonstick spray. Set it in the heated machine and air-fry *undisturbed* for 15 minutes. Remove the cooking tray or the basket. Use two flatware forks to *gently* pry the onion open to reveal more of the (hot!) interior sections of the onion, thereby letting some of the existing crumbs fall deeper down inside. Ⓓ

6. Increase the temperature to 375°F or 190°C. Continue air-frying about 5 more minutes, until browned and crunchy. Use a nonstick-safe spatula (and perhaps a rubber spatula in the other hand for balance) to transfer the onion to a wire rack. Cool for several minutes before serving warm. Ⓔ

Up-Market Garlic Bread

We've added a little more flavor to traditional garlic bread with dried herbs and some onion powder in the coating. Why not use fresh herbs? Because fresh herbs turn black and bitter as they "fry" in the butter and it melts into the bread. But dried herbs can withstand the heat and air currents better, giving you a more present and even "fresher" flavor in a light coating like this one.

We've also upped the game by using ciabatta rolls, rather than the more common sliced Italian bread. We love the crunchy texture the ciabatta gets when it's buttered and air-fried. Look for ciabatta rolls in the bakery section of almost all supermarkets.

2 ciabatta rolls

2 tablespoons or 30 grams butter, softened to room temperature

2 medium garlic cloves, peeled and minced (about 2 teaspoons)

½ teaspoon table salt

¼ teaspoon dried basil

¼ teaspoon dried oregano

¼ teaspoon onion powder

½ ounce (¼ cup) or 15 grams grated Parmigiano-Reggiano

Master the Method

Did you know you can make toast in an air fryer? Set the slices in a single layer without touching in a 375°F or 190°C air fryer and toast for 3 to 4 minutes, turning once.

RAISE THE BAR

Use olive ciabatta rolls, rather than plain.

Mix up to 1 tablespoon olive tapenade, minced sun-dried tomatoes, or pesto into the butter mixture.

1. With the basket in the machine or the tray set at the center level in a toaster-oven-style model, heat an air fryer to 400°F or 200°C on the air fryer setting.

2. Slice the rolls in half as if you're cutting an English muffin into two disks. **A**

3. Mix the softened butter, garlic, salt, basil, oregano, and onion powder in a small bowl until uniform. **B**

4. Spread this mixture evenly onto the cut sides of the rolls. **C**

5. Set the rolls buttered side up and in a single layer without touching in the heated machine. Work in batches as necessary. Air-fry for 4 minutes, or until the bread is browning at the edges and getting crisp. Do not turn. Sprinkle about a quarter of the grated cheese evenly over the top of each slice. **D**

6. Continue air-frying for about 1 minute, or until the cheese melts and even begins to brown. Use nonstick-safe tongs to transfer the garlic bread to a wire rack, cool for a couple of minutes, and serve warm. **E**

Garlic Lover's Garlic Knots

We're only friends with people who double the garlic in a recipe. You, too? If so, the double kick of fresh garlic and garlic powder in these crunchy-outside-soft-inside garlic knots is sure to satisfy your cravings.

They're made with raw pizza dough, often available in the refrigerator or dairy case of large supermarkets. Buy the dough that comes in plastic bags rather than cans. For the best results, let the dough sit out an hour or two at room temperature before using as it will be softer and easier to work with.

3 tablespoons or 45 milliliters olive oil

2 medium garlic cloves, peeled and minced (about 2 teaspoons)

1 teaspoon table salt

½ teaspoon onion powder

½ teaspoon garlic powder

1 pound or 450 grams raw regular or whole wheat pizza dough

Master the Method

Never skip the heating step in a recipe unless the recipe asks you to set something in a cool machine before turning it on. A hot machine sets crusts and edges more quickly so they can get crunchier as a result.

RAISE THE BAR

For more garlic flavor, stir together the olive oil mixture in advance, leaving it out on the counter for at least 1 hour or up to 6 hours.

Sprinkle the knots lightly with finely grated Parmigiano-Reggiano before the last 1 to 2 minutes of their cooking time.

1. With the basket in the machine or the tray set at the center level in a toaster-oven-style model, heat an air fryer to 400°F or 200°C on the air fryer setting.

2. Stir the oil, garlic, salt, onion powder, and garlic powder in a small bowl until uniform. **A**

3. Set the pizza dough on a cutting board. Use clean fingers to flatten the dough to a 6 x 4-inch or 15 x 10-centimeter rectangle. Slice it widthwise into twelve ½-inch or 1¼-centimeter thick trips. **B**

4. Roll one strip of dough with your clean palms into a 6-inch or 15-centimeter log. Tie it into a simple but loose overhand knot and set aside. Roll and tie the remaining slices of dough. **C**

5. Brush the oil mixture evenly over the tops of the knots. **D**

6. Set the knots oiled side up in the air fryer in a single layer with at least 2 inches or 5 centimeters between each. You *must* work in batches, even in the largest machines. **E**

7. Air-fry *undisturbed* for 8 minutes, or until golden-brown and firm. Transfer the knots to a wire rack with a nonstick-safe spatula. Cool them for a few minutes before serving warm. **F**

Fried Pizza Slices

What's better than pizza? Air-fried, crumb-coated, crunchy pizza slices. Talk about the answer to midnight munchies! Or the perfect snack on the next Netflix night with the kids!

This recipe *only* works with a frozen pizza because the slices must slowly heat in the machine as the crust sets. You can indeed use a gluten-free pizza and gluten-free seasoned bread crumbs, but one note: Stay away from vegetable-based crusts, as they fall apart, even frozen, once they're dipped in the eggs.

One 13- to 18-ounce or 365- to 510-gram frozen pizza with any toppings (*do not thaw*)

3 large eggs

¼ cup or 60 milliliters water

2 cups or 225 grams Italian-seasoned dried bread crumbs

Olive oil spray

Master the Method

White smoke from an air fryer means it hasn't been cleaned properly. Black smoke is a more serious matter. Unplug the machine. There may be food or oil splattered on the heating element (above or below, depending on your model). Cool, then gently wipe off the gunk with a clean paper towel. If the machine still produces black smoke, replace it.

RAISE THE BAR

Mix up to 1 teaspoon red pepper flakes into the bread crumbs.

For a garlic kick, use a garlic-flavored cooking spray.

1. With the basket in the machine or the tray set at the center level in a toaster-oven-style model, heat an air fryer to 325°F or 165°F on the air fryer setting.

2. Cut the frozen pizza into six even wedges. Ⓐ

3. Whisk the eggs and water in a shallow soup plate, small pie plate, or medium food storage container until uniform with no bits of egg white floating in the mix. Spread the bread crumbs in a second shallow soup plate, small pie plate, or medium food storage container. Ⓑ

4. Set a slice of pizza, crust side down, in the egg mixture. Use a spoon or a pastry brush to coat the top of the slice with egg mixture. Ⓒ

5. Set the slice in the bread crumbs crust side down. Gently press down to get the crumbs to adhere to the bottom, then spoon or sprinkle the top of the slice with bread crumbs, pressing gently to make an even crust. Pick up the slice, gently shake off any excess, and set aside. Ⓓ

6. Repeat steps 4 and 5 with the remaining five pizza slices. Then lightly coat the slice tops and bottoms with olive oil spray. Ⓔ

7. Set the slices crust side down in a single layer without touching in the heated machine. Work in batches as necessary. Air-fry *undisturbed* for 8 minutes, then increase the temperature to 375°F or 190°C. Continue air-frying *undisturbed* for 6 minutes, or until crisp and golden brown. Transfer the slices to a wire rack with a nonstick-safe spatula. Cool for a few minutes before serving hot. (If you're working in batches, remember to lower the temperature to 325°F or 165°C at the start of each new batch.) Ⓕ

Toasted Ravioli

This recipe uses standard frozen ravioli to make a tasty, crunchy snack for before dinner, or even in the afternoon when the kids come home. Think of it as a next-level version of pasta chips.

Although we offer the simplest choice of cheese ravioli, you can substitute meat, spinach and cheese, or even butternut squash ravioli. Do not use mini ravioli or extra large ones, as the timing won't work. Also, do not use those with sauce already in the bag (that is, the sort that can be microwaved in the bag, sauce and all).

1½ cups or 75 grams Italian-seasoned panko bread crumbs

½ ounce (¼ cup) or 15 grams finely grated Parmigiano-Reggiano

1 teaspoon red pepper flakes

2 large eggs

1 tablespoon or 15 milliliters balsamic vinegar

One 12-ounce or 340-gram bag of frozen unsauced *square* cheese ravioli (20 to 24 pieces), *thawed*

Olive oil spray

Jarred marinara sauce, purchased pesto, or ranch dressing, for dipping

Master the Method

When you open a drawer-style air fryer to check on food or turn items, make sure you push the basket fully into the machine again or it won't start cooking again.

RAISE THE BAR

To make a tasty homemade marinara dip, cook a chopped small yellow or white onion with a splash of olive oil in a small saucepan until the onion has wilted, stirring often, about 3 minutes. Add 2 peeled and minced medium garlic cloves (about 2 teaspoons), ½ teaspoon dried oregano, ½ teaspoon dried thyme, and ⅛ teaspoon red pepper flakes. Stir well, then add one 14-ounce or 400-gram can of crushed tomatoes (do not drain). Bring to a simmer, then reduce the heat to low and simmer gently, stirring often, until thickened, about 20 minutes. Stir in 1 tablespoon or 15 milliliters balsamic vinegar and about ½ teaspoon table salt. Serve warm.

1. With the basket in the machine or the tray set at the center level in a toaster-oven-style model, heat an air fryer to 400°F or 200°C on the air fryer setting.

2. Mix the bread crumbs, cheese, and red pepper flakes in a shallow soup plate, small pie plate, or medium food storage container. Whisk the eggs and vinegar in a medium bowl until there are no bits of egg white floating in the mix. **A**

3. Pour the ravioli into the egg mixture. Stir well until thoroughly and evenly coated. **B**

4. Pick the ravioli one by one and set them in the bread crumb mixture. You can use your clean hands or two forks. Turn and press the ravioli gently to coat evenly and thoroughly. Set aside on a cutting board as you coat more. **C**

5. Generously coat *both sides* of the ravioli with olive oil spray. **D**

6. Arrange the ravioli in a single layer without touching in the heated machine. Work in batches as necessary. Air-fry for 4 minutes, then gently turn them over with nonstick-safe tongs. **E**

7. Continue air-frying for 2 more minutes, or until golden brown and crispy. Use those tongs to transfer the ravioli to a wire rack to cool for at least 5 minutes before serving warm with marinara sauce, pesto, or ranch dressing as a dip. **F**

Spicy Bacon-Wrapped Pineapple Bites

Bacon-wrapped dates have been done time and again (even by us—a spicy version in *The Essential Air Fryer Cookbook* and a mild one in *The Instant Air Fryer Bible*). Wanting to try something new, we substituted pineapple chunks for the dates. The results are naturally sweeter, which we balance with both spicy pickled jalapeño rings and a little diced pimiento.

There's no doubt that fresh pineapple chunks taste better—although fresh pineapples can be a bit of a gamble at the supermarket. Just remember: If a pineapple doesn't smell like anything, it won't taste like anything. So if you can't find a pineapple with a discernable perfume, you're better off with canned chunks.

12 thin strips of U.S.-style bacon, each halved widthwise

24 fresh, peeled, cored 1-inch or 2½-centimeter pineapple chunks; or 24 canned pineapple chunks (one 20-ounce or 567-gram can), packed in juice but *drained*

24 jarred pickled jalapeño rings

About 2 tablespoons or 24 grams *drained* jarred diced pimientos

Master the Method

When reheating foods, turn to the air fryer more than the microwave. Anything off the grill or any roast can be sliced and quickly reheated with better results in an air fryer.

RAISE THE BAR

For a sweeter finish, brush the bacon with maple syrup before the last minute of air-frying.

For a hotter version, brush the bacon with sriracha or chili crisp before the last minute of air-frying.

For a more piquant flavor, use pepper bacon (but do not use thick-cut U.S.-style bacon).

1. With the basket in the machine or the tray set at the center level in a toaster-oven-style model, heat an air fryer to 400°F or 200°C on the air fryer setting.

2. Set one of the halved bacon strips on a clean work surface. Set a pineapple chunk at one end of the strip. **A**

3. Set a jalapeño ring on top of the pineapple chunk, then fill the center of that jalapeño ring with a few bits of diced pimiento. **B**

4. Roll up the pineapple chunk in the bacon strip. Set aside and continue making the remainder of the bacon packets, following the instructions in steps 2 through 4. **C**

5. Lay the packets seam side down in the heated machine in a single layer without touching. Work in batches as necessary (particularly in drawer-style machines). **D**

6. Air-fry *undisturbed* for about 12 minutes, or until the bacon is browned, sizzling, and crisp without being hard. Transfer the packets to a wire rack with nonstick-safe tongs. Cool for at least 5 minutes before serving warm. **E**

Crispy Avocado Halves

These are not air-fried avocado wedges. These are a far more substantial "nibble," each a half of a pitted and peeled avocado with more creaminess per bite than the usual air-fried wedges and a nice indentation that can be filled with salsa (or many other creamy or saucy things—your imagination is your only limit, although we give you some options in Raise the Bar). Because these halves are large, they'll require more than just napkins—a knife and fork, in fact (and a plate, of course).

    Avocados have a lot of fat—which means that when hot, they can give you a bad pizza burn. Cool these for at least 5 minutes before you serve them.

4 medium ripe Hass avocados

1 cup all-purpose flour or 120 grams plain flour, or a gluten-free flour alternative

2 large egg whites

2 tablespoons or 30 milliliters lemon juice (fresh is best)

2 cups or 225 grams Italian-seasoned dried bread crumbs or gluten-free Italian-seasoned dried bread crumbs (do not use panko bread crumbs)

Nonstick spray

2 cups or 500 milliliters salsa of any sort

Master the Method

Although you should sometimes bring eggs to room temperature in baking recipes for better loft in a cakes or quick breads, you needn't do so in many air-frying recipes. In fact, cold eggs out of the fridge help to slow down the crisping process in the heated machine. The coating can get crunchy while the food underneath gets properly done.

RAISE THE BAR

Top the salsa in the halves with sour cream.

Or skip the salsa and fill the indentations with French onion dip, ranch dressing, blue cheese dressing, or just crumbled blue cheese with a drizzle of balsamic vinegar.

1. With the basket in the machine or the tray set at the center level in a toaster-oven-style model, heat an air fryer to 400°F or 200°C on the air fryer setting.

2. Halve, pit, and peel the avocados. Ⓐ

3. Pour the flour into a shallow soup plate, small pie plate, dinner plate, or medium food storage container. Whisk the egg whites and lemon juice in a second shallow soup plate, small pie plate, or medium food storage container until quite foamy. Finally, pour the bread crumbs into a third shallow soup plate, small pie plate, dinner plate, or medium food storage container. Ⓑ

4. Dip an avocado half in the flour and coat on all sides, even in the indentation. Transfer to the egg whites and coat on all sides, even spooning some of the egg mixture into the indentation. Ⓒ

5. Let the excess egg slip off the avocado half, then set in the bread crumbs and turn to coat it well on all sides, even spooning or sprinkling the bread crumbs into its indentation. Press gently so the bread crumbs adhere. Set aside and repeat this three-dip process with the remaining avocado halves. Ⓓ

6. Generously coat the crumbed avocado halves with nonstick spray *on all sides*. Set them *rounded side up* in a single layer without touching in the heated machine. Work in batches as necessary. Air-fry for 4 minutes, then use nonstick-safe tongs to flip them over. Ⓔ

7. Continue air-frying for 4 more minutes, or until crunchy and browned. Use a nonstick-safe spatula to transfer them to a wire rack. Cool for at least 5 minutes, then spoon ¼ cup salsa into the indentation of each half before serving warm. Ⓕ

Old-School Tostones

These are a traditional snack or even a side dish in many Caribbean restaurants. The green plantains have a distinctly firm, sour, even bitter edge to their flavor, a nice contrast to their creamy interiors and also a more sophisticated pop that pairs perfectly with sweet drinks, particularly a daiquiri or piña colada.

2 green unripe plantains, about 6 ounces or 170 grams each

Nonstick spray

Salt for garnishing, preferably kosher salt or a crunchy coarse sea salt

Master the Method

Although air fryers are loud, don't be tempted to cover them in any way. They get hot and can burn any sort of cover. And don't be tempted to put them in a back pantry to cook unattended. They're essentially a countertop oven and need monitoring. You're saving fat yet getting crunchy food. You can put up with a little noise.

RAISE THE BAR

Here's a fiery and smooth jalapeño dip for these plantain rounds: Boil 1 peeled and quartered medium onion; 6 to 8 stemmed, halved, and seeded fresh medium jalapeños; and 5 peeled medium garlic cloves in a medium saucepan of water set over high heat for about 15 minutes. Drain and put the vegetables in a food processor. Cool for 15 minutes, then add ½ cup or 125 milliliters vegetable oil and 1 teaspoon table salt. Cover and process until smooth, stopping the machine occasionally to scrape down the canister's inside. Add water in 1-tablespoon or 15-milliliter increments if the mixture is too thick. This sauce can stay covered in the fridge for up to 1 week.

1. With the basket in the machine or the tray set at the center level in a toaster-oven-style model, heat an air fryer to 400°F or 200°C on the air fryer setting.

2. Use a paring knife to cut the ends off each unpeeled plantain and make a slit along the length of the peels. Ⓐ

3. Use a flatware spoon to strip back the peel from each plantain. Ⓑ

4. Slice the peeled plantains into 1-inch or 2½-centimeter segments. Ⓒ

5. Generously coat the plantains with nonstick spray on all sides, even the edges. Set them in a single layer without touching in the heated machine. Work in batches as necessary. Air-fry for 6 minutes, *shaking the basket or rearranging them on the cooking tray twice*. Transfer the plantains to a cutting board with nonstick-safe tongs. Use the back of a metal spatula or the bottom of a small saucepan to mash them down to about ½-inch or 1¼-centimeter thick rounds. Ⓓ

6. Coat the plantains *again* with nonstick spray. Return them to the machine in a single layer without touching. Work in batches as necessary. Continue air-frying, *shaking or rearranging once*, for 5 more minutes, or until crispy and well browned. Transfer them to a wire rack with tongs and cool for at least 5 minutes before sprinkling with salt and serving warm. Ⓔ

Fried Sardines

This recipe is *not* what you think. It's *not* the fried sardines that are often served as a first course in Italian or Spanish restaurants. Rather, these are canned sardines that are breaded and air-fried to create crunchy, briny little nibbles, best with ice-cold shots of vodka.

Without a doubt, the quality of the canned sardines will affect the success of this recipe. Although there are lots of downscale canned sardines available in every supermarket, splurge on Provisions London or King Oscar canned sardines packed in oil.

Two 4¼-ounce or 125-gram cans or tins of sardines packed in olive oil, preferably boneless, skinless sardines

1½ cups or 170 grams Italian-seasoned dried bread crumbs

Olive oil spray

Crunchy sea or kosher salt, for garnishing

Lemon wedges, for serving

Master the Method

Fishy smells are the hardest to get out of an air fryer. Soak the basket or the cooking tray in soapy water for an hour or so—and wipe out the inside of the machine once it's cool.

RAISE THE BAR

Sprinkle minced fresh chives, minced fresh oregano leaves, and/or minced fresh parsley leaves over the fried sardines before serving them with the salt and lemon wedges.

1. With the basket in the machine or the tray set at the center level in a toaster-oven-style model, heat an air fryer to 400°F or 200°C on the air fryer setting.

2. Open the cans and remove the sardines but do not blot them dry. They should remain quite oily. **A**

3. Pour the bread crumbs into a large bowl. Add the oily sardines and toss well to coat them on all sides. Transfer the coated sardines to a cutting board. **B**

4. Lightly coat the sardines *on all sides* with olive oil spray. **C**

5. Set the sardines in a single layer without touching in the heated machine. Work in batches as necessary. Air-fry for 4 minutes, then use nonstick-safe tongs to *gently* turn the sardines over. **D**

6. Continue air-frying for 3 more minutes, or until browned and crispy. Use a nonstick-safe spatula to transfer the sardines to a wire rack. Cool for a few minutes, then serve with sea or kosher salt for sprinkling and lemon wedges for squeezing over the crunchy bits. **E**

Classic Chicken Egg Rolls

Although these egg rolls are modeled on the American Chinese standard, we've used rotisserie chicken for a much easier filling and a light finish in each bite, although we're still providing that classic flavor and beloved crunch.

We lace the filling with hoisin sauce, a thick, slightly sweet condiment that is often served as the sauce in the pancakes for moo shu pork. It's sometimes made of sweet potatoes, sometimes with other root vegetables, all thickened and loaded with spices. It's usually got gluten in the mix; so look for gluten-free alternatives from online suppliers if you're concerned.

2½ cups or 190 grams bagged undressed cole slaw mix

⅔ cup or 100 grams skinned, deboned, and chopped rotisserie chicken meat (white and/or dark)

¼ cup or 35 grams *roasted* unsalted shelled peanuts, chopped

2 teaspoons or 10 milliliters regular or reduced-sodium soy sauce

2 teaspoons or 10 milliliters unseasoned rice vinegar

2 teaspoons or 10 grams hoisin sauce (see the headnote for more information)

1½ teaspoons cornstarch

½ teaspoon onion powder

¼ teaspoon five-spice powder (see Raise the Bar, page 132)

¼ teaspoon garlic powder

8 fresh egg roll wrappers (or thawed frozen egg roll wrappers; do not use spring roll wrappers)

Nonstick spray

Master the Method

If you resist working in batches for recipes, consider buying two air fryers! A large one and a medium-sized model would be a great pairing. Or only make a smaller, half batch, where some recipes in this book indicate you can.

1. With the basket in the machine or the tray set at the center level in a toaster-oven-style model, heat an air fryer to 400°F or 200°C on the air fryer setting.

2. Stir the slaw mix, chicken, peanuts, soy sauce, vinegar, hoisin sauce, cornstarch, onion powder, five-spice powder, and garlic powder in a medium bowl until well combined. Ⓐ

3. On a clean, dry work surface or cutting board, set one egg roll wrapper with one of its corners pointing toward you. Put about ⅓ cup or 40 grams of the chicken mixture in a log-ish line between the halfway point in the wrapper and the point that's closest to you. Ⓑ

4. Run a clean, wet finger around the outer edge of the wrapper. Fold the corner closest to you up and over the filling mixture. Then fold the two corners at either end of the filling mixture up and over the filling (without covering it completely). Press lightly to seal and roll the egg roll closed, pressing the seam to seal it, too. Set aside and continue making the remaining egg rolls. Ⓒ

5. Generously coat the egg rolls on all sides with nonstick spray. Ⓓ

6. Set them seam side down in a single layer without touching in the heated machine. Work in batches as necessary. Air-fry for 4 minutes, then turn them *gently* with nonstick-safe tongs. Ⓔ

7. Continue air-frying for 4 more minutes, or until golden brown and crisp. Use those same tongs to transfer the egg rolls to a wire rack. Cool for at least 5 minutes before serving warm. Ⓕ

RAISE THE BAR

Swap out the peanuts for chopped slivered shelled almonds or cashews.

Egg rolls need a dipping sauce. So-called "duck" or "sweet-and-sour orange" sauce is traditional in American Chinese food, but you can also try hot Chinese mustard, sweet red chili sauce, or even a 50/50 blend of Worcestershire sauce and balsamic vinegar (or better yet, Chinese black vinegar).

Copycat Tex-Mex Egg Rolls

Yep, this recipe is a copycat for the famed egg rolls served at the Cheesecake Factory. They contain a flavorful mix of ingredients that you'd normally put in a burrito, but they're stuffed into egg roll wrappers and fried. Or air-fried, in our case, which means they're healthier, too.

Don't want the hassle of skinning and deboning rotisserie chicken meat? Substitute sliced deli turkey or deli skinless chicken breast. Ask for thicker slices than you'd use in sandwiches for better texture inside the egg rolls.

3 ounces (¾ cup) or 85 grams shredded mild American cheddar or Monterey Jack cheese

½ cup or 75 grams skinned, deboned, chopped rotisserie chicken meat (white and/or dark)

⅓ cup or 60 grams drained and rinsed canned black beans

⅓ cup or 45 grams drained canned corn kernels

Half of a 4-ounce or 115-gram jar of diced pimientos (do not drain)

1 small single-lobe shallot, peeled and minced

½ teaspoon ground coriander

½ teaspoon ground cumin

½ teaspoon standard chili powder

½ teaspoon garlic powder

½ teaspoon table salt

Ground black pepper, to taste (maybe about ½ teaspoon)

8 fresh egg roll wrappers (or thawed frozen egg roll wrappers; do not use spring roll wrappers)

Nonstick spray

Master the Method

Deciding between a wooden spoon or a rubber spatula to stir ingredients? It really doesn't make a great difference, although a rubber spatula works better with wetter, saucier mixes.

RAISE THE BAR

Dip these egg rolls in jarred salsa, or in a 50/50 combo of salsa and sour cream.

Have pickled jalapeño rings and/or jarred spicy okra spears on the side.

1. With the basket in the machine or the tray set at the center level in a toaster-oven-style model, heat an air fryer to 400°F or 200°C on the air fryer setting.

2. Stir the cheese, chicken, beans, corn, pimientos, shallot, coriander, cumin, chili powder, garlic powder, salt, and pepper in a medium bowl until well combined. **A**

3. Set one egg roll wrapper on a clean, dry work surface or cutting board with one of the corners pointing toward you. Run a clean, wet finger around the outer edge of the wrapper. **B**

4. Put about ⅓ cup or about 40 grams of the chicken mixture in a log-ish line between the halfway point in the wrapper and the point that's closest to you. **C**

5. Fold the corner closest to you up and over the filling mixture. Then fold the two corners at either end of the filling mixture up and over the filling (without covering it completely). Press lightly to seal and roll the egg roll closed, pressing the seam lightly to seal it, too. Set aside and continue making the remaining egg rolls. **D**

6. Generously coat the egg rolls *on all sides* with nonstick spray. Set them in the heated machine, seam side down in a single layer and without touching. Work in batches as necessary. **E**

7. Air-fry for 4 minutes, then flip them over *gently* with a nonstick-safe spatula. Continue air-frying for about 4 more minutes, or until golden brown and crisp. Transfer the egg rolls to a wire rack with a *clean* nonstick-safe spatula. Cool for at least 5 minutes before serving warm. **F**

Crunchy Chicken Summer Rolls

Summer rolls are a lighter, even crunchier version of egg rolls. They're made with dried rice paper rounds, which become irresistibly crisp and delicate in an air fryer. Because the wrappers have such a mild flavor and offer little "competition" to the filling, we made the filling more assertive, both sweet and savory, with red chili sauce and peanut butter.

The dried paper rounds are found in most supermarkets near the soy sauce or other Asian foods. Look for a clear container of opaque-white rounds that are not chipped or broken. The dried rounds can stay in their sealed container in a cool, dry pantry for up to 1 year.

1½ cups or 225 grams skinned, deboned, and chopped rotisserie chicken *white* meat

1½ cups or 150 grams fresh soy or mung bean sprouts

2 tablespoons or 30 milliliters sweet red chili sauce

2 tablespoons or 30 milliliters regular or reduced-sodium soy sauce

1½ tablespoons or 23 milliliters lime juice

1 tablespoon or 15 grams smooth peanut butter

½ teaspoon yellow curry powder

Warm water as needed

8 dried round opaque-white rice paper wrappers

Nonstick spray

Master the Method

A lot of people line the bottoms of their air fryers with aluminum foil to make cleanup easier. We do not recommend doing this. Foil can impede proper air flow unless it's scrupulously flat against the bottom. (And in some models, the heating element is on the bottom!) Yes, cleanup can be a pain. But the point of an air fryer is the air circulation. Best not to block it!

1. With the basket in the machine or the tray set at the center level in a toaster-oven-style model, heat an air fryer to 400°F or 200°C on the air fryer setting.

2. Stir the chicken and bean sprouts in a large bowl to combine. Add the chili sauce, soy sauce, lime juice, peanut butter, and curry powder. **A**

3. Stir this mixture well until uniform. Fill a pie plate with *warm* tap water, then set a rice paper wrapper in it. Soak until soft, less than 30 seconds. **B**

4. Spread the wrapper on a cutting board. Put a scant ⅓ cup or a scant 55 grams of the chicken mixture in the center of the wrapper and make a fairly compact log out of that filling with about 2 inches or 5 centimeters of space from *each* end of the log to the edge of the wrapper. **C**

5. Roll up the wrapper by first folding half of the wrapper over the filling log, then folding in the sides at the ends of the log (without covering it fully). **D**

6. Roll the wrapper closed. Repeat with the remaining wrappers and chicken mixture, creating eight rolls. Generously coat the rolls *on all sides* with nonstick spray. Set them in the heated machine, seam side down and in a single layer without touching. Work in batches as necessary. Air-fry for 8 minutes, then use nonstick-safe tongs to turn the rolls over. **E**

7. Continue air-frying for 8 more minutes, or until visibly crunchy and speckled *light* brown. Use those tongs or a nonstick-safe spatula (if you notice any breaking open) to transfer the rolls to a wire rack. Cool for at least 5 minutes before serving warm. **F**

RAISE THE BAR

Serve these summer rolls with bottled peanut sauce or more sweet red chili sauce.

Substitute 1 tablespoon or 15 milliliters fish sauce for 1 tablespoon or 15 milliliters of the soy sauce for a more assertive and savory flavor.

Use Thai red curry paste instead of the more common curry powder to amp up the spice.

Air-Fried Deviled Eggs

Imagine if you could take a luscious deviled egg and give it a crisp coating. It's such a great treat: creamy and crunchy all at once. To get the job done, we take the hard-cooked whites, bread them, get them crunchy in the machine, and *then* fill them with the creamy egg-yolk mixture. This recipe is a dream come true, no?

6 *cold* large eggs

2 tablespoons or 30 grams regular or low-fat mayonnaise

1 tablespoon or 3 grams minced fresh chives or the green part of a scallion

2 teaspoons or 10 milliliters jarred prepared white horseradish

½ teaspoon table salt

Several dashes of a thin red hot sauce, preferably Tabasco sauce, optional

½ cup all-purpose flour or 60 grams plain flour

2 tablespoons or 30 milliliters sriracha

1½ cups or 170 grams Italian-seasoned dried bread crumbs

Nonstick spray

Mild paprika, for garnishing

Master the Method

We hate washing kitchen utensils while we cook, so we invest in several pairs of nonstick-safe tongs and a couple of nonstick-safe spatulas. It's a small investment that save us time and energy in the kitchen.

RAISE THE BAR

Add up to 2 teaspoons minced stemmed fresh thyme and/or oregano leaves with the chives. Or sprinkle these minced herbs over the deviled eggs just before serving.

1. With the basket in the machine or the tray set at the center level in a toaster-oven-style model, heat an air fryer to 250°F or 120°C on the air fryer setting.

2. Set four eggs in the heated machine. Air-fry for 17 minutes. Transfer the eggs with nonstick-safe tongs to a colander set in the sink. Rinse repeatedly and well with cool tap water to stop the cooking. Peel the eggs, then halve them longways, tip to rounded end. **A**

3. Pick out the yolks and set them in a small bowl. Add the mayonnaise, chives or scallions, horseradish, salt, and thin red hot sauce (if using). Mix gently until well combined and fairly smooth. **B**

4. Increase the air fryer's temperature to 400°F or 200°C. Pour the flour in a shallow soup plate, dinner plate, small pie plate, or food storage container. Whisk the remaining two raw eggs with the sriracha in a second shallow soup plate, small pie plate, or food storage container until no bits of egg white are floating in the mix. Spread the bread crumbs in a third shallow soup plate, dinner plate, small pie plate, or food storage container. Dip a peeled egg half into the flour and turn it to coat on all sides. Transfer it to the egg mixture and turn to coat well. **C**

5. Transfer the egg to the bread crumbs; turn and press gently to get an even coating. Then *return* the breaded egg white to the egg mixture and coat it well again—and then set it back in the bread crumbs and roll it around again to create a thick coating. In other words, the steps to coat the eggs are: flour, eggs, bread crumbs, eggs, bread crumbs. Set aside and continue dipping the remaining egg halves with this same five-step process. **D**

6. Generously coat the egg halves on all sides with nonstick spray. Set them in the heated machine, rounded side down in a single layer without touching. Air-fry for 4 minutes. Turn them over with nonstick-safe tongs. **E**

7. Continue air-frying for 3 more minutes, or until golden and crunchy. Use a nonstick-safe spatula to transfer them to a wire rack. Cool for 5 minutes before filling the indentations with the egg-yolk mixture. Sprinkle the eggs with mild paprika as a garnish. **F**

Crab-Stuffed Mushroom Caps

Stuffed mushrooms are such an old-school treat. And the air fryer makes them even better than the oven! The hot air currents dry out the mushroom caps a bit, concentrating their flavors without letting them sit and stew in their own juices (thereby offering better taste without squishy bottoms).

This nibble could easily be a light dinner for four on your deck or patio if you've got some chips and a tangy dip on the side as well.

2 slices of white or whole wheat sandwich bread (do not remove the crusts)

8 ounces or 225 grams lump or backfin crabmeat, picked over for shells and cartilage

⅓ cup or 75 grams regular or low-fat mayonnaise (do not use fat-free mayonnaise)

1 medium scallion, trimmed and minced (white part, too)

2 tablespoons minced fresh dill fronds

2 tablespoons or 25 grams drained jarred diced pimientos

½ teaspoon Old Bay seasoning

20 medium brown or white mushrooms, stemmed

Nonstick spray

½ ounce (¼ cup) or 15 grams finely grated Parmigiano-Reggiano

Master the Method

Having a deck party? Bring an air fryer right out onto the deck so you don't have to leave your guests. Make sure you keep children and pets clear of the hot machine.

RAISE THE BAR

Substitute 8 ounces or 225 grams shelled lobster meat, finely chopped, for the crabmeat.

Swap out the Old Bay seasoning for lemon-pepper seasoning.

Add up to ½ teaspoon red pepper flakes with the crabmeat.

1. With the basket in the machine or the tray set at the center level in a toaster-oven-style model, heat an air fryer to 375°F or 190°C on the air fryer setting.

2. Tear the bread slices and put them in a food processor. Cover and pulse repeatedly to make fresh bread crumbs. Pour them into a large bowl. Ⓐ

3. Add the crabmeat, mayonnaise, scallion, dill, pimientos, and Old Bay. Stir well but gently to keep from turning the crabmeat into mush. Ⓑ

4. Use a small flatware spoon or even a melon baller to scoop out more of the centers from the stemmed mushroom caps. Ⓒ

5. Gently pack about 1 tablespoon or 20 grams of the crab mixture into each of the mushroom caps. Ⓓ

6. Lightly coat the filling and tops of the mushroom caps with nonstick spray. Place the caps rounded side down and sprinkle a little cheese over each. Ⓔ

7. Set them in the heated machine in single layer without touching. Work in batches as necessary. Air-fry *undisturbed* for about 9 minutes, or until browned and crunchy. Transfer the stuffed caps to a wire rack with a nonstick-safe spatula. Cool for a few minutes before serving warm. Ⓕ

2

SANDWICHES & WRAPS

A hot lunch is almost always better than a cold lunch. And an air fryer makes a hot sandwich or wrap in minutes. So there's no excuse to eat a cold sandwich.

Better yet, there's no need for another kitchen gadget like a panini press when you've got an air fryer. By spreading the outside of the sandwich with mayonnaise or butter, or just coating it with nonstick spray, you can turn almost any sandwich into a crunchy delight. In other words, lunch can be about comfort food, too—but with way less effort.

That said, the fillings in sandwiches have to be able to withstand the machine's heat vortex. And admittedly, it's hard to get a gooey filling in a sandwich to stand up in an air fryer because the filling melts and runs out. So we swapped things up a bit in a couple of these recipes and used a thick sauce on the *outside* of the sandwich. We wanted to let the machine do the things it does best—that is, browning and crisping.

Before you head off to the recipes and photographs, one note about the bread: Better bread means a better sandwich. Yes, we call for a lot of sliced sandwich loaves in this chapter, but you should aim for the best you can comfortably afford. Cheaper sliced white bread is often loaded with sugar and can burn more quickly in the machine. And char is no substitute for crunch.

The Banging Best Grilled Cheese

Yes, you can make a grilled cheese with American cheddar or Swiss. But life's too short! Here's our candidate for a crazy-great grilled cheese, made with cheddar and Brie and layered with a little jam for a sweet-tangy pop. There's no way you can eat this sandwich without a quaff in hand. Cream soda? Iced tea? Bourbon? (Hey, you're an adult.)

Slicing gooey Brie can be a pain. Yes, you can just go ahead and maul it. (It's going to melt anyway.) Or you can be more precise. Freeze the Brie for 15 minutes, just to firm it up. Then spray your knife with nonstick spray to keep the sticking to a minimum.

2 slices of sandwich-style *white* sourdough bread, preferably a country-style or farmhouse-style bread

Butter at room temperature, for smearing

Two 1-ounce or 30-gram slices of mild American-style cheddar cheese

3 ounces or 90 grams herbed or plain Brie, rind removed, the remainder thinly sliced

1½ tablespoons or 30 grams fig or raspberry jam, preferably fig, although it's admittedly hard to find

Master the Method

Anything with cheese and/or a sweet condiment like jam must be cooled a few minutes before serving. An air fryer superheats melty things.

RAISE THE BAR

Spread a thin layer of chili crisp (such as Lao Gan Ma or—better!—Sze Daddy) on the bread before you spread on the jam.

Go swanky by swapping in Camembert (rind removed) for the Brie.

1. With the basket in the machine or the tray set at the center level in a toaster-oven-style model, heat an air fryer to 400°F or 200°C on the air fryer setting.

2. Set the two slices of bread on a cutting board or a clean work surface. Generously butter the exposed side of each slice. **Ⓐ**

3. Flip one of the slices over (buttered side down). Top it evenly with the cheddar and Brie. **Ⓑ**

4. Spread the jam on the unbuttered side of the other slice of bread. Set it jam side down (or buttered side up) on top of the other half. **Ⓒ**

5. Transfer the sandwich to the heated basket or tray. Air-fry for 3 minutes. Flip the sandwich with a nonstick-safe spatula. (And perhaps a rubber spatula, the back of a wooden spoon, or even a flatware tablespoon in your other hand to steady the sandwich.) **Ⓓ**

6. Continue air-frying until the sandwich is browned and crisp with melty cheese galore, about 3 more minutes. Use the nonstick-safe spatula to transfer the sandwich to a wire rack. Cool for a couple of minutes before slicing in half (on the diagonal, unless you're an animal) and serving warm. **Ⓔ**

Super Crunchy Pimento Cheese Sandwiches

Don't @ us. We know pimento cheese is not traditionally made with cream cheese in many parts of the U.S. But for the *best* air-fried pimento cheese sandwich, we need cream cheese! It lets the filling get velvety inside the crunchy bread. One bite and you'll forgive us for our gaffe.

If you don't want to make your own pimento cheese, use about ½ pound or 225 grams of purchased pimento cheese. But we *strongly* suggest you find a pimento made with cream cheese.

3 ounces or 90 grams regular or low-fat cream cheese (do not use fat-free), at room temperature

1½ ounces (3 tablespoons) or 45 grams shredded sharp or extra-sharp American-style cheddar cheese

Half of a jarred whole roasted red pepper, blotted dry and *minced* (seriously)

⅛ teaspoon onion powder

⅛ teaspoon cayenne

⅛ teaspoon table salt

4 slices of sandwich-style white or whole wheat bread

2 tablespoons or 30 grams regular or low-fat mayonnaise (do not use fat-free)

Master the Method

Work gently with coated sandwiches when they're on the cutting board or your work surface before they're cooked. Don't press down or move them around—or else you'll wipe off the exterior coating.

RAISE THE BAR

Add ⅛ teaspoon garlic powder to the pimento cheese.

Or go nuts and add up to 2 tablespoons or 20 grams minced sun-dried tomatoes to the mix.

Although we call for white or whole wheat bread, you haven't lived until you've had a fried pimento cheese sandwich with seedy rye bread.

1. With the basket in the machine or the tray set at the center level in a toaster-oven-style model, heat an air fryer to 400°F or 200°C on the air fryer setting.

2. Stir the cream cheese, cheddar, red pepper, onion powder, cayenne, and salt in a medium bowl until uniform *but not* mushy. Ⓐ

3. Set the slices of bread on a cutting board or clean work surface. Spread about a quarter of the mayonnaise across the exposed side of each slice of bread. Ⓑ

4. Turn two slices over so they're mayo-ed side down. Evenly pile and smooth half of the cheese mixture onto each slice of bread. Ⓒ

5. Set a second slice of bread mayo-ed side up over each sandwich. Ⓓ

6. Transfer the sandwiches to the air fryer. Air-fry for 3 minutes. Flip the sandwiches with a nonstick-safe spatula. (And perhaps another spatula, the back of a wooden spoon, or even a flatware tablespoon in your other hand to steady the sandwich.) Ⓔ

7. Continue air-frying until the sandwiches are golden brown but not runny, about 2 more minutes. Use the nonstick-safe spatula to transfer the sandwiches to a wire rack. Cool for a few minutes before slicing and serving. Ⓕ

Crumb-Coated Ham and Cheese

The better the ham, the better the ham-and-cheese sandwich. At an up-market deli counter, look for a salty, baked whole ham that can be sliced for sandwiches. There are, of course, packaged varieties, but they vary greatly in quality.

The pickles may be a surprise addition to this classic. Trust us: They add a sweet-tart pop. You can leave them out, but only if you insist. You can also swap out the cheese on this one for another sort you prefer, so long as you stick with a semi-firm slicing cheese (like sharp American-style cheddar or Muenster).

4 slices of sandwich-style, white, country-style, or farmhouse-style bread, crusts removed

Four 1-ounce or 30-gram slices of deli ham

Four 1-ounce or 30-gram slices of Swiss cheese

8 bread-and-butter pickle "chips" or rounds, blotted dry

2 large eggs, well beaten in a shallow soup plate, shallow food storage container, or small pie plate

1 cup or 50 grams plain panko bread crumbs, spread in a second shallow soup plate, shallow food storage container, or small pie plate

Nonstick spray

Master the Method

Never stack sandwich bread slices on top of each other to slice off the crusts. You can tear the bread or mush the edges.

RAISE THE BAR

Spread a thin coating of deli mustard on the bread before you top it with the ham and cheese.

And/or spread a thin layer of chutney over the bread before you top it.

Whisk up to 1 tablespoon or 15 milliliters sriracha or the pickled brine from a jar of pickled jalapeño rings into the beaten eggs before you use them for the coating.

1. With the basket in the machine or the tray set at the center level in a toaster-oven-style model, heat an air fryer to 375°F or 190°C on the air fryer setting.

2. Set the crustless bread slices on a cutting board or clean work surface and use a rolling pin to roll them to half their original thickness. **A**

3. Trim the ham and cheese slices so they'll fit on two of the rolled bread slices with a ¼-inch or ½-centimeter border of bread all around. Lay the trimmed ham and cheese evenly on two rolled slices of bread. Top evenly with the trimmed bits of ham and cheese. **B**

4. Top the ham and cheese with four pickle "chips" or rounds on each sandwich. Set a second slice of rolled bread on top of each sandwich. **C**

5. Set one sandwich in the beaten eggs, then turn it over to coat it well. (Your clean hands work best.) Lift it up to let any excess egg drip off. Then set the egged sandwich in the bread crumbs and press gently to coat well and partially seal the edges of the sandwich, turning the sandwich over and in all directions to make sure it's evenly coated. It will never completely seal but pinch the edges a bit without tearing them. Set aside and repeat with the second sandwich. **D**

6. Coat the sandwiches *on all sides* with nonstick spray. Transfer the sandwiches to the heated machine. Air-fry for 5 minutes, then flip the sandwiches with nonstick-safe tongs. **E**

7. Continue air-frying the sandwiches until golden brown and absurdly crunchy, about 3 minutes. Use the nonstick-safe spatula to transfer the sandwiches to a wire rack and cool for a few minutes before serving. (Because they're so crunchy, they don't slice very well.) **F**

Fried Bologna and Cheese Sandwiches

Some of us grew up with fried bologna sandwiches. For those not in the know, the bologna was fried, not the sandwich. For this recipe, we've upped the game considerably.

We also got the idea for this cheesy potato-chipped bologna sandwiches from those served at the Labor Day Fair in our rural New England town. (You can enjoy one during the frog-jumping contest.)

By heating the bologna in the air fryer before it goes into the sandwich, we get it hot to help melt the cheese more quickly, so that the sandwich becomes even more irresistible.

4 slices of sandwich-style rye bread

2 tablespoons or 30 grams regular or low-fat mayonnaise (do not use fat-free)

Eight 1-ounce or 30-gram slices of mild American cheese (often sold as squares in individually wrapped packets)

2 tablespoons or 30 grams purchased spicy or sweet pickle relish, dill pickle relish, jalapeño relish, or chowchow (do not use a super wet relish like corn relish)

6 ounces or 170 grams thinly sliced bologna

½ ounce or 15 grams plain potato chips (10 to 12 chips)

Master the Method

Melty cheese glues other ingredients in place in a sandwich. For the best sandwiches, always top or underlay loose ingredients with a slice of cheese because it melts and holds everything in place.

RAISE THE BAR

Although packaged sliced bologna might seem a natural for this sandwich, you can make better sandwiches with hand-sliced bologna from the deli counter. Ask for thin (but *not* paper thin) slices.

Or go nuts and use thinly sliced mortadella.

1. With the basket in the machine or the tray set at the center level in a toaster-oven-style model, heat an air fryer to 400°F or 200°C on the air fryer setting.

2. Set the bread slices on a cutting board or a clean work surface. Smear a quarter of the mayonnaise on the exposed side of each slice. Ⓐ

3. Flip two slices over (mayo-ed side down). Top these flipped slices each with two slices of cheese. Evenly spread the cheese with half of the relish or chowchow. Ⓑ

4. Divide the bologna in two stacks and set each in the heated air fryer. Ⓒ

5. Air-fry for about 3 minutes, until the top piece is sizzling and has begun to curl. Use nonstick-safe tongs to transfer the hot bologna stacks to each of the topped slices of bread, folding the bologna to fit as necessary. Ⓓ

6. Now top each with half of the potato chips and two more slices of cheese. Ⓔ

7. Set the other slice of bread mayo-ed side up on top of the sandwich. Press down gently to lightly crush the potato chips. Transfer the sandwiches to the air fryer. Air-fry for 4 minutes, then flip the sandwiches with nonstick-safe tongs. Continue air-frying for about 3 minutes, until browned and nicely crunchy at the edges. Use the nonstick-safe spatula to transfer the sandwiches to a wire rack and cool for a few minutes before slicing and serving. Ⓕ

Patty Melts

Our only problem with patty melts is the amount of cheese. Or more specifically, the lack thereof. Listen, the cheese should be gooey enough that it almost becomes the star of the sandwich. Almost. Sure, there's a hamburger patty in there. But the cheese is the thing. So we've increased the amount here to include both American-style cheddar and Swiss for the biggest cheese-to-burger proportions possible (before the sandwich falls apart under the sheer weight of its cheese).

1 small sweet yellow or white onion (preferably a Vidalia), peeled, halved, and sliced into thin half-moons

1 tablespoon or 15 grams butter, melted and cooled

12 ounces lean ground beef or 340 grams lean beef mince (at least 85% or even leaner—no worries about a dry sandwich with all the cheese)

1 tablespoon or 15 milliliters Worcestershire sauce

½ teaspoon ground black pepper

¼ teaspoon table salt

4 slices of sandwich-style rye bread (preferably a seedy rye)

8 teaspoons or 40 grams regular or low-fat mayonnaise (do not use fat-free)

Four 1-ounce or 30-gram slices of mild American-style cheddar cheese

Four 1-ounce or 30-gram slices of Swiss cheese

RAISE THE BAR

For a crisper and more buttery patty melt, swap out the mayonnaise and spread melted butter on the outside of the sandwiches. You'll need about 3 tablespoons or 45 grams butter, melted and cooled for a few minutes.

1. With the basket in the machine or the tray set at the center level in a toaster-oven-style model, heat an air fryer to 350°F or 180°C on the air fryer setting.

2. Toss the onions and melted butter in a small bowl until well coated. Spread the coated onions in the heated air fryer and cook for 6 minutes, tossing once or twice, until softened and a bit browned at the edges. Transfer the onions to a bowl (you can use the same bowl they were originally in). Ⓐ

3. Increase the air fryer's temperature to 375°F or 190°C. Mix the ground beef or beef mince, Worcestershire sauce, pepper, and salt in a medium bowl until uniform. (Your clean hands work best.) Form this mixture into two patties, each about the size of one of the slices of the rye bread. Ⓑ

4. Transfer the patties to the air fryer. Cook for 3 minutes, then flip the patties with a nonstick-safe spatula. Continue air-frying until browned and sizzling, about 3 more minutes. Ⓒ

5. Set the bread slices on a cutting board or a clean work surface. Slather the exposed side of each slice with about a quarter of the mayonnaise. Flip two slices over (now mayo-ed side down). Top each of these slices with half of the American cheese and half of the softened onions. Add a patty to each, then top each with half of the Swiss cheese. Close each sandwich with a second slice of bread, mayo-ed side up. Ⓓ

6. Transfer the sandwiches to the machine. Air-fry for 5 minutes, then flip the sandwiches over (with perhaps another spatula or the back of a wooden spoon in your other hand to steady the sandwich). Turning them is admittedly tricky. You can push the sandwiches back into shape if they slip off-kilter as they're turned. Ⓔ

7. Continue air-frying until lightly browned in spots and crispy, about 3 more minutes. Transfer the sandwiches to a wire rack and cool for a few minutes, then get them onto a cutting board, slice on the diagonal, and serve warm. Ⓕ

Tuna Melts

Tuna melts are often (and depressingly) just a toasted sandwich topped with canned tuna salad and maybe a perfunctory slice of American cheese for . . . color? Anyway, we wanted to make this sandwich the showstopper it can truly be, so we made a quick but super cheesy version of Mornay sauce in the microwave, mixed tuna salad ingredients into it, then used that mixture to top the sandwiches that are air-fried into a warm, melty fantasia on comfort food.

These are open-faced sandwiches, the better to get the cheesy mixture browned and bubbly. And they're a knife-and-fork meal because they're truly gooey, rich, and ever so satisfying.

½ cup plus 2 tablespoons or 155 milliliters whole or 2% milk

1 tablespoon all-purpose flour or 8 grams plain flour

3 ounces (¾ cup) or 85 grams shredded mild American-style cheddar cheese

One 5-ounce or 140-gram can of tuna packed in oil, preferably yellowfin, drained

2 tablespoons or 20 grams minced celery

1 tablespoon or 20 grams minced red onion

1 teaspoon or 5 milliliters Dijon mustard

½ teaspoon ground black pepper

¼ teaspoon table salt

2 slices of sandwich-style white, whole wheat, or rye bread

Nonstick spray

Master the Method

There's no worry about dropping the temperature if you repeatedly check on things in an air fryer. Because the internal area is small, the temperature doesn't drop drastically, especially in drawer-style machines.

1. With the basket in the machine or the tray set at the center level in a toaster-oven-style model, heat an air fryer to 375°F or 190°C on the air fryer setting.

2. Whisk the milk and flour in a large (at least 2-cup or 500-milliliter), microwave-safe measuring cup or bowl until smooth. Microwave on high in 30-second increments, whisking thoroughly after each, until thick and bubbling, about 1½, maybe 2 minutes in all, depending on the wattage of your microwave oven. Whisk in the cheese and cool for 5 minutes. (Do not stint on the cooling at this step.) Ⓐ

3. Mix the tuna, celery, onion, mustard, pepper, and salt in a large bowl. Pour in the cheese sauce and stir well. Ⓑ

4. Lightly coat one side of each slice of bread with nonstick spray. Set the bread slices sprayed side up in the machine and air-fry until *lightly* toasted, 2 to 3 minutes. Ⓒ

5. Transfer the bread, sprayed side down, to a cutting board. Spoon and spread half of the tuna mixture on top of each slice of bread. Ⓓ

6. Transfer the sandwiches, tuna side up, back to the air fryer. Air-fry *undisturbed* until brown and bubbling, about 5 minutes. Transfer the sandwiches to serving plates with a nonstick-safe spatula. (They're too drippy for a wire rack). Cool for a few minutes before serving with a knife and fork. Ⓔ

RAISE THE BAR

Add up to 1 peeled and minced medium garlic clove (about 1 teaspoon) with the celery and onion.

Swap in minced shallot for the red onion.

For more crunch, double the celery.

Add up to ¼ teaspoon grated nutmeg and/or ¼ teaspoon cayenne with the cheese.

Honest-to-Goodness Croque Monsieurs

We're not sure how a croque monsieur got designated as street food. It was once a sit-down bistro favorite sandwich. We've improved on the classic by making it more saucy, more decadent. Why not, if you're going to sit down and enjoy it?

We have, however, modified the recipe for simplicity. Rather than battering the sandwich, we've topped it with a rich, creamy sauce in the air fryer. We've also made that béchamel sauce in a microwave, rather than on the stovetop, in a bid for lots of rich goodness with little fuss.

⅔ cup or 160 milliliters whole or 2% milk

1 tablespoon or 15 grams butter

1 tablespoon or 8 grams all-purpose flour

¼ teaspoon table salt

¼ teaspoon ground black pepper

⅛ teaspoon grated nutmeg or a pinch of ground nutmeg

4 slices of sandwich-style white bread

1 tablespoon or 15 grams Dijon mustard

Eight 1-ounce or 30-gram slices of Swiss or Gruyère cheese

Four 1½-ounce or 45-gram slices of deli ham

Nonstick spray

RAISE THE BAR

Stir up to ¼ teaspoon dried thyme into the sauce.

Sprinkle the cheese-covered sandwiches with mild paprika before air-frying.

And/or dot the sauce with a few dashes of red hot sauce before adding the cheese and air-frying.

1. Put the milk and butter in a large (at least 2-cup or 500-milliliter), microwave-safe measuring cup or bowl. Microwave on high for 1 minute, until the butter has melted and the milk is hot. Whisk in the flour, salt, pepper, and nutmeg. Microwave on high in 20-second increments, whisking well after each, until thickened a bit and bubbling, 1 minute, maybe less, depending on the wattage of your microwave. Ⓐ

2. With the basket in the machine or the tray set at the center level in a toaster-oven-style model, heat an air fryer to 400°F or 200°C on the air fryer setting.

3. Set two slices of bread on a cutting board or a clean work surface. Smear half of the Dijon across one side of each slice of bread. Ⓑ

4. Set the bread, mustard side up, on a cutting board. Set two slices of cheese and two slices of ham on top of each sandwich. Set the second slice of bread on top of the sandwich. Generously spray the bread on the top of the sandwich with nonstick spray. (Do not spray both sides of the sandwich.) Ⓒ

5. Transfer the sandwiches, sprayed side up and without touching, to the air fryer. Work in batches if necessary. Air-fry for 2 minutes, then flip the sandwiches with a nonstick-safe spatula. (And perhaps another spatula, the back of a wooden spoon, or even a flatware tablespoon in your other hand to steady the sandwich.) Ⓓ

6. Spread half of the prepared milk sauce (or béchamel) on top of each sandwich. Top each sandwich with two slices of cheese. Ⓔ

7. Air-fry *undisturbed* for about 7 more minutes, until the cheese on top and even some of the sauce underneath the cheese is lightly browned and bubbling. Use the spatula to transfer the sandwiches to serving plates. Cool for at least 5 minutes before serving with a knife and fork. Ⓕ

A

B

C

D

E

F

Hot Browns

Talk about rich! This variation on a Welsh rarebit was invented at the Brown Hotel in Louisville, Kentucky, during the roaring 1920s when a splurge always seemed in order. It's made with Mornay sauce, a cheesy variation on béchamel.

We've made things easier by developing a microwave version of the classic sauce, although the sandwich is still a decided splurge. Keep plenty of paper napkins on hand for the inevitable drips.

4 thick-cut slices of U.S.-style bacon, halved widthwise

1 cup or 250 milliliters whole or 2% milk

1½ tablespoons all-purpose flour or 10 grams plain flour

½ teaspoon table salt

½ teaspoon ground black pepper

¼ teaspoon grated nutmeg or a pinch of ground nutmeg

1 ounce (¼ cup) or 30 grams grated Swiss cheese

2 slices of country- or farmhouse-style white sandwich bread

Four 1½-ounce or 40-gram slices of deli turkey

Two 1½-ounce or 40-gram slices of deli ham

1 medium ripe tomato, thickly sliced

Master the Method

If you need extra balance when transferring gooey things or heavy dishes to a rack, use the back of a large wooden spoon in your other hand to balance the food or the dish by holding it *on the side*, rather than smooshing down the melty bits on top.

RAISE THE BAR

Substitute shredded Gruyère for the Swiss.

Whisk up to ⅛ teaspoon cayenne into the sauce with the cheese.

Although *not* traditional, we like hot browns with thin dill pickle slices interlayered with the tomato slices before the sauce is added.

1. With the basket in the machine or the tray set at the center level in a toaster-oven-style model, heat an air fryer to 400°F or 200°C on the air fryer setting.

2. Set the bacon slices in a single layer in the air fryer and air-fry until cooked through, about 4 minutes (maybe a little less if you like softer bacon, more if you like a little carbon). Transfer the bacon to a plate using nonstick-safe tongs. Ⓐ

3. Whisk the milk, flour, salt, pepper, and nutmeg in a large (2-cup or so), microwave-safe measuring cup or bowl until the flour dissolves. Microwave on high in 15-second increments, whisking well after each, until bubbling, 1½ to 2 minutes in all, depending on the wattage of your microwave. Add the cheese while the sauce is very hot and whisk until smooth. Ⓑ

4. In a 6-cup or 1½-liter air fryer–safe baking dish, set two slices of bread and top each with two slices of turkey, one slice of ham, and a tomato slice. Ⓒ

5. Pour or spoon the cheese sauce evenly over the top of each sandwich. (Scrape out every drop!) Ⓓ

6. Set the baking dish in the heated machine and air-fry for about 8 minutes, or until lightly browned and bubbling. Use hot pads to transfer the hot (!) baking dish to a wire rack. Top each sandwich with an equal portion of the bacon. Cool for a couple of minutes, then use a spatula to transfer the sandwiches to serving plates. Serve warm with a knife and fork. Ⓔ

French Dip

Time was, a French dip sandwich was the height of lunch elegance—with a martini, natch. These days, we're too old to handle distilled pleasures in the middle of the day; but we do know how to make this old-school favorite easy enough to whip up at lunch, with a little help from the air fryer.

First off, we've got to get the right spice blend for the classic taste. But the real secret is the addition of packaged onion soup mix in the dip. It gives the dip just the right flavor. However, onion soup mix can be extremely salty, so we tested this recipe with a low-sodium mix and much preferred it.

½ teaspoon ground rosemary

½ teaspoon dried oregano

½ teaspoon dried thyme

½ teaspoon garlic powder

½ teaspoon ground black pepper

1 teaspoon or 5 milliliters Worcestershire sauce

6 ounces or 170 grams thinly sliced rare deli roast beef, cut widthwise into ½-inch or 1-centimeter wide strips

1 medium yellow or white onion, peeled, halved, and cut into thin half-moons

Nonstick spray

Two 4-inch or 10-centimeter sections of a crusty baguette, split lengthwise into halves

2 tablespoons or 30 grams butter

¾ cup or 185 milliliters beef broth, preferably low-sodium broth

1½ tablespoons or 10 grams onion soup mix

2 tablespoons or 30 milliliters beer, ale, or dry sherry

½ teaspoon granulated white sugar

RAISE THE BAR

Although deli roast beef is an easy ingredient to find, these sandwiches are delicious with leftover London broil or even prime rib. Make sure the meat is sliced into very thin strips.

1. With the basket in the machine or the tray set at the center level in a toaster-oven-style model, heat an air fryer to 400°F or 200°C on the air fryer setting.

2. Combine the rosemary, oregano, thyme, garlic powder, and black pepper in a small bowl until uniform. Pour the Worcestershire sauce into a large bowl and stir in about half of this dried spice mixture. Put the beef in that large bowl and toss well to coat. Ⓐ

3. Generously coat the onion half-moons with nonstick spray, set them in the air fryer, and cook for 3 minutes, tossing once, until somewhat softened. Push the onions to one side of the air fryer basket or cooking tray. Set the beef in the empty part of the basket or tray. Ⓑ

4. Air-fry for 5 minutes, until the beef is sizzling and cooked through, tossing the beef and onions separately at least once. Ⓒ

5. Transfer the beef and onions to a clean bowl. Lay the baguette sections cut side up on a cutting board. Smear the cut side of each with a quarter of the butter. Set the sections buttered side up in the air fryer and cook about 2 minutes, or until crusty at the edges and a little browned in the centers. Ⓓ

6. Transfer the baguette sections cut side up to a wire rack with nonstick-safe tongs. Cool for a few minutes, then top the two bottom baguette sections evenly with the beef and onions. Set a second "top" slice cut side down on each to close the sandwich. Ⓔ

7. To make the dipping sauce, whisk the remaining dried spice mixture into the broth in a small microwave-safe bowl. Whisk in the onion soup mix, the beer or its substitute, and the sugar. Heat in the microwave on high until simmering, 1 to 1½ minutes, depending on the wattage of your microwave. Serve along with the sandwiches. Ⓕ

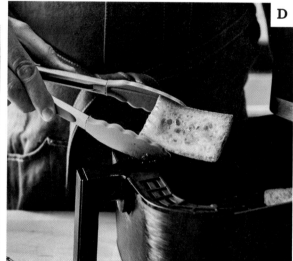

Butter Burgers

Culver's, the U.S. chain originally from the Midwest, started a craze decades ago for butter burgers. How could we resist creating a version for the air fryer? But we couldn't just top patties with butter, lest it melt too quickly, run off the burger, and burn in the tray or drawer. Rather, we needed to create patties with grated butter mixed into the meat.

You'll need to start early in the day because the shredded butter has to be good and cold inside the patty when it goes into the air fryer.

We suggest using lean ground beef (or beef mince), preferably ground sirloin, because of, well, all the butter. But the drier meat will not make a successful burger at medium-well or well-done. Make these patties a little rarer so the butter stays inside and the meat stays unbelievably decadent.

4 tablespoons (½ stick) or 60 grams *cold* butter

12 ounces lean ground beef or 340 grams lean beef mince, preferably ground sirloin

1 tablespoon or 5 grams minced dehydrated onion

½ teaspoon table salt

½ teaspoon ground black pepper

¼ teaspoon garlic powder

2 plain hamburger buns, preferably brioche buns

Condiments of your choice, such as mustard, mayonnaise, ketchup, iceberg lettuce leaves, and/or sliced tomatoes

Master the Method

The space inside an air fryer is so small that you don't need to worry about hot and cool spots. When you heat a standard oven, it's always best to let it rest at the desired temperature for perhaps 5 minutes before you begin cooking or baking to make sure the larger space is evenly heated. Not so with a small air fryer.

RAISE THE BAR

Brush the cut side of each burger bun with the juices that have dripped into the bottom of the basket or onto the drip tray in toaster-oven-style machines. Set the buns cut side up in the machine and air-fry until lightly toasted, about 1 minute.

1. Grate the butter through the large holes of a box grater into a bowl. Ⓐ

2. Crumble the ground beef into the bowl. Add the dehydrated onion, salt, pepper, and garlic powder. Mix until well combined, either using a rubber spatula or your clean hands. The butter should still be in distinct threads. Ⓑ

3. Divide this mixture in half and form into two patties about 4 inches or 10 centimeters in diameter and slightly thicker at the centers than the edges. Set them on a small cutting board or plate, cover with plastic wrap, and refrigerate for at least 2 hours or up to 6 hours. Ⓒ

4. With the basket in the machine or the tray set at the center level in a toaster-oven-style model, heat an air fryer to 400°F or 200°C on the air fryer setting.

5. Set the patties in the machine with a little space between them. Air-fry for 4 minutes, then flip the burgers over with a nonstick-safe spatula or tongs. Ⓓ

6. Continue air-frying for 2 more minutes, or until medium-rare to medium inside. An instant-read meat thermometer inserted into one burger will register 130°F or 55°C for medium-rare (not USDA approved) or 140°F or 60°C for medium (USDA approved). Transfer the patties to a cutting board and build two burgers with the buns and the condiments of your choice. Ⓔ

Juicy Lucys

A Juicy Lucy is an inside-out cheeseburger, the cheese tucked inside the meat patty. Although it's something of a fad now, we're not really following a trend for this recipe: This sort of cheeseburger actually works better than a standard, cheese-topped patty in an air fryer because the cheese doesn't bubble and burn in the heat.

Use lean ground beef (or beef mince). The less fat, the less chance the meat will shrink and open up to let the cheese escape during cooking.

Take care to cool these sandwiches a bit before serving. That melted cheese inside is scalding hot!

12 ounces lean ground beef or 340 grams lean beef mince, preferably 90% lean or more

½ teaspoon onion powder

½ teaspoon table salt

½ teaspoon ground black pepper

¼ teaspoon garlic powder

Four 1-ounce or 30-gram slices of mild or sharp American-style cheddar, Swiss, or Monterey Jack cheese

2 regular or whole wheat hamburger buns

Condiments of your choice, such as mayonnaise, ketchup, mustard, Russian dressing, relish of any sort, lettuce, tomatoes, thinly sliced red onion, and/or pickle slices

Master the Method

Burger patties can make quite a mess. Clean your air fryer well after a recipe like this one to avoid a smoking machine in the future.

RAISE THE BAR

Use a fancier cheese, like thin slices of Brie (rind removed) or Camembert.

Toast the buns: Set them cut side up in a 400°F or 200°C air fryer for 1 to 2 minutes. Even better, brush them with softened butter first.

1. With the basket in the machine or the tray set at the center level in a toaster-oven-style model, heat an air fryer to 400°F or 200°C on the air fryer setting.

2. Mix the ground beef, onion powder, salt, pepper, and garlic powder in a large bowl until the spices are uniform throughout. (Your clean hands work best.) Divide this mixture into four even balls. On a cutting board or a clean work surface, flatten each into a patty that's 5 inches or 13 centimeters in diameter. **Ⓐ**

3. Set two slices of cheese on top of each of two of the patties, folding over or even breaking the corners and setting the extra on top to make the cheese slices fit on the patty with a distinct edge of meat all around. **Ⓑ**

4. Cover each cheese-topped patty with a second patty. Seal the edges well by pinching them together all around. **Ⓒ**

5. Transfer the patties to the air fryer. Air-fry for 5 minutes, then flip the patties with a nonstick-safe spatula (and maybe a rubber spatula in the other hand for balance). **Ⓓ**

6. Continue air-frying until cooked through, about 5 more minutes. Transfer the patties to the buns and cool for at least 5 minutes, especially if you're offering them to children. Serve with all the condiments of your choice. **Ⓔ**

Super Juicy Chicken Burgers and Veggie Tot Dinner

Here's a full meal, right out of an air fryer! Admittedly, chicken burgers can be depressingly dry because ground chicken is so low in fat. But we've solved that problem by adding shredded zucchini to the mix. In fact, zucchini is so loaded with water that the shreds *must* be squeezed dry before cooking to make sure the patties don't get soggy. But we can then guarantee these burgers stay moist for the long haul in the machine.

Because undercooked ground chicken presents distinct health concerns, use an instant-read meat thermometer to make sure the burgers are cooked through.

1 small zucchini

12 ounces ground chicken or 340 grams chicken mince (do not use only white meat chicken)

1 small single-lobe shallot, peeled and minced

1 tablespoon or 15 milliliters lemon juice

1 medium garlic clove, peeled and minced (about 1 teaspoon)

½ teaspoon dried thyme

½ teaspoon table salt

½ teaspoon ground black pepper

Nonstick spray

One 14-ounce or 400-gram bag of frozen veggie tots, such as cauliflower and sweet potato tots (*do not thaw*)

2 regular or whole wheat hamburger buns

Condiments of your choice, particularly mustard, chutney, chowchow, jalapeño relish, or dill pickle relish

Master the Method

Never spritz nonstick spray (or any oil spray) directly into an air fryer. The droplets will go everywhere and coat everything inside, eventually causing the machine to smoke.

RAISE THE BAR

Sprinkle a dried barbecue rub on the tots before you air-fry them.

Drizzle the crunchy tots with syrupy balsamic vinegar.

1. With the basket in the machine or the tray set at the center level in a toaster-oven-style model, heat an air fryer to 400°F or 200°C on the air fryer setting.

2. Shred the zucchini through the large holes of a box grater onto a cutting board. Squeeze the zucchini threads dry in small handfuls over a bowl or the sink before transferring them to a medium bowl. **A**

3. Crumble in the ground chicken. Add the shallot, lemon juice, garlic, thyme, salt, and pepper. Mix until uniform. (Your clean hands work best.) **B**

4. Divide this mixture into two even balls and form them into patties about 4 inches or 10 centimeters in diameter. Coat the patties generously with nonstick spray *on both sides*. **C**

5. Transfer the patties to the air fryer. Air-fry for 4 minutes, then turn the patties over and move them to one side of the basket or the cooking tray. Pile the veggie tots in a low mound on the other side of the basket or the cooking tray. **D**

6. Continue air-frying, tossing the tots twice, for about 10 more minutes, or until an instant-read meat thermometer inserted into one of the patties registers 165°F or 75°C. Transfer the patties to the buns and cool for a couple of minutes. Serve with the condiments of your choice and the tots on the side. **E**

Thanksgiving Turkey Burgers

Even if these patties boast the flavors of our favorite holiday, we can enjoy them all year. They're super juicy, thanks to the way the cornbread stuffing mix absorbs the turkey "juices" as the patties cook, and the little bit of canned sweet potatoes adds a nice touch of holiday flavor. (Freeze each of the remaining canned sweet potatoes in small sealed bags, so you can make the burgers anytime you want.)

Although ground white-meat turkey is certainly leaner, it won't make as successful a burger patty here because we're not adding an egg or other fat to the mix. We want the meat to be a little fattier to make a better meal.

½ cup or 30 grams purchased dry cornbread stuffing mix

1½ pounds or 680 grams ground turkey, preferably a combination of white and dark meat

2 rounded tablespoons or 20 grams dried cranberries, chopped

2 packed tablespoons or 30 grams canned sweet potatoes

2 tablespoons or 15 grams minced red onion

½ teaspoon ground sage

½ teaspoon table salt

¼ teaspoon celery seeds

¼ teaspoon grated nutmeg or a pinch of ground nutmeg

Nonstick spray

4 regular or whole wheat hamburger buns

Whole berry cranberry sauce and Dijon mustard, for condiments

Master the Method

Chopping dried fruit can be a pain. Coat a chopping knife with nonstick spray to make the job easier.

RAISE THE BAR

Although we suggest cranberry sauce and mustard as the condiments, swap these out for chutney and mayonnaise or ginger jam and chili crisp.

1. With the basket in the machine or the tray set at the center level in a toaster-oven-style model, heat an air fryer to 400°F or 200°C on the air fryer setting.

2. Put the cornbread stuffing mix in a food processor or a turbo blender, cover, and process or blend until finely ground but not powdery. Pour the ground stuffing mix into a large bowl. **A**

3. Crumble the ground turkey into the bowl. Add the dried cranberries, sweet potatoes, onion, sage, salt, celery seeds, and nutmeg. Mix well until uniformly combined. **B**

4. Form this turkey mixture into four even patties, each about 5 inches or 13 centimeters in diameter. **C**

5. Generously coat *both sides* of the patties with nonstick spray. **D**

6. Set the patties in the machine without touching. Work in batches as necessary. Air-fry for 10 minutes. Flip the patties with a nonstick-safe spatula. Continue air-frying for about 10 more minutes, or until browned and sizzling—and most importantly, until an instant-read meat thermometer inserted into the center of one patty registers at least 165°F or 75°C. **E**

7. Slather the buns with the cranberry sauce and mustard. Transfer the patties to the buns and serve warm. **F**

Choose-Your-Bean Burgers

This recipe lets you customize bean burgers to your heart's content. You can use any sort of bean as well as any sort of chopped shelled nut you prefer. But here's one important note: Dried beans that are cooked from scratch will unfortunately not be soft enough for success. You must use drained and rinsed *canned* beans.

The rolled oats are crucial to these patties. Flour or cornstarch tend to make bean burgers gummy, but oats provide the "adhesion" with better texture.

1 large single-lobe shallot, peeled and quartered

Nonstick spray

One 15-ounce or 425-gram can of pinto, white, black, kidney, Great Northern, or cannellini beans, drained and rinsed in a colander to get rid of the slimy foam

½ cup or 70 grams raw shelled almonds, walnuts, pecans, or cashews

½ cup or 45 grams standard rolled oats (do not use quick-cooking or steel-cut oats)

1 large egg

1 teaspoon table salt

½ teaspoon ground cinnamon

½ teaspoon ground cumin

½ teaspoon ground black pepper

4 regular or whole wheat hamburger buns

Condiments of your choice, including mayonnaise, iceberg lettuce leaves, sliced tomato, and/or thinly sliced red onion

Master the Method

Since air fryers work by desiccating food in a hot wind, a little fat is almost always helpful. An easy and natural way to add it to patties (as here) or even crumb coatings is to add some ground or finely chopped shelled nuts.

RAISE THE BAR

Even crazier condiments include fig jam, sriracha, drained salsa, and/or pickled jalapeño rings.

Make slightly healthier bean burgers by using only 1 large egg *white*.

1. With the basket in the machine or the tray set at the center level in a toaster-oven-style model, heat an air fryer to 400°F or 200°C on the air fryer setting.

2. Generously coat the shallot quarters with nonstick spray. Set the quarters in the air fryer and air-fry until softened and browned at the edges, about 10 minutes. Ⓐ

3. Transfer the shallot to a food processor and cool for a few minutes. Add the beans, nuts, oats, egg, salt, cinnamon, cumin, and black pepper. Ⓑ

4. Cover and process into a thick paste, scraping down the inside of the canister at least once. Ⓒ

5. Scrape down and remove the blade. Form the bean mixture into four even patties, each about 4 inches or 10 centimeters in diameter. Generously coat them on both sides with nonstick spray. Ⓓ

6. Set the patties in the air fryer and cook for 4 minutes. Flip them over with a nonstick-safe spatula and continue air-frying for 4 minutes, or until the patties are a bit browned and firm. Ⓔ

7. Smear the cut sides of the buns with mayonnaise. Transfer the patties to the buns and add the lettuce, tomato, and/or red onion as desired. Serve warm. Ⓕ

Copycat Fried Chicken Sandwiches

This recipe is a copycat of the famous chicken sandwiches sold at Popeyes. You know: the sandwiches people line up for miles to order. Our air fryer version is perhaps simpler than you might expect, but let's face it: The original is actually not all that complex. It's the simple mix of a tangy coating, mayonnaise, and zippy pickles that does the trick.

That said, you want to aim for a generous, thick coating on the chicken breasts before air-frying. And by the way, briny pickles are *the* essential condiment for the classic flavor.

1 cup or 250 milliliters regular or low-fat buttermilk (do not use fat-free)

1 cup all-purpose flour or 120 grams plain flour

3 tablespoons or 20 grams cornstarch

1 tablespoon mild smoked paprika

1½ teaspoons table salt

1 teaspoon garlic powder

1 teaspoon onion powder

¼ teaspoon cayenne

Ground black pepper, to taste

Four 5- to 6-ounce or 140- to 170-gram boneless skinless chicken breasts

Nonstick spray

¼ cup or 55 grams regular, low-fat, or fat-free mayonnaise

2 teaspoons or 10 milliliters sriracha, Texas Pete, or other thick red hot sauce

4 brioche buns

Dill pickle strips, for garnishing

Master the Method

If you don't want to use your clean hands, nonstick-safe tongs work best for dredging cuts of meat or vegetables in various coatings. But don't forget to coat the part of the food that is grasped by the tongs. Set the food down in the liquid or dry ingredients, then pick it up at another spot for an even coating.

1. With the basket in the machine or the tray set at the center level in a toaster-oven-style model, heat an air fryer to 400°F or 200°C on the air fryer setting.

2. Pour the buttermilk into a shallow soup plate, small pie plate, or medium food storage container. Whisk the flour, cornstarch, smoked paprika, salt, garlic powder, onion powder, cayenne, and black pepper in a second shallow soup plate, small pie plate, or food storage container until uniform. **A**

3. Submerge one chicken breast in the buttermilk, turning to coat on all sides. Do not let the excess buttermilk run off; immediately transfer the chicken breast to the flour mixture and dredge it generously on all sides to get a decent coating. **B**

4. Set aside this coated chicken breast on a cutting board and do the same with the remaining chicken breasts. Generously coat the breasts *on all sides* (even the edges) with nonstick spray. **C**

5. Set the coated chicken breasts in the machine. Air-fry for 7 minutes, then gently flip the chicken pieces over with nonstick-safe tongs. (Be gentle: Try not to disturb the coating.) Continue air-frying for 7 minutes, or until browned, crispy, and cooked through. **D**

6. Transfer the chicken breasts to a wire rack. Again, be gentle to preserve the coating. Whisk the mayonnaise and hot sauce in a small bowl until uniform. Smear this mixture over the cut sides of the brioche buns. **E**

7. Lay dill pickle strips on the bottom halves of the buns. Top with the chicken breasts. (You can cut the breasts to fit the buns or let the chicken overhang at will.) Close the sandwiches with the bun tops before serving warm. **F**

Crispy Fish Fillet Sandwiches

Battered or crumbed? That's always the question when it comes to the fillets in fried fish sandwiches. Why decide? We opted for both for a rich, maximum crunch.

We developed a creamy batter that will stick to the fillets (thanks to the flour in the mix). Then we dredged the fillets in panko bread crumbs for tons of crunch per bite from an air fryer. Thus, we get the best of both worlds: an irresistibly rich *but still* crunchy coating.

2 cups or 100 grams plain panko bread crumbs

2 large eggs

¼ cup or 55 grams regular or low-fat mayonnaise (do not use fat-free)

1 tablespoon or 15 grams Dijon mustard

1 tablespoon all-purpose flour or 8 grams plain flour

½ teaspoon mild paprika

½ teaspoon onion powder

½ teaspoon tablespoon salt

½ teaspoon ground black pepper

Four 4- to 6-ounce or 115- to 140-gram cod fillet sections (thawed if frozen)

Nonstick spray

4 white burger buns, preferably potato buns

Purchased tartar sauce (or for a homemade version, see Raise the Bar, page 194), as a condiment

Master the Method

How toasted bread should be is a matter of personal taste. One of us likes a little carbon with every sandwich; the other, none. Open the machine repeatedly to check on the state of bread or buns.

RAISE THE BAR

Add a slice of sharp American-style cheddar cheese to each sandwich.

Sprinkle the crispy fish fillets with malt vinegar before building the sandwiches.

1. With the basket in the machine or the tray set at the center level in a toaster-oven-style model, heat an air fryer to 400°F or 200°C on the air fryer setting.

2. Spread the bread crumbs in a shallow soup plate, small pie plate, or medium food storage container. Whisk the eggs, mayonnaise, mustard, flour, paprika, onion powder, salt, and pepper in a second shallow soup plate, small pie plate, or medium food storage container until uniform. **A**

3. Set all of the fish fillets in the egg mixture and turn them to coat. If your containers or bowls are small, you'll need to work in batches in this step. **B**

4. Pick up one coated fillet from the egg mixture and set in the bread crumbs. Turn repeatedly, pressingly gently, to coat all sides with the bread crumbs. Transfer to a cutting board and repeat with the remaining fillets. **C**

5. Generously coat the fillets *on all sides* with nonstick spray. **D**

6. Set the fillets without touching in the heated machine and air-fry *undisturbed* for 10 minutes, or until browned with a crisp coating. Gently transfer the fillets to a wire rack. Be careful to keep the coating intact. Lightly coat the cut side of the buns with nonstick spray. Set them cut side up in the machine and air-fry for about 2 minutes, or until very lightly toasted. (Be careful: They can dry out.) Work in batches as necessary. **E**

7. Transfer the buns cut side up to a cutting board. Slather the bottom halves with tartar sauce and top each with a fish fillet. Close the buns and serve with more tartar sauce on the side for dipping. **F**

Shrimp Po'Boy Sandwiches

What could be bad about a fried shrimp sandwich? Not much—except (depending on your preferences) the *very* spicy heat in some traditional versions of a Louisiana po'boy and all the salt from both the shrimp and the spice blend. Check that your Cajun blend isn't just mildly seasoned cayenne. It should have a range of spices, not just the burn. And if salt is near the top of the list of the ingredients, cut down on the amount that goes into the flour mixture.

Since you'll be eating the shrimp in a sandwich, make sure they're fully peeled—that is, no little remainder of shell at the very ends of their tails.

¾ cup or 120 grams yellow cornmeal

¾ cup all-purpose flour or 90 grams plain flour

1 tablespoon dried Cajun seasoning blend

1 teaspoon table salt

½ teaspoon ground black pepper

1 cup or 250 milliliters regular or low-fat buttermilk (do not use fat-free)

1 tablespoon plus 2 teaspoons or 25 milliliters sriracha, Texas Pete, Frank's RedHot, or other thick red hot sauce

1 pound or 450 grams medium shrimp (20 to 24 shrimp), peeled and deveined

Nonstick spray

½ cup or 115 grams regular, low-fat, or fat-free mayonnaise

2 tablespoons or 30 grams pickle relish

Up to 1 small single-lobe shallot, minced

4 French bread rolls

Shredded iceberg lettuce and thinly sliced ripe tomatoes, for garnishing

RAISE THE BAR

Although not traditional by any means, we've been known to add dill pickle sandwich slices or pickled jalapeño rings to the sandwiches with the lettuce and tomato.

1. With the basket in the machine or the tray set at the center level in a toaster-oven-style model, heat an air fryer to 400°F or 200°C on the air fryer setting.

2. Whisk the cornmeal, flour, Cajun seasoning, salt, and pepper in a shallow soup plate, small pie plate, or medium food storage container until uniform. Whisk the buttermilk and 1 tablespoon or 15 milliliters of the hot sauce in a second pie plate or shallow soup plate until uniform. Add the shrimp to the buttermilk mixture. Ⓐ

3. Stir the shrimp well but gently to coat them. Transfer them one by one to the flour mixture. Turn and press gently to coat well on all sides. Transfer the coated shrimp to a cutting board and continue dredging the remaining shrimp in the flour mixture. Ⓑ

4. Generously coat *both sides* of the dredged shrimp with nonstick spray. Transfer the shrimp to the machine in as much of a single layer as possible. (Some tails can lie under other tails.) Ⓒ

5. Air-fry for 4 minutes, then gently flip the shrimp with nonstick-safe tongs. Continue air-frying for 3 more minutes, or until lightly browned and crunchy. Transfer the shrimp to a wire rack. Ⓓ

6. Make the sauce by whisking the mayonnaise, relish, shallot, and remaining 2 teaspoons or 10 milliliters red hot sauce in a small bowl until uniform. Ⓔ

7. Make the sandwiches by opening the rolls, then lining them with lettuce and tomato, as well as equal portions of fried shrimp. Generously dollop the sauce on each sandwich to serve, reserving more of the sauce for extra bites. Ⓕ

Artichoke and Olive Gyros

Sure, you can roast a leg of lamb for authentic gyros. But why take all day to make a simple pita sandwich? This easy recipe uses the air fryer to make a heavily seasoned lamb "meat loaf" that you then slice into wedges to put into pita pockets.

We also provide a basic tzatziki recipe, an essential element to that classic gyro flavor. But if you want to make your life easier, look for ready-made tzatziki at the deli counter of a larger or high-end supermarket.

If you don't need to make four sandwiches at once, you can cool the lamb meat loaf, set it on a plate, seal under plastic wrap, and refrigerate for up to 3 days. Warm up slices in a microwave for 30 seconds or so to take the chill off.

12 ounces ground lamb or 340 grams lamb mince

¼ pound lean ground beef or 115 grams lean beef mince, at least 90% lean or more

3 canned artichoke hearts packed in water, *squeezed dry* and chopped

¼ cup or 40 grams black pitted olives, chopped

1 tablespoon or 15 grams tomato paste

1 teaspoon dried oregano

½ teaspoon ground cinnamon

½ teaspoon dried thyme

1 teaspoon table salt

¾ teaspoon ground black pepper

1 medium cucumber, peeled, seeded, and chopped

1 cup or 230 grams regular or low-fat plain yogurt (do not use Greek yogurt)

1 tablespoon or 15 milliliters lemon juice

1½ teaspoons dried dill

4 regular or whole wheat pita pockets

Thinly sliced red onion rings

Chopped cherry or plum tomatoes, for garnishing

1. With the basket in the machine or the tray set at the center level in a toaster-oven-style model, heat an air fryer to 375°F or 190°C on the air fryer setting.

2. Crumble the ground lamb and beef into a large bowl. Add the artichoke hearts, olives, tomato paste, oregano, cinnamon, thyme, ½ teaspoon of the salt, and ½ teaspoon of the pepper. Mix well until uniform. (Your clean hands work best.) Form this meat mixture into a 6 x 4-inch or 15 x 10-centimeter loaf. Ⓐ

3. Transfer the loaf to the machine. Air-fry for 15 minutes. Use a large nonstick-safe spatula as well as nonstick-safe tongs to turn the loaf over. Ⓑ

4. Continue air-frying for 10 more minutes, or until cooked through and an instant-read meat thermometer inserted into the center of the loaf registers 165°F or 75°C. Transfer the loaf to a cutting board. Ⓒ

5. Stir the cucumber, yogurt, lemon juice, dill, remaining ½ teaspoon salt, and remaining ¼ teaspoon pepper in a medium bowl until well combined. Ⓓ

6. Carve the loaf into ½-inch or 1-centimeter thick slices. (There will be inevitable crumbling. No worries: It's all going in pita pockets.) Fill the pita pockets with some sliced red onion, then slices (and crumbles) of the loaf. Garnish with the chopped tomatoes and the cucumber sauce. Ⓔ

RAISE THE BAR

Substitute pickled red onion slices for the raw. To make them, thinly slice 1 peeled large red onion and pack the rings into a quart-sized or 1-liter canning jar. Bring ¾ cup or 185 milliliters apple cider vinegar, ¼ cup or 60 milliliters water, 1½ tablespoons or 18 grams granulated white sugar, and 1 teaspoon kosher salt to a boil in a medium saucepan, stirring constantly until the sugar dissolves. Pour this hot mixture over the onion slices and let stand for 30 minutes. Use at once or cover and refrigerate for up to 2 weeks.

Super Crispy Burritos

Sure, we love to cook plain ol' frozen burritos in an air fryer. But why not use this kitchen tool to its max? We give those frozen burritos a crunchy coating, all in a bid to turn them into newfangled, easier versions of old-fashioned chimichangas.

We tested this recipe with frozen beef-and-bean burritos, but any sort will do well so long as you keep the size the same.

For the coating, use plain salty tortilla chips, rather than flavored ones, so the burrito filling has no competition.

---

2 large eggs

2 tablespoons or 30 milliliters sriracha, Texas Pete, Frank's RedHot, or other thick red hot sauce

½ teaspoon ground cumin

6 ounces or 170 grams tortilla chips

Six 4-ounce or 115-gram frozen burritos (*do not thaw*)

Nonstick spray

Master the Method

When frozen items need to get into an air fryer at once, have everything else prepped and ready so that you can work quickly. Many items thaw quickly at room temperature.

RAISE THE BAR

Want sweeter burritos with less heat? Substitute any smooth barbecue sauce for the hot sauce.

Garnish the warm burritos with sour cream, salsa, pickled jalapeño rings, and/or shredded cheese.

1. With the basket in the machine or the tray set at the center level in a toaster-oven-style model, heat an air fryer to 375°F or 190°C on the air fryer setting.

2. Whisk the eggs, red hot sauce, and cumin in a shallow soup plate, small pie plate, or medium food storage container until uniform with no bits of egg white floating in the mix. **A**

3. Grind the tortilla chips in a closed food processor until fine crumbs but not dust. Pour the ground chips into a second shallow soup plate, small pie plate, or medium food storage container. **B**

4. Dip a frozen burrito in the egg mixture, turning it to coat on all sides. Pick it up to let the excess drain off, then set it in the ground chips. Gently roll it around to coat all sides (even the ends). **C**

5. Transfer the coated burrito to a cutting board and repeat the process in step 4 for the remaining burritos. Generously coat them with nonstick spray *on all sides* (even the ends). **D**

6. Transfer the burritos to the heated machine and place in a single layer without touching. Work in batches if necessary. Air-fry for 8 minutes. Gently flip over the burritos with nonstick-safe tongs (to preserve the coating) and *continue* air-frying for about 8 more minutes, until browned and crispy. Transfer the burritos to a wire rack to cool for at least 5 minutes before serving warm or at room temperature. **E**

Fried Philly Cheesesteak Wrap

Why a wrap and not just the traditional sandwich for this classic? Because the air fryer is all about crunch. And putting a tortilla wrap in the machine lets us get the maximum crunch, thereby honoring what the machine does best while preserving the flavors of the real Philly.

We know there are great debates among American-style cheddar fans, provolone fans, and Cheez Whiz fans. You can see our choice. Otherwise, talk among yourselves and adjust the recipe to your liking.

6 ounces or 170 grams thinly sliced rare deli roast beef

½ teaspoon table salt

Ground black pepper, to taste

1 medium yellow or white onion, peeled and thinly sliced

Nonstick spray

Two 10-inch or 25-centimeter "burrito-size" flour tortillas

2 tablespoons or 30 grams butter, softened to room temperature

¼ teaspoon garlic powder

4 thin round slices of provolone cheese (about 3 ounces or 85 grams total weight)

Master the Method

When tossing or rearranging thin, wiggly, or small items (like the beef and onions here), nonstick-safe tongs always work better than a nonstick-safe spatula.

RAISE THE BAR

Drizzle the meat with a chipotle sauce like Cholula after air-frying and before the meat goes in the wrap.

Sprinkle minced fresh oregano leaves over the cheese before closing the wraps.

1. With the basket in the machine or the tray set at the center level in a toaster-oven-style model, heat an air fryer to 400°F or 200°C on the air fryer setting.

2. Lay the roast beef slices on a cutting board and cut them widthwise into thin strips. Mound them up. Add the salt and pepper. **A**

3. Toss the beef strips well to season them. Push them to the side of the cutting board and mound the onion slices in the open space on the board. Coat them generously with nonstick spray, toss well, and spray again, and maybe even a third time, tossing after each spraying, until well coated. **B**

4. Pile the onions on one half side of the basket or the cooking tray in the machine. Air-fry for 3 minutes. Toss the onions well and add the beef in a mound to the other half of the basket or tray. **C**

5. Air-fry for 5 more minutes, *tossing both once*, until the beef is well done and sizzling at the edges. **D**

6. Transfer the beef and onions to a clean cutting board. Spread one side of each tortilla with half of the butter. Sprinkle ⅛ teaspoon garlic powder over the butter on each tortilla. Top the buttered side of each tortilla with half the beef and half the onions, then with two slices of cheese. Fold two "sides" up and over the filling in one tortilla, then roll the tortilla closed like an egg roll. Repeat with the other tortilla. **E**

7. Generously coat the wraps with nonstick spray *on all sides*. Transfer them to the machine seam side down with a little space between them for air flow. Air-fry *undisturbed* for 8 minutes, or until browned and crisp. Use nonstick-safe tongs to transfer the wraps to a wire rack and cool for 5 minutes before serving warm. **F**

Reuben Rolls

We thought we'd reinvent the wheel just for the fun of it. We took the classic deli sandwich and encased it in puff pastry to make it unexpectedly elegant. You can even serve the rolls as appetizer bites, particularly if you cut them in halves or thirds widthwise.

If you want to make a more standard Reuben sandwich, follow the air-frying technique for our Patty Melts (page 68), using the ingredients listed here but coating the outside of the rye bread slices with mayonnaise as happens in that recipe. The timing will be in keeping with the Patty Melt recipe.

4 ounces or 115 grams purchased corned beef, chopped

½ loosely packed cup or 70 grams *drained* purchased sauerkraut

1 ounce (¼ cup) or 30 grams shredded Swiss cheese

2 tablespoons or 30 milliliters bottled Russian salad dressing

1 large sheet of frozen puff pastry (half of a 14.25-ounce or 410-gram box), thawed but cold (best to thaw it in the fridge overnight)

All-purpose or plain flour, for dusting

1 large egg, whisked until uniform in a small bowl

Master the Method

Although a pastry brush is the easiest way to get an egg wash or other slippery coating on food items, your clean fingers can work just as well (if you don't mind playing with your food).

RAISE THE BAR

Make your own Russian dressing: Whisk ½ cup or 115 grams regular or low-fat mayonnaise, 2 tablespoons or 28 grams ketchup-style chili sauce, 1 tablespoon or 9 grams *minced* yellow or white onion, ½ teaspoon or 3 milliliters Worcestershire sauce, ½ teaspoon or 3 milliliters thick red hot sauce (such as Frank's RedHot), and ¼ teaspoon table salt in a bowl until uniform. Save the leftovers, covered, in the fridge for up to 1 week.

1. With the basket in the machine or the tray set at the center level in a toaster-oven-style model, heat an air fryer to 400°F or 200°C on the air fryer setting.

2. Mix the corned beef, sauerkraut, cheese, and Russian dressing in a medium bowl until uniform. Ⓐ

3. Dust a cutting board or a clean work surface with flour. Lay the sheet of puff pastry on top. Cut the sheet into six even rectangles by making two cuts widthwise and one cut lengthwise in the center. Ⓑ

4. Separate the rectangles and dust the surface again with flour. Put one of these rectangles on the surface, dust it lightly with flour, and roll it out to a 5 x 4½-inch or 13 x 11-centimeter rectangle. Set aside and do the same with the remaining rectangles of puff pastry. Ⓒ

5. Put one rolled rectangle on the surface with a long side towards you. Place about ⅓ cup or about 40 grams of the corned beef mixture in a line about ½ inch or 1 centimeter from the edge of the long side nearest you and leaving about ½ inch or 1 centimeter of space on either end of this "log." Roll the log closed from the long side. Seal the sides closed with the tines of a fork. (Be very careful to seal it well.) Set aside and continue to make five more rolls. Ⓓ

6. Brush the tops of the rolls with the beaten egg to coat them well but not drench them. Ⓔ

7. Set the rolls coated side up in the air fryer with a little space between each. Work in batches as necessary. Air-fry for 8 minutes, then turn the rolls over with nonstick-safe tongs. *Continue* air-frying for about 3 more minutes, or until lightly browned and puffed. Transfer the rolls to a wire rack and cool for 5 minutes before serving warm. Ⓕ

The Easiest-Ever Stromboli Rolls

With purchased pizza dough and sauce, you can make stromboli anytime you want! We've modified the original shape (which tends to burn on the outside without cooking on the inside) to create a stromboli "log" that cooks more evenly in the air fryer. We've also cut it in half to allow the heat to get inside the filling as the pastry cooks.

Our technique involves parchment paper, an admittedly fussy baking item, for rolling out the dough. We do this because adding flour to the work surface for rolling toughens the dough (and results in a much less successful stromboli). Look for parchment paper by the aluminum foil and wax paper, or maybe in the baking aisle.

One 13.8-ounce or 390-gram tube of refrigerator pizza dough

Parchment paper

¼ cup or 60 milliliters jarred pizza sauce

3 ounces (¾ cup) or 85 grams shredded semi-firm mozzarella (do not use fresh mozzarella)

12 thin slices of salami (about 2½ ounces or 70 grams in total)

12 fresh basil leaves

Master the Method

Whenever you turn heavy rolled items, figure out which way the seam lies (that is, which side is the overlap). Never slip the spatula toward that overlap as the spatula will open the seam. Instead, slip the spatula from the other side so it slides underneath the overlapping portion.

RAISE THE BAR

Add up to 2 tablespoons or 16 grams chopped pitted black olives with the salami.

Substitute purchased sun-dried tomato pesto for the pizza sauce.

1. With the basket in the machine or the tray set at the center level in a toaster-oven-style model, heat an air fryer to 350°F or 180°C on the air fryer setting.

2. Open the dough tube and lay the dough on a sheet of parchment paper on a clean work surface. Roll the dough into a 9 x 13-inch or 23 x 33-centimeter rectangle. Ⓐ

3. Spread the pizza sauce over the dough, leaving a ½-inch or 1-centimeter border all around. Top evenly with the cheese, salami slices, and basil leaves, leaving that empty border intact. Ⓑ

4. Starting at one long side, roll the dough into a log. It helps to lift a long side of the parchment paper with the dough, then peel back the paper as you begin to roll, still using the parchment occasionally to push the roll along. Ⓒ

5. Cut the log in half widthwise. Make four slashes across the top of each half. Ⓓ

6. Transfer the two stromboli seam side down to the machine and air-fry for 7 minutes. Flip the stromboli using nonstick-safe tongs. If you're working with the cooking basket in a toaster-oven-style machine, the logs may have stuck a bit because the basket's surface may not be nonstick. Slip a spatula under the logs to gently loosen them. Ⓔ

7. Continue air-frying for 5 more minutes, or until the stromboli are browned and bubbling inside. Transfer the stromboli to a wire rack and cool for 5 minutes before serving warm. Ⓕ

3

CHICKEN & TURKEY

"Air-frying" sounds great: the promise of less fat, the expectation of crispy bits. Except the technique's proper name should be "hot-air-desiccating"—which truly doesn't sound so great and is bad news when it comes to modern poultry. Time was, farm-raised chickens and turkeys were fattier than today's kin, which are bred to be super lean. In other words, poultry can dry out quickly in an air fryer.

You might think an air fryer was made for boneless skinless chicken breasts. Health breeds more health, right? Nope. The hot air currents can actually produce a pile of chicken shards.

The solution is twofold: 1) a good coating. It protects the meat inside. It seals in the "juices" (a combination of subcutaneous and interstitial fat, as well as natural cellular moisture) to render the meat far tastier. And/or 2) a salty marinade. It forces more moisture into the meat's fibers through osmosis, rendering modern cuts a better fit for the machine.

We've used both techniques in this chapter because we suspect that a lot of people want to cook chicken in an air fryer but haven't had good results up until now.

One note: Watch the size of the cuts, particularly when it comes to chicken breasts. They're sold in a wide range of weights these days, from super-large, greater-than-1-pound bone-in breasts to small, individually packaged, 5-ounce boneless skinless breasts. Make sure you have the cut in hand that works with the recipe you've chosen.

Skip-the-Drive-Through Chicken Nuggets

McDonald's sets the golden nugget standard with a prized, crunchy exterior *and* an incredibly luxurious interior. To get as close to theirs as possible, we use ground chicken to mimic the texture. That ground chicken makes the little nugget disks pretty sticky, so you'll get messy as you form them. But you won't need to give them an egg-white wash to get the panko bread crumbs to adhere to them.

Must you use two types of bread crumbs? Yes! The seasoned (but otherwise standard) bread crumbs in the chicken mixture offer a smoother, interior bite. The panko crumbs on the outside yield a better exterior crunch.

1 pound ground chicken or 450 grams chicken mince (preferably white meat only)

⅓ cup or 35 grams Italian-seasoned dried bread crumbs or seasoned gluten-free dried bread crumbs

3 tablespoons or 45 milliliters milk of any sort

½ teaspoon ground sage

½ teaspoon mild paprika

½ teaspoon garlic powder

¼ teaspoon table salt

Ground black pepper, to taste

1 cup or 50 grams plain panko bread crumbs or plain gluten-free panko bread crumbs

Nonstick spray

Master the Method

Everyone knows to wash their hands before cooking. But continue washing them while you're cooking. There's unsavory residue from raw meat on, say, the handle of your air fryer or on any tools you're using. It ends up on your hands, then in your food.

RAISE THE BAR

To make a barbecue dipping sauce for the nuggets, whisk all of the following in a small bowl until smooth: ¼ cup or 55 grams mayonnaise of any sort; 2 tablespoons or 30 milliliters smooth plain barbecue sauce; ½ tablespoon or 10 grams honey; 1 teaspoon prepared yellow mustard; ¼ teaspoon garlic powder; and ¼ teaspoon table salt (optional).

1. With the basket in the machine or the tray set at the center level in a toaster-oven-style model, heat an air fryer to 400°F or 200°C on the air fryer setting.

2. Crumble the ground chicken into a large bowl. Stir and/or fold in the seasoned bread crumbs, milk, sage, paprika, garlic powder, salt, and ground black pepper to taste until uniform. **A**

3. Wash your hands and rinse them, but keep them wet. Scoop up some of the chicken mixture, about the size of an unshelled walnut. Form it into a flattened oval disk about ¾ inch or 2 centimeters thick. Set aside and continue to make about 19 more. Dampen your hands when the chicken mixture starts to stick to your fingers. **B**

4. Clean and dry your hands. Spread the panko bread crumbs on a dinner plate, shallow soup plate, shallow food storage container, or small pie plate. Dip each disk in the panko, sprinkling on the crumbs and pressing gently to coat the nugget well on all sides (even around the perimeter), without flattening or deforming the disk. **C**

5. Coat *both sides* of the nuggets with nonstick spray. **D**

6. Set the nuggets in the heated air fryer in a single layer without touching. Work in batches as necessary. Air-fry for 6 minutes, then flip the nuggets over with a nonstick-safe tongs (and perhaps a rubber spatula in the other hand for balance). **E**

7. Continue air-frying for about 6 more minutes, or until firm and well browned. Use clean tongs to *gently* transfer the nuggets to a wire rack. Cool for a few minutes before serving warm. **F**

Super Crunchy Chicken Fingers

The best chicken fingers are *not* made from giant chicken breasts, the 1-pound or ½-kilo monsters that show up in the butcher case at many supermarkets. The best are made with the smaller 5- to 6-ounce or 140- to 170-gram boneless skinless chicken breasts that often show up individually packed and in big bags at big-box stores (in so-called "family packs") or sometimes in the freezer case of more standard supermarkets.

If you can't find these smaller chicken breasts, buy 12-ounce or 340-gram boneless skinless breasts but set them on a cutting board and slice them "horizontally" into two fairly even pieces (as if you were trying to turn each piece into an open book). Then open the "book" and divide it into equal portions along its "spine."

We do not recommend using precut chicken fingers (often designated for stir fries) to make chicken fingers. Those strips are too thin and get overcooked before the coating is set.

Four 5- to 6-ounce or 140- to 170-gram boneless skinless chicken breasts

½ cup all-purpose flour or 60 grams plain flour (or any gluten-free flour blend)

3 large eggs

3 cups or 150 grams Italian-seasoned panko bread crumbs or Italian-seasoned gluten-free panko bread crumbs

Nonstick spray

Master the Method

Fingers get messy during any three-bowl-dipping process. Make sure you wash *and dry* your hands repeatedly.

RAISE THE BAR

We love a creamy, spicy sauce with chicken tenders. Whisk all of the following in a medium bowl until smooth: ½ cup or 55 grams mayonnaise of any sort; 2 tablespoons or 30 grams ketchup; 2 tablespoons or 30 milliliters thick red hot sauce such as Texas Pete or Frank's RedHot; ½ teaspoon table salt; ¼ teaspoon onion powder; and ¼ teaspoon garlic powder. If you really want to go over the top, add up to 1 tablespoon or 15 grams pickle relish or jalapeño relish and/or 1 very finely minced tinned anchovy fillet.

1. With the basket in the machine or the tray set at the center level in a toaster-oven-style model, heat an air fryer to 400°F or 200°C on the air fryer setting.

2. Slice the chicken breasts lengthwise into 1-inch or 2½-centimeter wide strips. **A**

3. Spread the flour in a shallow soup plate, shallow food storage container, or small pie plate. Beat the eggs *well* in a second shallow soup plate, shallow food storage container, or small pie plate. Spread the seasoned panko bread crumbs on yet another shallow soup plate, shallow food storage container, or small pie plate. Now set these two plus the beaten eggs in a three-bowl or -plate arrangement like this: flour, eggs, bread crumbs. **B**

4. Dip a slice of chicken into the flour and turn it to coat all sides evenly and well. Transfer to the beaten eggs and gently turn to coat on all sides without knocking off the flour. **C**

5. Transfer the egg-coated strip to the bread crumbs and gently press into them to coat on all sides, even the ends. Set aside and continue dipping all the strips in this three-step process. **D**

6. Generously spray the strips *on both sides* with nonstick spray. **E**

7. Arrange the strips in the heated machine in a single layer without touching. Work in batches as necessary. Air-fry *undisturbed* for 12 minutes or until firm, browned, and sizzling. Use nonstick-safe tongs to transfer the strips from the fryer to a wire rack. Cool for a few minutes before serving warm. **F**

Popcorn (Seriously!) Chicken

We've got recipes for the more standard batter- and crumb-coated popcorn chicken in *The Essential Air Fryer Cookbook* and *The Instant Air Fryer Bible*. This time, we thought we'd go over the top and use honest-to-goodness popcorn as the coating for chicken pieces, thereby fulfilling the name of the dish as no one ever has.

Why? Because ground popcorn gets super crunchy and brilliantly tasty in the air fryer, creating a little bit of corny goodness on each piece of chicken. Just watch carefully to make sure the coating doesn't burn. Remove any pieces the moment you see any blackening along the edges.

6 heaping cups or 400 grams of popped popcorn

1½ pounds or 680 grams boneless skinless chicken breasts

1 large egg

1 teaspoon mild smoked paprika

½ teaspoon onion powder

½ teaspoon garlic powder

½ teaspoon table salt

Nonstick spray

Master the Method

The cooking surface in drawer-style air fryers is often coated with a nonstick finish. It can get nicked over time. Replace this surface if you see it chipped or too gunked to clean properly.

RAISE THE BAR

Make a honey-butter drizzle for the popcorn chicken: Microwave to melt 2 tablespoons or 30 grams butter in a microwave-safe bowl on high for about 1 minute, stirring at least once. Cool for a few minutes, then whisk in 1 tablespoon or 20 grams honey, 1 tablespoon or 15 milliliters apple cider vinegar, and 1 tablespoon or 15 milliliters soy sauce or tamari. Drizzle this sauce over the hot chicken pieces.

1. With the basket in the machine or the tray set at the center level in a toaster-oven-style model, heat an air fryer to 375°F or 190°C on the air fryer setting.

2. Use a food processor to grind the popcorn until the consistency of panko bread crumbs. Work in batches as necessary in smaller machines. If there are still a few larger bits, it's better than having a finely ground powder in the machine. Ⓐ

3. Cut the chicken breasts into 1-inch cubes. If they're thick, large breasts, they should be sliced lengthwise into 1-inch wide strips, then each of these strips cut lengthwise in half, which are *then* each cut widthwise into 1-inch chunks. Smaller breasts won't need that intermediate step of cutting the long strips lengthwise into halves. Ⓑ

4. Whisk the egg, smoked paprika, onion powder, garlic powder, and salt in a large bowl until uniform. Add the chicken pieces and toss well to coat evenly and thoroughly. There should very little liquid pooling in the bowl. Ⓒ

5. Add the ground popcorn and fold or toss to coat each piece well and thoroughly. Ⓓ

6. Pick up a piece of chicken with nonstick-safe tongs, coat it on all sides with nonstick spray, and set in the heated machine. Continue spraying the remaining pieces and placing them in a single layer without touching. Work in batches as necessary. Ⓔ

7. Air-fry *undisturbed* for 10 minutes, or until the coating is brown, the bits of visible chicken are white, and the pieces are firm. Use clean nonstick-safe tongs to transfer the pieces to a wire rack. Cool for a few minutes before serving warm. Ⓕ

Healthier Herb-Marinated Chicken Breasts

These chicken breasts have some oil in their marinade, but they're otherwise low-carb (or no-carb if you use breasts that haven't been injected with certain stabilizers—aka wheat fillers). These chicken breasts can be the center of a healthy meal any night of the week.

Because the recipe is so simple—really, just breasts dunked in a marinade and refrigerated to bump up their flavors—we felt free to create a slightly more elaborate herb mix to give them as much flavor as possible. Can you use a bottled spice blend, like a dried Italian seasoning blend? Of course: Use the garlic as we suggest, then add about 1 tablespoon or 3 grams.

If you can find only giant 12-ounce to 1-pound or 340- to 450-gram boneless skinless chicken breasts, follow the instructions for halving them in the headnote for Super Crunchy Chicken Fingers on page 108.

¼ cup or 60 milliliters red wine vinegar

3 tablespoons or 45 milliliters olive oil

2 medium garlic cloves, peeled and minced (about 2 teaspoons)

2 teaspoons dried oregano

1 teaspoon dried dill

1 teaspoon fennel seeds

½ teaspoon table salt

¼ teaspoon ground cinnamon

¼ teaspoon red pepper flakes

Four 6- to 8-ounce or 170- to 225-gram boneless skinless chicken breasts

Master the Method

Although it's convenient to take boneless skinless chicken breasts right out of the fridge and slip them into the air fryer, they'll cook more evenly if they're close to room temperature. For this recipe, take the breasts out of their marinade and leave them on a cutting board for 10 minutes before you heat the machine.

1. Whisk the vinegar, oil, garlic, oregano, dill, fennel seeds, salt, cinnamon, and red pepper flakes in a 9-inch or 23-centimeter nonreactive square baking pan or other medium-sized baking dish. **A**

2. Slip the breasts into the vinegar mixture and turn them with tongs a couple of times to coat them well. Cover and refrigerate for at least 2 or up to 6 hours. **B**

3. With the basket in the machine or the tray set at the center level in a toaster-oven-style model, heat an air fryer to 400°F or 200°C on the air fryer setting.

4. Transfer the breasts to the heated machine in a single layer without touching, although just a hair's breadth of distance between is fine. Work in batches if necessary. **C**

5. Air-fry for 6 minutes. Use clean nonstick-safe tongs to turn the breasts over. **D**

6. Continue air-frying for about 6 more minutes, or until an instant-read meat thermometer inserted into the thickest part of one breast registers 165°F or 75°C. Use clean tongs to transfer the breasts to a serving platter or plate. Cool for a couple of minutes before serving hot. **E**

RAISE THE BAR

These breasts are great over a simple salad, dressed right in the bag! Buy a 9-ounce or 255-gram bag of chopped *crunchy* lettuce, like iceberg and romaine. (Soft arugula or mesclun mix won't work for this hack.) Dress the salad right in the bag with a mixture of 3 parts olive oil and 2 parts vinegar, as well as a little dried oregano, table salt, and ground black pepper. Or add whatever creamy dressing you prefer, again right in the bag. Gently massage the lettuce in the bag with the dressing, then serve it up. (Just make sure the bag has no air holes in it before you try this!)

The Best Buttermilk Fried Chicken

A wet batter proves difficult in an air fryer. Before the batter can set, the air currents blow it into uneven waves or even completely off of larger cuts like bone-in chicken pieces. However, by coating the chicken in flour, it can then hold a buttermilk marinade in the machine.

Since bone-in, skin-on chicken pieces make the best fried chicken, thighs are your best bet for a juicy, irresistible meal. Bone-in, skin-on breasts tend to be too large; the crust burns before the meat is cooked through.

That said, you *can* substitute bone-in skin-on breasts here if you lay them on a cutting board and slice each one (while raw, of course) into *even* halves *widthwise* (that is, widthwise but a bit on the diagonal to get the same amount of meat on each piece).

1 cup or 250 milliliters regular or low-fat buttermilk

Up to 6 medium garlic cloves, peeled and minced (up to 2 tablespoons)

2 teaspoons table salt

Four 8-ounce or 225-gram bone-in skin-on chicken thighs

2 cups all-purpose flour or 240 grams plain flour

1 tablespoon mild paprika

1 tablespoon onion powder

Lots of ground black pepper (maybe 1 tablespoon), to taste

Nonstick spray

Master the Method

For the best air-fried chicken in almost any recipe, slice off any overhanging skin or fat. The remaining skin and fat should be tight to the meat. Excess bits tend to burn.

RAISE THE BAR

Serve the fried chicken with a sweet corn salad: Drain a 15-ounce or 425-gram can of corn kernels and set them in a large bowl. Add a 4-ounce or 115-gram jar of diced pimientos (do not drain); 1 to 2 trimmed and thinly sliced scallions; a splash of olive oil as well as another of apple cider vinegar; and a sprinkling of sugar, salt, and even less ground cumin. Toss well before serving.

1. Mix the buttermilk, garlic, and salt in a 9- to 10-inch or 23- to 25-centimeter square glass baking dish or other medium-sized nonreactive baking dish. Add the chicken thighs and turn several times to coat. Cover and refrigerate for 1 hour or up to 4 hours, turning the chicken pieces at least once. Ⓐ

2. With the basket in the machine or the tray set at the center level in a toaster-oven-style model, heat an air fryer to 350°F or 180°C on the air fryer setting.

3. Mix the flour, paprika, onion powder, and black pepper in a shallow soup plate, shallow food storage container, or small pie plate. Ⓑ

4. Pick up a chicken thigh with nonstick-safe tongs and gently shake off some of the excess buttermilk while leaving the thigh wet. Set it in the flour mixture, press gently, and turn repeatedly to get an even and uniform coating, even on the sides. Set aside. Ⓒ

5. Repeat the dredging process with the remaining thighs. Generously coat them *on all sides* with nonstick spray. Ⓓ

6. Set them in the heated machine and air-fry *undisturbed* for 14 minutes. If any of the exposed (or top side) of the coating has remained white, it needs another spritz of nonstick spray to get crisp. Very gently pick the piece up with clean tongs and spritz it *outside of the machine.* Now flip all the thighs over with those tongs. (There will still be white spots on the undersides.) Ⓔ

7. Continue air-frying *undisturbed* for 14 more minutes, or until the coating is browned and crunchy and the chicken has cooked through—that is, an instant-read meat thermometer inserted into the thickest part of the meat without touching bone registers 165°F or 75°C. Use clean tongs to gently transfer the thighs to a wire rack. Cool for a few minutes before serving warm. Ⓕ

Chicken-Fried Chicken with Easy Cream Gravy

If you don't know what "chicken-fried" meat is, hie thee to Texas. If you can't, we'll fill you in: The name refers to a way of frying any cut (usually cube steak but even pork chops or—yes!—bacon) in a thick batter, the way you'd normally fry a piece of chicken in an old-school recipe.

In general, the batter coating for chicken-fried *steak* is a little thicker than that used for traditional fried chicken because the beef needs more protection while it's submerged in hot oil. That accommodation also works great for chicken in an air fryer because the thicker coating then protects even chicken from the machine's insistent heat.

This recipe comes the closest of any in this book to traditional fried chicken because of the double-dipping process for a thick coating. For the best results, you *must* generously spray the thighs once they're coated and you must *gently* flip them to keep the still-unset crust intact.

2 cups or 500 milliliters regular or low-fat buttermilk

2 cups plus 2 tablespoons all-purpose flour or 255 grams plain flour

2½ teaspoons table salt

1 teaspoon onion powder

1 teaspoon garlic powder

½ teaspoon cayenne

½ teaspoon celery seeds

Four 6-ounce or 170-gram boneless skinless chicken thighs, opened up "flat"

1 cup or 250 milliliters whole milk (do not use low-fat or fat-free)

¼ teaspoon ground black pepper

⅛ teaspoon dried thyme

Nonstick spray

Master the Method

Wash and dry any kitchen utensils that have previously touched raw meat or poultry before you use those utensils again in a recipe.

RAISE THE BAR

Spice up the gravy with the addition of up to ½ teaspoon cayenne.

And/or give it a distinctly more sophisticated twist with up to 1 tablespoon or 15 milliliters dry sherry and/or ¼ teaspoon grated or ground nutmeg.

1. With the basket in the machine or the tray set at the center level in a toaster-oven-style model, heat an air fryer to 400°F or 200°C on the air fryer setting.

2. Pour the buttermilk into a shallow soup plate, shallow food storage container, or small pie plate. Whisk 2 cups or 240 grams flour, 2 teaspoons salt, the onion powder, garlic powder, cayenne, and celery seeds in a second shallow soup plate, shallow food storage container, or small pie plate. Ⓐ

3. Use your clean fingers or tongs to dip a chicken thigh into the buttermilk, turning it to coat it thoroughly. Pick it up to let any excess drain off, then set it in the flour mixture. Press gently and turn repeatedly to get an even coating across the meat, even along the sides. Ⓑ

4. Now repeat this same double-dipping process with the *same* chicken thigh: buttermilk, then flour mixture. Ⓒ

5. Set the thigh aside and repeat this double dip-dredge maneuver with the remaining chicken thighs. Very generously coat the thighs *on all sides* with nonstick spray. Ⓓ

6. Set them in a single layer without touching in the heated machine. Work in batches as necessary. Air-fry for 17 minutes, *carefully turning about halfway through the cooking process*, until the coating is browned and crunchy and the meat is cooked through. Use nonstick-safe tongs to *gently* transfer the thighs to a wire rack to cool while you make the gravy. Ⓔ

7. Whisk the milk, black pepper, thyme, the remaining 2 tablespoons or 15 grams flour, and the remaining ½ teaspoon salt in a microwave-safe 2- to 4-cup or 500-milliliter to 1-liter measuring cup or tall glass container. Microwave on high for 2 to 3 minutes, whisking at least twice, until thickened and creamy. Serve the gravy alongside the chicken thighs. Ⓕ

A

B

C

D

E

F

Chicken in Chips

By coating chicken breasts in ground potato chips, we create a crunchy and salty coating that pairs well with cold beer or iced tea. We also use egg whites rather than whole eggs to achieve a lighter flavor, letting the potato chips really shine.

The tricks for success are 1) grinding those chips so they're like bread crumbs rather than dust, and 2) turning the chicken pieces very gently in the air fryer so that you don't disturb the coating before it sets. As always, nonstick-safe tongs in one hand and a rubber spatula in the other offer you the best balance for careful turning.

One 8-ounce or 225-gram bag of potato chips or potato crisps, preferably salt and vinegar or barbecue chips or crisps

1 cup or 115 grams potato starch or cornstarch

3 large egg whites

Two 12-ounce or 340-gram boneless skinless chicken breasts, cut into 8 even chunks

Master the Method
Don't store an air fryer on your stove. You might forget, turn on a burner, and ruin both the machine and your cooktop.

RAISE THE BAR

Ever tried a green bean slaw? Start with haricots verts, those super thin green beans found in most produce sections. Blanch them in boiling water for about 20 seconds, then drain thoroughly and refresh under cold, running water. Mix them with carrot matchsticks and thin strips of red bell pepper, both of which you can find precut in most produce sections (although you may have to slice the bell pepper strips in half lengthwise to make them super thin). Mix the three vegetables with your favorite creamy dressing, even a traditional cole slaw dressing. Make sure you use lots of ground black pepper. (And maybe a generous sprinkle of salt, if there's little in the dressing.)

1. With the basket in the machine or the tray set at the center level in a toaster-oven-style model, heat an air fryer to 400°F or 200°C on the air fryer setting.

2. Pour the potato chips into a large food processor. (Work in batches in a smaller model.) Cover and pulse repeatedly to create bread crumb–like bits, not a ground powder at all. Pour these chips into a shallow soup plate, shallow food storage container, or small pie plate. **A**

3. Spread the potato starch or cornstarch in a second shallow soup plate, shallow food storage container, or small pie plate. Whisk the egg whites until very foamy in a third shallow soup plate, shallow food storage container, or small pie plate. **B**

4. Set these ingredients in this order on your work surface: potato starch or cornstarch, egg whites, chips. Dip one piece of chicken in the potato starch or cornstarch. Press gently but firmly, turning repeatedly, to coat evenly but not too thickly. Transfer the piece of chicken to the egg whites and gently turn several times to thoroughly coat. **C**

5. Transfer the chicken piece to the potato chip crumbs. Press gently and turn repeatedly to get an even coating all over the meat, even along its edges. Set aside. **D**

6. Repeat this three-dip process with the remaining pieces of chicken. Set them in the heated machine in a single layer without touching. Air-fry for 6 minutes, then *gently* flip them over with nonstick-safe tongs (and probably a rubber spatula in your other hand for deft balance). **E**

7. Continue air-frying for about 6 more minutes, until the chicken is golden brown and cooked through (that is, until an instant-read meat thermometer inserted into the center of a thick piece registers 165°F or 75°C). Use clean tongs to transfer the pieces to a wire rack to cool for a few minutes before serving warm. **F**

Sticky-Spicy Chicken Wings

This recipe for chicken wings asks you to glaze them with a honey mixture during the last minutes so they get extra crunchy. Watch out that the ends don't burn, particularly on the drumettes. If they start getting dark, shake the basket much more often during the last 5 minutes of cooking.

These days, you can usually find packages of either wingettes or drumettes (and sometimes both). If you can find only whole wings, buy 2¼ pounds or 1 kilogram, then slice each wing through the joint and into its three component sections. Discard the so-called "flapper" sections (without much meat) or freeze them in a sealed bag for the next time you make chicken stock.

2 pounds or 900 grams chicken wingettes and/or drumettes

1½ teaspoons baking powder

1 teaspoon table salt

1 teaspoon or 5 milliliters honey

1 teaspoon or 5 milliliters sriracha

1 teaspoon or 5 milliliters lemon juice

Master the Method

The inner cooking tray in drawer-style machines can fall out if you turn the drawer upside-down over a rack or a platter. To prevent the mishap, hold that tray in place with nonstick-safe tongs or a rubber spatula.

RAISE THE BAR

For vinegary cucumbers as a side dish, thinly slice 1 long seedless "English" cucumber into ¼-inch or ½-centimeter thick rounds. Set in a bowl and add ⅔ cup or 160 milliliters distilled white vinegar, ⅓ cup or 80 milliliters water, 1 tablespoon or 12 grams granulated white sugar, 1 teaspoon table salt, and up to ½ teaspoon red pepper flakes. Cover and refrigerate for at least 1 hour or up to 1 week.

1. With the basket in the machine or the tray set at the center level in a toaster-oven-style model, heat an air fryer to 400°F or 200°C on the air fryer setting.

2. Toss the wing parts, baking powder, and salt in a big bowl until the meat is evenly and thoroughly coated. **A**

3. Set the wing parts into the heated machine. They can touch in spots or even be loosely piled on each other. **B**

4. Air-fry for 10 minutes, then toss well. In basket-style machines, you can remove the basket and shake it well, about like flipping things in a skillet. In toaster-oven-style machines, you'll need to use nonstick-safe tongs to rearrange the wings. *Continue* air-frying for 10 more minutes. Meanwhile, use a fork to mix the honey, sriracha, and lemon juice in a small bowl until smooth. **C**

5. Brush the honey mixture over the wings. **D**

6. Continue air-frying for about 5 more minutes, or until the wing parts are golden-brown and shiny-glazed. Pour out onto a serving platter or a wire rack and cool for a couple of minutes before serving hot. **E**

Buffalo Chicken Wings

Butter and chicken wings. Is there a finer combination? We probably have to thank every bar in North America for showing us all how fantastic it is! But here's the air-fryer problem: If you add all the butter to the wings up front, you'll end up with a burned coating in the intense heat. So it's best to put just a little butter on the meat with the spices, just enough fat to keep those spices in place until the wings are crunchy and delectable. After that, make a buttery, spicy *dip* for the wings when they're served. Now there's enough butter in the preparation to match the modern classic!

For more information about buying and cutting up chicken wings, see the headnote for Sticky-Spicy Chicken Wings on page 120.

By the way, you *cannot* easily halve the amount for chicken wings in an air fryer. The timing changes dramatically with the reduced portions.

2 pounds or 900 grams chicken wingettes and/or drumettes

9 tablespoons (1 stick plus 1 tablespoon) or 125 grams butter, melted and cooled a couple of minutes

1 teaspoon celery seeds

1 teaspoon garlic powder

1 teaspoon table salt

Up to ½ teaspoon cayenne

¼ cup or 60 milliliters Frank's RedHot, Texas Pete, or other thick red hot sauce

2 tablespoons or 30 milliliters apple cider vinegar

2 tablespoons or 40 grams honey

Master the Method

Like any other appliance, air fryers can go out of whack over time. Test that yours is maintaining the correct temperature by putting an oven thermometer inside to see if indeed your machine gets up to (and doesn't surpass!) the set temperature.

1. With the basket in the machine or the tray set at the center level in a toaster-oven-style model, heat an air fryer to 400°F or 200°C on the air fryer setting.

2. Toss the wing parts, 1 tablespoon or 15 milliliters melted butter, the celery seeds, garlic powder, ½ teaspoon salt, and the cayenne (to taste) in a large bowl until the wing parts are glistening and evenly coated in the spices. Ⓐ

3. Pour the wings into the heated machine. Make sure they're loosely piled on each other, not compacted or layered. Ⓑ

4. Air-fry for 10 minutes. Toss well. In basket-style machines, you can use tongs (as Bruce does in the picture) or you can remove the basket and shake it well, like chefs do when they're flipping things in a skillet. In toaster-oven-style machines, you *must* use nonstick-safe tongs to rearrange the wings. Ⓒ

5. Continue air-frying for another 10 minutes. Again, toss well. Ⓓ

6. Continue air-frying for about 5 more minutes, or until the wings are crispy and brown. Meanwhile, whisk the remaining butter, the hot sauce, vinegar, honey, and remaining ½ teaspoon salt in a medium bowl until smooth. Ⓔ

7. Pour the wings onto a serving platter or plates. Cool for a few minutes and serve with the sauce on the side. Ⓕ

RAISE THE BAR

Miss the blue cheese? Crumble about 2 ounces or 55 grams into the dip when you whisk it together. Or crumble the cheese right over the hot wings so it melts a bit before you serve them.

Get even more classic by serving the wings with celery stalks (preferably halved lengthwise, then cut widthwise into smaller segments) and baby carrots.

Pretzel-Coated Chicken and Broccoli Dinner

Pretzel crumbs make an *excellent* coating for chicken. The coating gets crunchy quickly but is nicely salty, a tasty option when you're looking for something beyond the ordinary.

We turn these breasts into a full meal by adding broccoli florets to the machine halfway through the cooking process. That means you can make only two servings at once, but the recipe's quick enough that cooking in batches won't slow you down that much.

To keep the chicken pieces warm and crunchy, set an oven-safe rack on a lipped baking sheet and keep the cooked breasts on that rack in a 250°F or 120°C oven while you make a second (or third) batch. You can reheat all the broccoli for a minute or two in a 325°F or 165°C air fryer when you're ready to serve everything.

6 ounces or 170 grams pretzel nuggets (a little more than a third of a standard 16-ounce or 450-gram bag)	1 tablespoon or 15 grams Dijon mustard (gluten-free, if desired)
½ cup all-purpose flour or 60 grams plain flour or any gluten-free flour alternative	Two 6- to 8-ounce or 170- to 225-gram boneless skinless chicken breasts
2 large eggs	Nonstick spray
	9 ounces or 255 grams (about 3 cups) medium-sized (about 1½-inch or 4-centimeter) broccoli florets

1. With the basket in the machine or the tray set at the center level in a toaster-oven-style model, heat an air fryer to 375°F or 190°C on the air fryer setting.

2. Put the pretzels in a large food processor. Work in batches in smaller machines. Cover and process until ground to the consistency of panko bread crumbs, not sand or powder. Pour the ground pretzels into a shallow soup plate, shallow food storage container, or small pie plate. Pour the flour into a second shallow soup plate, shallow food storage container, or small pie plate. Whisk the eggs and mustard in a third shallow soup plate, shallow food storage container, or small pie plate so that the mixture is uniform, with no bits of egg white floating in it. **Ⓐ**

3. Set the bowls up in this order on your work surface: flour, egg mixture, and pretzel crumbs. Use tongs to set a chicken breast in the flour and turn it several times to coat it thoroughly, even along the sides. Transfer the breast to the egg mixture and gently turn several times to coat it well. **Ⓑ**

4. Pick the breast up, let the excess egg run off, and set it in the pretzel crumbs. Press gently, turning repeatedly, to coat it well, even along the sides. Set the breast aside and repeat this process with the second chicken breast. Generously coat *both sides* of the chicken breasts with nonstick spray. **Ⓒ**

5. Set the chicken breasts in the heated machine in a single layer without any overlap. Work in batches as necessary. Air-fry for 8 minutes, then flip the breasts over with nonstick-safe tongs and move them to one side of the basket or the cooking tray. Squishing them together a bit at this point is fine. **Ⓓ**

6. Lightly coat the florets with nonstick spray, tossing them several times and spraying repeatedly to get an even coating. (If you're working in batches, only add half of the broccoli now, reserving the remainder for the second batch.) Pile the florets into the machine in the cleared space. Don't let any sit on top of the crunchy coating on the chicken. **Ⓔ**

7. Continue air-frying for about 8 more minutes, until the chicken is brown, crunchy, and cooked through (an instant-read meat thermometer inserted into the middle of the thickest part of one breast registers 165°F or 75°C). Use clean tongs to transfer the breasts to serving plates or a platter. Pile the broccoli florets onto the plates or the platter with the chicken. **Ⓕ**

Master the Method

Just because we call for two or three shallow soup plates, shallow food storage containers, or small pie plates doesn't mean you have to use three of the same thing. Use one pie plate and two soup plates, for example. Flat plates work better for dry ingredients; bowls or plates with rounded edges, for wet ingredients.

RAISE THE BAR

Make a chocolate fondue for dipping the remaining pretzel nuggets for dessert: Melt 4 ounces or 115 grams of chopped dark chocolate (or dark chocolate chips) with ¼ cup or 60 milliliters heavy cream in a small saucepan over very low heat, stirring constantly. Stir in ½ teaspoon vanilla extract, or ½ tablespoon or 7 milliliters of sweet liqueur of some sort (such as Grand Marnier, Frangelico, Amaretto, or crème de menthe). Serve warm with those nuggets.

Chicken Adobo and Green Bean Dinner

Here's a healthy, simple dinner with big flavors, modeled on those of Filipino adobo (as opposed to Southwestern chile-based adobo)—that is, vinegar, soy sauce, garlic, and bay leaves. Filipino adobo tends to be less sweet, which is perfect for the air fryer, as higher sugar contents can lead to burning or charring. In fact, our marinade includes no sugar at all!

For the best success, use fairly hefty boneless skinless chicken thighs. Trim off any excess blobs of fat that will melt and make a mess in the machine.

½ cup or 125 milliliters distilled white vinegar

½ cup or 125 milliliters regular or reduced-sodium soy sauce, or gluten-free tamari

6 medium garlic cloves, peeled and minced (about 2 tablespoons)

2 bay leaves

Four 6-ounce or 170-gram boneless skinless chicken thighs, trimmed

1 pound or 450 grams green beans, trimmed of their stems (if attached)

Master the Method

Although no manufacturer recommends that you clean the fan or the heating element in a machine with soapy water, you should *gently* wipe it down with a damp cloth once in a while.

RAISE THE BAR

For a more delicate flavor, swap out the distilled white vinegar for white balsamic or white wine vinegar.

Although cooked white rice might seem a go-to for this meal, consider cooked and drained wheat berries as a side.

Or serve the thighs and green beans in opened baked potatoes, all doused with a little more soy sauce and a dab of butter.

1. Whisk the vinegar, soy sauce, garlic, and bay leaves in a 9- to 10-inch or 23- to 25-centimeter square nonreactive baking pan or other medium-sized pan. Add the chicken thighs and turn repeatedly to coat. Cover and refrigerate for at least 1 hour or up to 4 hours. **A**

2. With the basket in the machine or the tray set at the center level in a toaster-oven-style model, heat an air fryer to 400°F or 200°C on the air fryer setting.

3. Remove the thighs from the marinade and set them in the heated machine in a single layer without touching. Work in batches as necessary. Reserve the marinade in the pan. **B**

4. Air-fry for 5 minutes. Meanwhile, put the green beans in the marinade and turn them to coat. **C**

5. Use nonstick-safe tongs to turn the thighs over. **D**

6. Continue air-frying for 4 minutes, then pile the green beans on and around the thighs. **E**

7. Continue air-frying for about 4 more minutes, or until the thighs are cooked through (an instant-read meat thermometer inserted into the middle of the thickest part of a thigh registers 165°F or 75°C). Use clean tongs to transfer the thighs to a serving platter or plates. Pile the green beans on and around the thighs and serve warm. **F**

Tandoori-Style Chicken Leg and Cauliflower Dinner

Another whole meal from the air fryer, this one with East Indian flavors and lots of vegetable crunch! We find that chicken legs have such thick meat on them that, without a heavy coating, the air fryer often burns the skin before the meat is cooked through. One solution is to strip off the skin—which then gives the meat a better chance to be cooked through. It also gives us a chance to use an aromatic marinade.

Jarred minced ginger is fine for this recipe (and any other in this book), so long as the minced bits are not watery or browned. Drain it to get the most ginger in the tablespoon.

4 chicken legs (or drumsticks), about 4 ounces or 115 grams each

2 tablespoons or 28 grams full-fat plain yogurt (*do not* use Greek yogurt)

1 tablespoon or 12 grams minced peeled fresh ginger

1 tablespoon standard yellow curry powder

½ teaspoon table salt

9 ounces or 255 grams (about 3 cups) medium-sized (1½-inch or 4-centimeter) cauliflower florets

2 tablespoons or 30 grams butter, melted and cooled for a few minutes

⅛ teaspoon ground dried turmeric

RAISE THE BAR

For a much spicier meal, substitute a spicy red or Madras curry powder for the standard yellow blend.

Serve these legs and the cauliflower with chutney and maybe a sambal of some sort, particularly sambal badjak, available at many Indian and Asian grocery stores.

An unusual "salad" for this meal would be stemmed, cored, and sliced firm pears, tossed with a little balsamic vinegar, a sprinkle of ground cardamom, and salt to taste.

1. With the basket in the machine or the tray set at the center level in a toaster-oven-style model, heat an air fryer to 375°F or 190°C on the air fryer setting.

2. Use a paper towel to grab the skin around the thick part of the chicken leg. Strip the skin off along the length of the leg, always holding it with the paper towel for a better grip. Repeat with the remaining legs. Discard the skins. **A**

3. Use a fork to make a paste out of the yogurt, ginger, curry powder, and salt in a small bowl. **B**

4. Rub this paste all over the skinned chicken legs. Set the legs in the heated machine in a single layer and without touching. **C**

5. Air-fry for 8 minutes. Meanwhile, mix the cauliflower, butter, and turmeric in a medium bowl until the florets are well coated. **D**

6. Turn the legs over with nonstick-safe tongs. Scatter the florets on and around the legs. **E**

7. Continue air-frying for 8 minutes, or until the cauliflower has browned a bit and the chicken is cooked through (an instant-read meat thermometer inserted into the thickest middle of a leg without touching bone registers 165°F or 75°C). If you notice any florets burning, either remove them from the machine or rescatter them in different spots with different bits exposed. Use clean tongs to transfer the legs to a serving platter or plates. Scatter the florets around the legs and serve. **F**

Master the Method

When you use an instant-read meat thermometer, make sure the probe isn't touching any bones. Bone will almost always be a lower temperature than the surrounding meat—which means that you'll overcook and dry out a cut if you go by the temperature of the bone itself.

Sweet-Spicy Chicken Patties and Buttery Carrots Dinner

These ground chicken patties are spiced with flavors reminiscent of Moroccan fare, slightly less complex than the spice blend on display in tagines and other North African stews but still robust and transportive. Alongside some buttery carrots, the patties make for a quick and elegant meal, fit even for a weekend supper with friends.

Cooked white rice might seem a go-to side dish, but check out our option for a chickpea salad in Raise the Bar.

8 ounces or 225 grams baby carrots

2 tablespoons or 30 grams butter, melted

½ teaspoon table salt

⅛ teaspoon cayenne, optional

12 ounces ground chicken or 340 grams chicken mince (do not use only white meat chicken)

1½ teaspoons or 7 milliliters balsamic vinegar

½ teaspoon light brown sugar

½ teaspoon ground coriander

½ teaspoon ground dried ginger

½ teaspoon garlic powder

¼ teaspoon ground cumin

Nonstick spray

RAISE THE BAR

Serve with a simple Moroccan-inspired chickpea salad: Drain and rinse one 15-ounce or 425-gram can of chickpeas and pour them into a medium bowl. Add a handful of dried currants or raisins, as well as some slivered almonds, much less minced shallot, and a bit of minced fresh mint leaves. If desired, add drained canned mandarin orange segments (maybe about half of a 15-ounce or 425-gram can). Dress the salad (taste as you go!) with olive oil, a generous splash of lemon juice, a little ground dried ginger, as well as salt and ground black pepper to taste.

1. With the basket in the machine or the tray set at the center level in a toaster-oven-style model, heat an air fryer to 400°F or 200°C on the air fryer setting.

2. Toss the carrots, melted butter, ¼ teaspoon salt, and the cayenne (if using) in a medium bowl until the carrots are well coated. **A**

3. Pour the carrots into the heated machine so that they're scattered about willy-nilly. Don't layer them or pack them in. **B**

4. Air-fry the carrots for 15 minutes, *tossing once or twice.* Meanwhile, crumble the ground chicken into that same bowl. Add the vinegar, brown sugar, coriander, ginger, garlic powder, cumin, and remaining ¼ teaspoon salt. Mix well, divide in half, and form the mixture into two compact patties, each about 4 inches or 10 centimeters in diameter. Generously coat the patties *on both sides* with nonstick spray. **C**

5. Push the carrots to one side of the cooking tray or the basket. Set the patties in the cleared space in the machine; they can touch a bit. **D**

6. Air-fry for 8 minutes, then flip the patties over with a clean nonstick spatula and rearrange the carrots. **E**

7. Continue air-frying for 7 more minutes, or until patties are sizzling and well browned and the carrots are shrunken a bit but still crisp-tender. Use that spatula to transfer the patties to serving plates and pile the carrots around them. **F**

Master the Method

Since the cooking basket in a toaster-oven-style machine has a limited amount of space, it's best to remove it from the machine when trying to flip *large* food items. Remember to set it on a wire rack or a heat-safe counter (because it's hot from the machine).

Spicy Chicken Skewers

Chicken skewers are always easy, maybe even more so in an air fryer, because the chunks on the skewers must be small enough to fit in the machine, so they cook super quickly.

We offer our version with a salty/spicy/sour sauce as a condiment. But you can skip our glaze and dipping sauce and use the general framework of this technique to make all sorts of chicken skewers, provided you do a few things: 1) Use boneless skinless chicken thigh meat, which holds up better to the heat, 2) make sure there's at least a tiny amount of oil on the meat so that it cooks more evenly, and 3) intersperse the meat on the skewers with vegetables like scallions, small broccoli or cauliflower florets, or even small chunks of zucchini or summer squash.

Five-spice powder is a blend of ground dried spices, often (in North America, at least) with cinnamon, cloves, fennel, star anise, and Sichuan peppercorns. Asian bottlings usually include Chinese cassia instead of the cinnamon and may also include ground dried orange peel, licorice, nutmeg, and/or ground dried turmeric. A basic blend is available in most supermarkets in the spice aisle; there's a more astounding array available from online spice purveyors. Or see Raise the Bar for a recipe to make your own.

1½ pounds or 680 grams boneless skinless chicken thighs

⅓ cup plus 1 tablespoon or 95 milliliters regular or reduced-sodium soy sauce

3 tablespoons or 45 milliliters unseasoned rice vinegar

1 teaspoon or 5 milliliters toasted sesame oil

½ teaspoon five-spice powder

Up to ½ teaspoon cayenne or red pepper flakes

Four 6-inch or 15-centimeter bamboo skewers

4 medium scallions, trimmed and cut into 2-inch or 5-centimeter pieces (white parts, too!)

½ cup or 135 grams *smooth* regular or natural-style peanut butter

Up to 2 tablespoons or 30 milliliters Frank's RedHot, Texas Pete, or other thick red hot sauce

1 tablespoon or 12 grams granulated white sugar

1 medium garlic clove, peeled and minced (about 1 teaspoon)

Water, as needed

Master the Method

There's rarely a need to soak skewers for air-frying. The cooking time is so quick and the skewers are so loaded that there's little chance they'll burn, although they may blacken at the tips.

1. With the basket in the machine or the tray set at the center level in a toaster-oven-style model, heat an air fryer to 400°F or 200°C on the air fryer setting.

2. Trim off and discard any blobs of fat from the chicken thighs. Cut the remaining pieces into 1½-inch or 4-centimeter pieces. **A**

3. Stir 1 tablespoon or 15 milliliters soy sauce, 1 tablespoon or 15 milliliters rice vinegar, the sesame oil, five-spice powder, and cayenne or red pepper flakes in a medium bowl until uniform. Add the chicken bits and stir or fold until the meat is uniformly coated. **B**

4. Alternate skewering the chicken pieces and scallion sections onto the bamboo skewers. The scallion pieces should be skewered widthwise (not down their lengths like a straw). **C**

5. Set the skewers in a single layer in the machine. Air-fry for 8 minutes, then turn the skewers over with nonstick-safe tongs (and perhaps a rubber spatula in your other hand for balance). **D**

6. Continue air-frying for about 7 more minutes, until browned and cooked through. Transfer the skewers to a wire rack to cool. Whisk the peanut butter, hot sauce, sugar, garlic, remaining ⅓ cup or 80 milliliters soy sauce, and remaining 2 tablespoons or 30 milliliters rice vinegar in a medium bowl until smooth, adding water in 1-tablespoon increments to thin out the sauce until it's the consistency of creamy salad dressing. Serve the sauce as a dip alongside the skewers. **E**

RAISE THE BAR

Make your own five-spice powder: Toast 2 tablespoons Sichuan peppercorns (or black peppercorns for a less piquant taste), 2 tablespoons fennel seeds, 10 whole cloves, 5 star anise pods, and a 2-inch or 5-centimeter cinnamon stick broken into several pieces in a dry skillet over medium heat, stirring constantly until aromatic and lightly browned, about 4 minutes. Cool to room temperature, then transfer to a spice grinder and grind until powdery. Pour through a mesh sieve to nix any hard bits. Store the sieved powder in a sealed jar in a cool, dark place for up to 6 months.

Cheesy Chicken Flautas

These flautas are an incredible treat: stuffed and deep-fried tortilla rolls, made relatively healthier in an air fryer. Flautas are usually filled with either a savory meat mixture or shredded cheese. We opt for both because we're foregoing the deep fryer, so we might as well indulge.

The best results come with pretty standard, supermarket corn tortillas—rather than high-end artisanal ones. The more economical ones are sturdier and better able to hold up to the natural dehydration in the machine. Even so, be generous in the amount of spray you give each roll.

¾ cup or 110 grams chopped skinned and boned rotisserie chicken meat (white and/or dark)

3 ounces (¾ cup) or 85 grams Tex-Mex shredded cheese blend

About half of a 4-ounce or 115-gram can of chopped green chiles, drained

½ teaspoon ground cumin

½ teaspoon onion powder

½ teaspoon garlic powder

¼ teaspoon table salt

Ground black pepper, to taste (we like lots!)

Six 6-inch or 15-centimeter corn tortillas

Nonstick spray

Master the Method

When you set the machine, always give it 10 or 15 minutes *more* than the stated timing of any recipe. You want ample time to prepare the dish as the machine heats and begins to run.

1. With the basket in the machine or the tray set at the center level in a toaster-oven-style model, heat an air fryer to 375°F or 190°C on the air fryer setting.

2. Stir the chicken meat, cheese, chiles, cumin, onion powder, garlic powder, salt, and pepper in a medium bowl until well combined. Ⓐ

3. Microwave the tortillas in a stack on high for 15 seconds to soften them a bit. Lay a tortilla on a cutting board or work surface. Place about ¼ cup or about 40 grams of the chicken mixture in the center. Spread the mixture to form a line with about ½ inch open space on either end. Ⓑ

4. Roll the tortilla up and set aside seam side down. Continue forming and rolling the remainder of the tortilla rolls. Ⓒ

5. Generously coat all of the tortilla rolls *on all sides* with nonstick spray. Ⓓ

6. Set them seam side down in the heated machine without their touching. Work in batches as necessary. Air-fry *undisturbed* for 8 minutes or until the tortillas are crunchy. Use a nonstick-safe spatula to transfer the flautas to a wire rack. Cool for a few minutes before serving. Ⓔ

RAISE THE BAR

Flautas need lots of condiments: chopped iceberg lettuce, chopped tomatoes, salsa, sour cream, guacamole, and/or jarred pickled jalapeño rings.

They may also need our easy version of Tex-Mex rice: Heat 2 tablespoons or 30 milliliters of vegetable oil in a medium saucepan set over medium heat. Add 1 cup or 200 grams uncooked long-grain white rice and stir a minute or so to coat the grains. Stir in 1¼ cups or 310 milliliters chicken broth, one 14-ounce or 400-gram can of diced tomatoes, one 4-ounce or 115-gram can of chopped green chiles, 2 teaspoons chili powder, ½ teaspoon ground cumin, and ½ teaspoon table salt. Bring to a simmer, cover, reduce the heat to low, and cook until the rice is tender, 20 to 25 minutes. Set aside, covered, for 5 minutes so the rice continues to absorb the liquids. Although optional, you can rinse the uncooked rice grains first in a mesh sieve set in the sink. Rinsing helps remove exterior starch and keeps the rice from getting too clumpy.

Chicken Saltimbocca

Saltimbocca is usually a prosciutto-wrapped veal cutlet topped with a buttery Marsala sauce. We've switched things up a bit with a boneless skinless chicken breast, which is easier to find and more affordable. Then we use the drippings right in the cooking tray or drawer as the "sauce."

Dry marsala is a dark, fortified wine, quite tasty as a tipple after dinner. Cork the bottle and keep it in the fridge for a few weeks. Avoid "cooking Marsala," which is loaded with salt.

1 very large (12- to 14-ounce or 340- to 400-gram) boneless skinless chicken breast

4 fresh sage leaves

1 medium garlic clove, peeled and minced (about 1 teaspoon)

½ teaspoon grated lemon zest

¼ teaspoon fennel seeds

¼ teaspoon table salt

Ground black pepper, to taste

4 thin slices of prosciutto

Olive oil spray

1 tablespoon or 15 grams butter

3 tablespoons or 45 milliliters dry Marsala wine or canned beef broth

RAISE THE BAR

Serve these with easy microwaved mashed potatoes: For two servings, quarter 3 medium Yukon Gold potatoes (about 1 pound or 450 grams—peeled or not, your choice), then set them in a small microwave-safe bowl along with 2 teaspoons or 10 milliliters water. Cover the bowl with plastic wrap. Microwave on high for 9 to 10 minutes, until the potatoes are fork tender. Remove the (hot!) bowl from the microwave and let it stand for 5 minutes. As the potatoes stand, combine ¼ cup or 65 milliliters milk of any sort and 1½ tablespoons or 25 grams butter in a large microwave-safe measuring vessel or small bowl. Microwave on high for 2 to 3 minutes, stirring occasionally, until the butter has melted. Uncover the potatoes, pour the hot milk over them, and mash with a fork, potato masher, or electric mixer until your preferred consistency. Season with salt and ground black pepper to taste.

1. With the basket in the machine or the tray set at the center level in a toaster-oven-style model, heat an air fryer to 400°F or 200°C on the air fryer setting.

2. Set the chicken breast on a cutting board. Starting at one side and with your knife parallel to the cutting board, halve the meat horizontally, about as if you were going to turn the breast into an open book—then slice it into two thinner fillets (as if you were dividing that open book into halves at its spine). Ⓐ

3. Set the fillets cut side up on your cutting board. Place two sage leaves widthwise on each. Sprinkle each evenly with the garlic, lemon zest, fennel, salt, and pepper. Ⓑ

4. Lay two slices of prosciutto the long way but overlapping by 2 inches on your cutting board. Lay one chicken fillet widthwise in the center on the prosciutto at the seam. Wrap the breast with the overlapping prosciutto. Set aside and repeat with the second two prosciutto slices and the remaining chicken fillet. Ⓒ

5. Generously coat the top of the wrapped breasts with olive oil spray. Ⓓ

6. Set the wrapped breasts in the heated machine without touching. Air-fry *undisturbed* for 10 minutes. Then place half of the butter on top of each and pour the wine over them without disturbing that butter. Ⓔ

7. Continue air-frying for 2 minutes, or until the chicken is cooked through and the prosciutto is sizzling, browned, and even crunchy in bits. Use a nonstick-safe spatula to transfer the chicken packets to serving plates. Remove the (hot!) cooking tray or rack as necessary from the machine. Spoon the "sauce" in the bottom of the cooking tray or the basket over each breast. Ⓕ

Master the Method
Once raw meat has touched a cutting board or other work surface, don't use it again until you've cleaned and dried it.

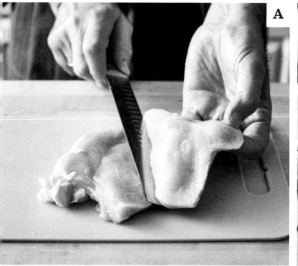

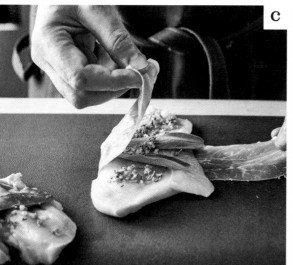

Chicken Kyiv

The point of chicken Kyiv is the butter! It's sealed inside a thin, coated chicken breast cutlet so that when the cutlet is cut on the plate, the butter runs out forming the, um, "sauce." You'll need mashed potatoes on the side, for sure: See our quick microwave mash in the Raise the Bar on page 136, but double the ingredient amounts and use a medium-sized microwave-safe bowl to make four servings.

Don't use purchased, flattened chicken cutlets. They're just too thin for success.

4 tablespoons (½ stick) or 60 grams butter

4 small (5- to 6-ounce or 140- to 170-gram) boneless skinless chicken breasts

2 teaspoons peeled and minced garlic (about 2 medium cloves)

1 teaspoon mild paprika

½ teaspoon table salt

Ground black pepper, to taste

4 large eggs, well beaten in a shallow soup plate, small pie plate, or medium food storage container

4 cups or 450 grams Italian-seasoned bread crumbs, spread out in a second shallow soup plate, small pie plate, or medium food storage container

Nonstick spray

RAISE THE BAR

How about a beet and carrot salad? Wearing kitchen gloves to protect your hands, grate 3 peeled, stemmed medium beets and 1 peeled medium carrot through the large holes of a box grater. Toss those shreds in a bowl with 2 tablespoons or 30 milliliters olive oil and 1 tablespoon or 15 milliliters red wine vinegar, as well as a little prepared yellow mustard, honey, and table salt to taste.

---

1. Cut the chunk of butter in half lengthwise, then turn these slices onto their sides and slice them in half (to make four rectangular "sticks"). Ⓐ

2. Wrap the cut butter in plastic wrap and freeze for 30 minutes. After a bit, with the basket in the machine or the tray set at the center level in a toaster-oven-style model, heat an air fryer to 400°F or 200°C on the air fryer setting.

3. Set one chicken breast between two slices of plastic wrap on a cutting board. Use the smooth side of a meat mallet or the bottom of a heavy saucepan to pound the breast to a 6 x 7-inch or 15 x 18-centimeter rectangle. Uncover the breast and repeat with the remaining breasts, using new plastic wrap if it tears in any spots. Ⓑ

4. Lay a flattened breast on a clean cutting board. Top with one of the unwrapped pieces of frozen butter, laying it lengthwise along the meat. Sprinkle the meat and butter evenly with ½ teaspoon minced garlic, ¼ teaspoon paprika, ⅛ teaspoon salt, and some ground black pepper. Repeat with the remaining breasts. Fold the "sides" of the meat of one breast over the ends of the butter, then roll the breast closed, starting with a side that's parallel to one long side of the butter slice. Repeat this folding and rolling with the remaining breasts. Ⓒ

5. Dip one rolled breast in the beaten eggs, turning to coat it thoroughly. Set in the bread crumbs and press gently, rolling it repeatedly to coat. Then *repeat this process with the same roll*: egg and bread crumbs again in that order for a thick coating. As you work, compact the breast into a fairly tight packet, about like a baked potato. Set aside. Continue with the egg, bread crumb, egg, bread crumb process with the other three chicken breasts. Ⓓ

6. Generously coat the breaded rolls *on all sides* with nonstick spray. Set them in the heated air fryer without touching. Air-fry for 7 minutes, then turn the breasts over with nonstick-safe tongs. Ⓔ

7. Continue air-frying for about 7 more minutes, or until the coating is very well browned and the meat has cooked through. (You cannot use an instant-read meat thermometer here because poking the breasts will cause the butter to run out.) Use clean tongs to transfer the breasts to a wire rack. Cool for a few minutes before serving warm. Ⓕ

Crispy Turkey Cutlets

Breaded turkey cutlets are one of our go-to weeknight dinners from an air fryer. Super tasty and satisfying—although they always seem like a much fancier meal.

Our simple technique in this recipe can actually be tweaked in lots of ways to make other crispy turkey cutlets. Skip the stuffing mix entirely and use Italian-seasoned dried bread crumbs (don't grind them). Or corn flake crumbs (again, don't grind them). Or grind Ritz crackers, Town House crackers, Wheat Thins, or bagel chips to make a crunchy coating for the meat.

One 6-ounce or 170-gram box of turkey stuffing mix of any flavor or variety

1 cup or 250 milliliters regular or low-fat buttermilk

Four 4-ounce or 115-gram turkey breast cutlets

Nonstick spray

Master the Method

With thin cuts like these turkey cutlets or, say, scaloppine, there's no way to tell if the coated meat is cooked through except by slicing it open and checking to make sure.

RAISE THE BAR

Easily up the flavors of these cutlets by using an olive oil spray or even a garlic-flavored spray.

Or up the flavors by adding more dried spices to the stuffing mix: up to 2 teaspoons dried basil, 2 teaspoons red pepper flakes, 1 teaspoon ground sage, and/or 1 teaspoon dried parsley.

For a side, try a loaded chopped salad with lots of arugula, a handful of chopped walnuts, fewer dried cranberries, a cored and chopped apple, and crumbled blue cheese, all dressed with a bottled Italian vinaigrette.

1. With the basket in the machine or the tray set at the center level in a toaster-oven-style model, heat an air fryer to 400°F or 200°C on the air fryer setting.

2. Pour the stuffing mix into a large food processor, cover, and pulse repeatedly until the consistency of coarse bread crumbs. Work in batches as necessary to keep from filling the canister more than half full. Pour the stuffing mix crumbs into a shallow soup plate, small pie plate, or medium food storage container. Ⓐ

3. Pour the buttermilk into a shallow soup plate, small pie plate, or medium food storage container. Dip a turkey cutlet in the buttermilk and turn it to coat it on both sides. Transfer the cutlet to the stuffing crumbs and press gently, turning repeatedly to coat on all sides. Ⓑ

4. Set the breaded cutlet aside on a cutting board or large piece of wax paper. Continue the buttermilk–stuffing crumb process with the remaining three cutlets. Coat them *on both sides* with nonstick spray. Ⓒ

5. Set them in a single layer in the heated machine. They shouldn't overlap but they can touch in spots. Work in batches as necessary. Air-fry for 4 minutes. Turn the cutlets over with nonstick-safe tongs. Ⓓ

6. Continue air-frying for about 3 more minutes, or until crispy-brown and cooked through. Use clean tongs to transfer the cutlets to a wire rack and cool for a minute or two before serving warm. Ⓔ

Sweet and Spicy Turkey Meatballs

These meatballs are a little sweet, thanks to the corn flake crumbs, but we've balanced that out with a savory blend of ground ginger and smoked paprika. The meatballs are super fragile until they have set in the air fryer: Make sure you compact the balls without smashing them as you form them and turn them gently in the machine so they stay together. Pull out the basket or take out the tray of a toaster-oven-style machine to give yourself plenty of room to work. A rubber spatula in your other hand can help balance the balls as you turn them.

1¼ pounds ground turkey or 575 grams turkey mince, preferably a mixture of white and dark meat

⅓ cup or 30 grams *finely* minced green parts of scallions

¼ cup or 7 grams corn flake crumbs

3 tablespoons or 45 milliliters sweet red chili sauce, such as Thai Kitchen or Mae Ploy

1 teaspoon ground dried ginger

1 teaspoon mild smoked paprika

Up to 1 teaspoon ground black pepper (to make the meatballs very spicy)

½ teaspoon garlic powder

Olive oil, as needed

RAISE THE BAR

Here's a tasty salad side: Melt 2 tablespoons or 30 grams butter in a medium nonstick skillet over medium heat. Add 1 cup or 50 grams plain panko bread crumbs and toast, stirring almost constantly, until golden and crisp, about 4 minutes. Immediately transfer the bread crumbs to a plate. Whisk ½ cup or 55 grams mayonnaise of any sort, 1 tablespoon or 15 grams Dijon mustard, 1 tablespoon or 15 milliliters lemon juice, 2 teaspoons or 10 milliliters Worcestershire sauce, ½ teaspoon table salt, and ¼ teaspoon garlic powder in a large bowl. Add a 12-ounce or 340-gram bag of chopped romaine lettuce, the toasted bread crumbs, and lots of shredded Parmigiano-Reggiano. Toss well and check for salt.

1. With the basket in the machine or the tray set at the center level in a toaster-oven-style model, heat an air fryer to 400°F or 200°C on the air fryer setting.

2. Crumble the ground turkey into a large bowl. Add the scallions, corn flake crumbs, chili sauce, ginger, smoked paprika, pepper, and garlic powder. Stir until uniform and well combined. Ⓐ

3. Pour a little olive oil into your clean hands and rub it around. Use your oiled hands to make 16 meatballs from the turkey mixture, each about the size of a golf ball. Repeat oiling your hands whenever the turkey mixture starts to stick. Ⓑ

4. Set the meatballs in the heated machine in one layer without touching. Work in batches as necessary. Ⓒ

5. Air-fry for 8 minutes, then turn the meatballs over with nonstick-safe tongs (and a helper rubber spatula in the other hand as necessary). Ⓓ

6. Continue air-frying for about 7 more minutes, or until an instant-read meat thermometer inserted into the center of one of the meatballs registers 165°F or 75°C. Use clean tongs to transfer the meatballs to a serving platter or plates. Cool for a couple of minutes before serving hot. Ⓔ

Master the Method

Although you shouldn't spray oil into the machine, it's tempting to oil or spray food in the drawer or the cooking basket *out* of the machine, before you put it in. However, excess oil even there can lead to a smoking machine.

A

B

C

D

E

Ginger-Spiced Turkey Tenderloins

Turkey tenderloins, the turkey version of pork tenderloins, are cut from the boneless breast meat. And they're a great choice for "roasted turkey" in the air fryer because they're leaner than pork but still quite tasty out of the machine. However, they can be hard to track down. If you can't find them, buy a 1½-pound or 680-gram boneless turkey breast roast and slice it lengthwise into two even halves.

Garam masala is a blend of "warm" (think "autumnal") spices, a common mélange in Indian cooking. There are dozens of blends available, especially from online spice suppliers. Read the ingredients: Some have more cinnamon or mace; others, more ground dried ginger or turmeric. Buy a blend that suits your taste.

1 tablespoon or 15 milliliters olive oil

1 tablespoon or 12 grams minced peeled fresh ginger

Up to 2 medium garlic cloves, peeled and minced (up to 2 teaspoons)

1 teaspoon garam masala

½ teaspoon ground dried turmeric

½ teaspoon table salt

Ground black pepper, to taste

Two 12-ounce or 340-gram turkey breast tenderloins

Master the Method

If you are using the wire rack in a toaster-oven-style air fryer, it can double as a cooling rack for many recipes. Simply use oven mitts to remove it from the machine (the rack is hot!) and set it on a heat-safe surface. Yes, it'll continue to cook the items a bit. Except for delicate foods (like shellfish and desserts), there's no worry about that bit of extra heat.

RAISE THE BAR

To make an easy couscous side dish, bring 1 cup or 250 milliliters chicken broth to a simmer in a small saucepan set over medium-high heat. Stir in ½ teaspoon table salt and ¼ teaspoon ground dried turmeric. Stir in 1 cup or 185 grams instant couscous, then immediately cover the saucepan and remove it from the heat. Set aside until the liquid has been absorbed, about 15 minutes. Fluff with a fork before serving.

1. With the basket in the machine or the tray set at the center level in a toaster-oven-style model, heat an air fryer to 375°F or 190°C on the air fryer setting.

2. Make a paste in a small bowl by using a fork to mash together the olive oil, ginger, garlic, garam masala, turmeric, salt, and pepper. Ⓐ

3. Smear this mixture all over the turkey tenderloins. Ⓑ

4. Use nonstick-safe tongs to set the tenderloins in the heated machine without touching. Ⓒ

5. Air-fry for 10 minutes, then flip the tenderloins over using clean tongs. Ⓓ

6. Continue air-frying for about 6 more minutes, or until an instant-read meat thermometer inserted into one of the tenderloins registers 165°F or 75°C. Transfer the tenderloins to a carving board. Cool for a few minutes before carving widthwise into 1-inch or 2½-centimeter thick slices. Ⓔ

4

BEEF & PORK

We filled this chapter with *basic* recipes you can turn to again and again for meals when friends or family drop by, or for moments when you're worn out from the day but still want to treat yourself right. Admittedly, recipes for air-frying beef and pork can sometimes get a bit complicated. We've opted overall for simple and more basic recipes (as throughout this book). Why go to quite so much fuss with a countertop appliance designed to cook quickly . . . and more healthily, to boot?

There are no burgers or sandwiches in this chapter. You'll find Patty Melts (page 68), Juicy Lucys (page 80), and the like in chapter 2, "Sandwiches and Wraps." Instead, this chapter focuses on comfort food—like Swedish Meatballs (page 168) and Crunchy-Cheesy Pork Loin Chops (page 174)—as well as lots of healthier fare, plus a few over-the-top but still simplified recipes like ours for Char Siu (page 188). With an air fryer, the cooking is easy, so we might as well up the game once in a while for the sheer joy of getting the most out of the machine.

Although we've mostly chosen lean cuts, like strip steaks and pork loin chops, you still want to buy cuts that have some visible fat. And don't trim off the fat before the steak or chop goes into the machine. If you want to get rid of extra fat, trim it *after* cooking. Let it stay on the cut to protect the meat from the hot air swirling around your dinner.

That way, you'll end up with juicy, tender steaks and chops, decadent ribs, and some pretty fine meatballs, all comforting options for any night of the week. In fact, recipes like these are the way you'll learn to use your air fryer to its fullest.

Strip Steaks with Garlic Butter

When it comes to a simple recipe for strip steaks, we took a cue from a traditional preparation for a leg of lamb. In that case, you often cut little pockets into the meat to hold garlic and herbs during roasting, the better to have those flavors permeate the meat. We've nailed down buttery, garlicky steak with the same technique.

One warning: It's easy to overcook strip steaks in an air fryer. The only way to get the job done to perfection is with an instant-read meat thermometer. Take the internal temperature when you first flip the steaks so you know about how much longer they need to stay in the machine. Don't worry: You won't cause "the juices" to run out, even if you poke each steak a couple of times.

2 medium garlic cloves, peeled

Two 10- to 12-ounce or 285- to 340-gram boneless strip steaks, each about 1 inch or 2½ centimeters thick

½ teaspoon table salt

At least ½ teaspoon ground black pepper (we prefer more!)

2 tablespoons or 30 grams butter, softened to room temperature

1 packed tablespoon stemmed fresh parsley leaves, minced

Master the Method

If you've got an air fryer on the counter, stock up at the supermarket on items when you see sales. A freezer with a few steaks in it will make dinner easier any weeknight.

RAISE THE BAR

Add up to 2 teaspoons minced fresh rosemary leaves or sage leaves to the garlic-butter mixture with the parsley.

For baked potatoes to go with these steaks, see the chart on page 227. Prepare the potatoes first, then reheat them in a 400°F or 200°C air fryer for 1 to 2 minutes.

1. With the basket in the machine or the tray set at the center level in a toaster-oven-style model, heat an air fryer to 375°F or 190°C on the air fryer setting.

2. Sliver *one* garlic clove lengthwise into 8 to 10 extremely thin strips. **A**

3. Using a paring knife, make five or six small slits across the surface of each steak. Tuck a garlic sliver into each slit. Season the two steaks evenly with the salt and pepper. **B**

4. Set the steaks garlic-ed side up with a little space between them in the heated machine. **C**

5. Air-fry for 12 minutes. Meanwhile, mince the remaining garlic clove (or put it through a garlic press) and mix it with the softened butter and parsley in a small bowl. **D**

6. Take the internal temperature of one of the steaks with an instant-read meat thermometer, just to see where you are in the cooking process. (Internal temperatures rise slowly at first, then pick up speed as the cooking continues. There's no real way to figure the exact algorithm for that rise but if the steak is at or above 90°F or 32°C, it's *no more* than 1 or 2 minutes from being done.) Flip the steaks with nonstick-safe tongs. Divide the butter mixture evenly over the steaks. **E**

7. Continue air-frying until an instant-read meat thermometer inserted into the center of a steak registers 145°F or 63°C (the USDA's notion of properly cooked beef), about 3 more minutes; or for less done, maybe just 1 or 2 more minutes, until the thermometer registers 130°F or 54°C for *our* notion of medium-rare. Transfer the steaks garlic-ed side up (that is, now flipped back over) to a serving platter or plates and cool for a few minutes to let the juices reincorporate into the meat. Spoon any melted butter and juices from the bottom of the drawer or the cooking tray over the steaks. **F**

Sirloin and Potato Dinner

This meat-and-potatoes meal will work with just about any cut of *boneless* sirloin: top sirloin, petit sirloin, sirloin tips, tri tips, petit sirloin flap (or *bavette*), or the much fancier *coulotte* (found at high-end butchers).

Most top sirloin steaks and many petit sirloin steaks will be about 1 pound or 450 grams each, which means you'll need to slice one in half widthwise to create the two steaks for this recipe.

8 ounces or 225 grams very small red- and/or white-skinned potatoes (each about 1½ inches or 4 centimeters in diameter)

1 tablespoon or 15 milliliters olive oil

1 teaspoon table salt

¼ teaspoon ground rosemary

¼ teaspoon garlic powder

Two 8-ounce or 225-gram boneless sirloin steaks (see the headnote for more information)

At least ½ teaspoon ground black pepper (we like more!)

Master the Method

Don't be tempted to poke holes in potatoes to speed up the cooking in an air fryer unless a recipe specifically says to do so. The spuds can lose moisture and petrify.

RAISE THE BAR

Put a pat of butter on each steak before serving.

Or drizzle them with a fine finishing olive oil.

To make an easy sauce, remove the rack or cooking basket from the machine. Pour 2 tablespoons or 30 milliliters red wine or beef broth right into the drawer or onto the cooking tray. Use a wooden spoon to scrape up any browned bits. Pour this mixture into a small, microwave-safe bowl or measuring cup. Add 1 tablespoon or 15 grams butter, 1 teaspoon or 5 milliliters Worcestershire sauce, and 1 teaspoon minced stemmed thyme leaves. Microwave on high for about 20 seconds, or until bubbling, then pour over the steaks.

1. With the basket in the machine or the tray set at the center level in a toaster-oven-style model, heat an air fryer to 400°F or 200°C on the air fryer setting.

2. Stir the potatoes, olive oil, ½ teaspoon salt, the rosemary, and garlic powder in a bowl until the potatoes are glistening and evenly coated. Ⓐ

3. Pour them into the heated machine, scraping any bits of herbs or oil from the bowl over the potatoes with a rubber spatula. Air-fry for 15 minutes. Meanwhile, season the steaks with the remaining ½ teaspoon salt and ground black pepper. Ⓑ

4. Move the potatoes to the side of the air fryer and set the steaks on the other side of the cooking basket or drawer. The steaks *can* touch but mustn't overlap. Work in batches as necessary. Air-fry for 6 minutes, then rearrange the potatoes *and* flip the steaks over with nonstick-safe tongs. Ⓒ

5. Continue air-frying until an instant-read meat thermometer inserted into the center of a steak registers 145°F or 63°C (the USDA's notion of properly cooked beef), about 4 more minutes; or for less done, maybe just 1 or 2 more minutes, until the thermometer registers 130°F or 54°C for our notion of medium-rare. If you (as we) like less-done steaks, take them out and let the potatoes continue to cook if they need more time, maybe 2 or 3 more minutes. Ⓓ

6. Transfer the steaks and potatoes to serving plates and cool for a few minutes before serving. Ⓔ

South Dakota Chislic Dinner

The curious name for this beef dish probably comes from a corruption of the Turkish word *shashlik*—that is, skewered meat, usually cooked over a fire. In South Dakota tradition, the meat is given a sweet and salty marinade, then cooked—if not indeed overcooked—until the steak pieces become almost jerky-like. To get that to happen in an air fryer, the steaks have to be cut into small pieces.

Chislic is often served with toothpicks to dip the bits into various condiments (like ketchup or ranch dressing), although we've added parsnips to turn this dish into a full meal. You can, of course, omit the parsnips. If so, cook the beef using its 15-minute timing.

1½ pounds or 680 grams boneless sirloin or tri tips, cut into *small* 1-inch or 2½-centimeter pieces

2 tablespoons or 30 milliliters Worcestershire sauce

1½ tablespoons or 20 grams dark brown sugar

1 tablespoon or 5 grams standard chili powder

1 teaspoon dried thyme

1 teaspoon *ground* sage

1 teaspoon onion powder

1 teaspoon garlic powder

½ teaspoon table salt

½ teaspoon ground black pepper

1½ pounds or 680 grams medium parsnips, peeled and cut into 1-inch or 2½-centimeter thick rounds

1½ tablespoons or 25 milliliters olive oil

Master the Method

For every recipe in this book, use only the air-fry button. Most machines come with lots of buttons. Many of those buttons do the same thing, only with adjustments to the preset timings and temperature. You bought an air fryer. Use the air-fry button!

RAISE THE BAR

Drizzle sriracha over the servings.

Serve this dinner with hot pretzel rolls and spicy deli mustard.

1. Stir the sirloin pieces, Worcestershire sauce, brown sugar, chili powder, thyme, sage, onion powder, garlic powder, salt, and pepper to taste in a large bowl until the beef is evenly coated in the spices and the brown sugar has dissolved. Cover and refrigerate for at least 1 hour or up to 4 hours. **A**

2. With the basket in the machine or the tray set at the center level in a toaster-oven-style model, heat an air fryer to 400°F or 200°C on the air fryer setting.

3. Mix the parsnips and oil in a second bowl until the vegetable pieces are glistening. Pour the parsnips into the heated machine in jumbled, overlapping pieces, nothing packed together or OCD-organized. **B**

4. Air-fry for 5 minutes. Stir the parsnips well and pour or set the meat pieces into the machine randomly around the vegetables. **C**

5. Air-fry for 5 more minutes. Toss the beef and parsnips well to rearrange all the pieces. *Continue* air-frying for yet 5 more minutes. *Again*, toss the beef and parsnips. **D**

6. Finally, air-fry for about 5 more minutes, or until the pieces of meat are crispy, crunchy, and deeply browned. Pour the beef and parsnips onto a serving platter. Cool for a few minutes before serving warm. **E**

Pickle- and Cheese-Stuffed Crispy Beef Rolls

These beef *rouladen* are a mix of briny pickles, melty cheese, and a crisp coating. They're terrific as a main course; but you can also cool them to room temperature, then slice into 1-inch or 2½-centimeter sections to make a substantial nibble on the deck or patio with a glass of rosé wine.

When you pound the beef to create the rolls, work firmly but gently. Don't smash the mallet or saucepan into the cut. Instead, calmly strike it with *glancing* blows, almost pushing the mallet or the saucepan away from yourself with each easy strike. Doing so will help keep the meat from tearing.

Four 6-ounce or 170-gram beef cube steaks

Six 1-ounce or 30-gram slices of Swiss cheese

Two 6-inch or 15-centimeter long dill pickles, halved lengthwise

½ teaspoon mild paprika

At least ¼ teaspoon ground black pepper

1 cup all-purpose flour or 120 grams plain flour (or a gluten-free flour alternative)

4 large eggs

3 cups or 335 grams Italian-seasoned or plain dried bread crumbs or Italian-seasoned or plain gluten-free dried bread crumbs

Nonstick spray

Master the Method

In a three-bowl set-up, it's tempting to coat all the rolls with, say, the flour, then coat them all in the eggs, then coat them all in the bread crumbs. However, doing so will inevitably lead to uneven crusts because the egg will continue to run off the rolls as they sit and wait to get into the bread crumbs. You must complete the process for each roll, cutlet, or chop before moving on to the next one.

RAISE THE BAR

Smear a little deli mustard on the meat before adding the cheese and pickle.

Substitute Emmenthaler for the more standard supermarket Swiss cheese.

1. With the basket in the machine or the tray set at the center level in a toaster-oven-style model, heat an air fryer to 375°F or 190°C on the air fryer setting.

2. Set a cube steak between sheets of plastic wrap on a large cutting board or clean work surface. Use the smooth side of a meat mallet or the bottom of a heavy saucepan to pound the cut into a 10 x 5-inch or 25 x 13-centimeter rectangle. The size is crucial to the proper roll. Ⓐ

3. Remove the plastic wrap. Place 1½ slices of cheese on the beef. Lay a pickle half lengthwise in the middle of the cheese. Sprinkle with a pinch of mild paprika and a smaller pinch of black pepper. Fold the ends of the beef at either end of the pickle up and over some of the filling. Ⓑ

4. Roll closed, sealing the pickle and cheese inside. Repeat steps 2 through 4 with the remaining pieces of beef to make three more rolls. Ⓒ

5. Pour the flour into a shallow soup plate, small pie plate, or medium food storage container. Whisk the eggs in a second shallow soup plate, small pie plate, or medium food storage container until no bits of egg white float in the mix. Finally, spread the bread crumbs in a third shallow soup plate, small pie plate, or medium food storage container. Ⓓ

6. Dip one roll into the flour and turn it to coat on all sides. Transfer it to the eggs and roll it to coat. Let the excess drip off and set it in the bread crumbs, rolling it to coat it evenly and well. (Press gently to gets lots of bread crumbs to adhere.) Set aside and repeat with the remaining three rolls. Ⓔ

7. Coat the rolls well on all sides with nonstick spray. Set them in the heated machine in a single layer without touching. Air-fry, *turning once*, for 12 minutes, or until browned and crispy. Use a nonstick-safe spatula (and maybe a rubber spatula in the other hand for balance) to transfer the rolls to a wire rack. Cool for a few minutes before serving warm. Ⓕ

Bulgogi-Style Beef Strips

We love Korean barbecue but have always struggled to find ways to easily pull it off at home. Sure, we can get close with an outdoor grill. But we were pleasantly surprised to find out that we could get even closer with an air fryer because of the way the intense heat concentrates the flavors of the rub and caramelizes them onto the steak.

For the best results here, look for boneless rib-eyes that are *not* loaded with fat. You want to see plenty of red meat in the steak. For that reason, grass-fed steaks might be a better choice, since they're usually leaner than more standard supermarket rib-eyes.

One 1½-pound or 680-gram boneless rib-eye steak, preferably a thicker cut rather than a long, flat one

¼ cup or 60 milliliters regular or low-sodium soy sauce

2 tablespoons or 25 grams dark brown sugar

2 tablespoons or 30 milliliters toasted sesame oil

3 medium garlic cloves, peeled and minced (about 1 tablespoon)

1 tablespoon or 15 milliliters sriracha

½ small hard pear, stemmed and seeded

4 medium scallions, trimmed and cut into 1-inch pieces

Master the Method

Box graters can be dangerous. They're sharp! And box graters don't come with cutting guard, the way mandolines do. Be extra careful when working with a box grater. If you're at all unsure, invest in cut-proof kitchen gloves to safeguard your knuckles.

RAISE THE BAR

Serve the strips over cooked long-grain white or brown rice.

Serve sliced Japanese pickles ("oshinko") and pickled sushi ginger on the side.

Or go all out at a Korean supermarket and serve the strips over rice with sticky-sweet strips of squid or baby shrimp, as well as lots of kimchi.

1. Set the steak on a cutting board and run your clean fingers across the cut to determine which way the fibers are running. Now slice the beef into ¼-inch or ½-centimeter thick strips *against* this grain (that is, at a 90-degree angle to it). Set aside. Ⓐ

2. Stir the soy sauce, brown sugar, sesame oil, garlic, and sriracha in a large bowl until the brown sugar dissolves. Grate the pear into the bowl through the large holes of a box grater. Ⓑ

3. Add the beef and toss well to coat the strips evenly. Set aside at room temperature for 15 minutes or cover and refrigerate for up to 2 hours. (If you do refrigerate the meat, let the bowl come back to room temperature for 20 minutes before proceeding with the recipe). Ⓒ

4. With the basket in the machine or the tray set at the center level in a toaster-oven-style model, heat an air fryer to 400°F or 200°C on the air fryer setting.

5. Pour the marinated beef into the heated machine. Air-fry for 4 minutes, then use nonstick-safe tongs to toss the beef to rearrange all the strips. Ⓓ

6. Continue air-frying for 8 more minutes, *tossing once more* at about the halfway mark. Toss the meat again, then scatter the scallions over the beef. Ⓔ

7. Continue air-frying for 1 more minute, then pour the beef and scallions into a serving bowl or platter and cool for just a minute or so before serving hot. Ⓕ

Skirt Steak Tostadas

This recipe is our homage to fajitas, but with a crispy tortilla shell under the toppings. Fajitas are traditionally made with very flavorful beef skirt steak. Unfortunately, that cut often smokes in an air fryer. So for this recipe we've built in time so that the meat sits in a marinade at room temperature. It'll then cook more quickly, with less chance of smoking.

This recipe even crisps a purchased soft tortilla for a tostada. Can you use a purchased fried tortilla? Of course! But it won't be as good.

The seeded juice of 1 medium orange

The seeded juice of 2 medium limes

1 small single-lobe shallot, peeled and minced

Up to 1 medium fresh jalapeño chile, stemmed, halved, seeded, and minced

1½ teaspoons ground cumin

1½ teaspoons table salt

1½ pounds or 680 grams beef skirt steak, sliced in half widthwise or even in three pieces, so that the pieces can lie flat in your air fryer without needing to be folded in any way

Four 4- to 6-inch or 10- to 15-centimeter round corn tortillas

Nonstick spray

2 ripe medium round or globe tomatoes, chopped

2 ripe medium Hass avocados, halved, pitted, peeled, and diced

1 tablespoon or 15 milliliters olive oil

Ground black pepper, to taste

RAISE THE BAR

Spread the tostadas with sour cream of any sort and/or warmed refried beans before adding the meat and avocado salsa.

Top the avocado salsa with pickled jalapeño rings, pickled onions, and/or fresh cilantro leaves.

1. Mix the orange juice, *half* of the lime juice, the shallot, jalapeño, 1 teaspoon cumin, and 1 teaspoon salt in a large bowl until well combined. Add the steak pieces and turn several times to coat well. Set aside at room temperature for 30 minutes while you make the tostadas. **A**

2. With the basket in the machine or the tray set at the center level in a toaster-oven-style model, heat an air fryer to 400°F or 200°C on the air fryer setting.

3. Lightly coat both sides of one tortilla with nonstick spray. Set it in the heated machine and air-fry, *turning after 2 minutes*, for 3 minutes total, or until crisp and lightly browned. Use nonstick-safe tongs to transfer the tortilla to a wire rack. Continue this process with the remaining three tortillas. Every once in a while, when you think about it, turn the steak pieces in the marinade. **B**

4. Remove the steak pieces from the marinade and set them *flat*, without touching or overlapping, in the heated machine. Work in batches as necessary. Air-fry for 15 minutes, *turning once about halfway through*, until well browned and sizzling. Transfer the steak pieces to a cutting board. Starting at a corner, slice each on the diagonal against the grain into ¼-inch or ½-centimeter thick strips. **C**

5. Gently toss the tomatoes, avocados, olive oil, remaining lime juice, remaining ½ teaspoon cumin, remaining ½ teaspoon salt, and ground black pepper to taste in a medium bowl to make an avocado salsa. **D**

6. Divide the meat among the crisp tostadas and top with the avocado salsa. **E**

Salisbury Steak with Mushroom Gravy

For this old-school comfort-food recipe, we suggest lean ground beef because excess fat in ground beef mostly just melts and runs out in an air fryer, making a mess and not adding much flavor. What's more, leaner ground beef lets all the warming flavors and sharp accents from the gravy really come through for a tastier meal.

The meat "ovals" are cooked with mushrooms, which become a side dish with a pan gravy poured over everything. Seems as if you need mashed potatoes, too, no? Try our easy microwave version in Raise the Bar on page 136.

1½ pounds lean ground beef or 680 grams lean beef mince (at least 90% lean)

½ cup or 25 grams plain panko bread crumbs or plain gluten-free panko bread crumbs

1 large egg

2 tablespoons or 30 milliliters Worcestershire sauce (gluten-free, if desired)

1 tablespoon or 15 grams pickle relish

1 tablespoon or 15 grams Dijon mustard

1 teaspoon onion powder

1½ teaspoons table salt

½ teaspoon ground black pepper

8 ounces or 225 grams sliced brown button, Baby Bella, or cremini mushrooms

Nonstick spray

1½ cups or 375 milliliters beef broth

1 tablespoon or 15 grams ketchup (gluten-free, if desired)

1 tablespoon or 7 grams cornstarch

¼ teaspoon dried thyme

¼ teaspoon ground sage

Master the Method

Set your air fryer back from the counter's edge. Never set the machine on a corner, lest it tip off.

1. With the basket in the machine or the tray set at the center level in a toaster-oven-style model, heat an air fryer to 400°F or 200°C on the air fryer setting.

2. Crumble the ground beef into a large bowl. Mix in the panko bread crumbs, egg, 1 tablespoon or 15 milliliters Worcestershire sauce, the pickle relish, mustard, onion powder, 1 teaspoon of the salt, and the black pepper to taste until uniform. **A**

3. Divide this mixture into (approximate) quarters and form each into a ball. On a cutting board, flatten the balls into ovals about 4 inches or 10 centimeters long. Put a thumbprint indentation into the middle of each oval. **B**

4. Set the ovals in the heated machine, flat side down in one layer and without touching. Work in batches as necessary. Air-fry for 8 minutes. **C**

5. Meanwhile, pour the mushrooms in a bowl and coat with nonstick spray, tossing several times and recoating them to get them shiny. After the ovals have air-fried for 8 minutes, pour the mushrooms on and around them. **D**

6. Continue air-frying for 5 minutes, until the meat is cooked through and the mushrooms have softened a bit. Transfer the meat and mushrooms to a serving platter. **E**

7. Pour the juices from the bottom of the air fryer drawer or in the cooking tray into a medium microwave-safe bowl. Stir in the broth, ketchup, cornstarch, thyme, sage, the remaining 1 tablespoon or 15 milliliters Worcestershire sauce, and the remaining ½ teaspoon salt. Microwave on high for about 4 minutes, stopping the machine to whisk three or four times, until thickened and bubbling. Pour the gravy over the meat and mushrooms before serving. **F**

RAISE THE BAR

Add up to 1 tablespoon or 15 milliliters dry sherry to the gravy mixture with the broth.

For a cheesy crust, coat the top of each oval with a little finely grated Parmigiano-Reggiano after they're cooked through and air-fry for 1 more minute. If you do this, make sure you knock any mushrooms off the ovals before you add the cheese.

Tater Tot Casserole

Why bake a Tater Tot casserole in an air fryer and not in the oven? Because the air currents brown these tots and turn them irresistibly crunchy, more so than in an oven.

Better yet, we can create a no-mess casserole by browning the ground beef right in the air fryer before we build the casserole in it. But to do so, note that the baking dish must get hot so the meat sizzles the moment it's crumbled inside.

1 tablespoon or 15 milliliters olive oil

10 ounces lean ground beef or 285 grams lean beef mince (at least 90% lean)

1 cup or 250 grams jarred chunky but plain salsa

4 ounces (1 cup) or 115 grams grated sharp American-style cheddar cheese

28 frozen Tater Tots (*do not thaw*)

1 tablespoon or 7 grams confectioners' sugar

Master the Method

How do you know if a baking dish is air fryer safe? Essentially, if it's broiler-safe, it's air-fryer-safe. Pyrex always works. Ceramics often do. Metal pans can work, provided they're heavy-duty. If a pan wouldn't warp under the broiler, it won't warp in an air fryer.

RAISE THE BAR

Stir up to a generous pinch of standard chili powder or even chipotle chile powder into the salsa before adding it to the meat.

Garnish the servings with sour cream of any sort or pickled onions. To make your own pickled onions, see Raise the Bar on page 94.

1. Put the basket in the machine or the cooking tray in the air fryer. (Because you'll be using a baking dish, you may need to set the rack in the bottom third of a toaster-oven-style model.) Set an air-fryer-safe, 6-inch or 15-centimeter square (or 7-inch or 18-centimeter round) baking dish in the machine. Heat the air fryer to 400°F or 200°C on the air fryer setting and let it stay at that temperature, thereby heating the dish, for 10 minutes. Pour the oil into the baking dish. Ⓐ

2. Crumble the ground beef into the oil. Air-fry for 2 minutes. Stir well with a fork to break up the meat. Ⓑ

3. Continue air-frying for 2 more minutes. *Again*, stir well. Then stir in the salsa. Ⓒ

4. Continue air-frying for 3 more minutes. Sprinkle the cheese evenly over the beef mixture. Ⓓ

5. Do not continue air-frying the casserole yet. Instead, toss the Tater Tots and confectioners' sugar in a medium bowl until they are well coated and place them in an even layer over the cheese in the (hot!) baking dish. Ⓔ

6. Air-fry for about 10 more minutes, or until the Tater Tots are browned and crisp. You can let the dish go longer if you want them really brown and crunchy. Use hot pads to transfer the baking dish to a wire rack. Cool for at least 5 minutes before serving up warm with a big spoon. Ⓕ

Cheeseburger-Filled Onion Rings

We wanted to make a meal with onion rings and cheeseburgers in the air fryer, but the rendered ground beef kept getting the coating on frozen onion rings soggy before they were crisp. So we combined the recipes and created rings of sliced onion that are filled with a cheesy ground beef mixture—a flight of fancy that'll be a hit at our next backyard party. Or you could serve them as a snack with drinks just about any weekend evening.

1 large white or yellow onion

12 ounces lean ground beef or 340 grams lean beef mince (at least 90% lean)

2 ounces (½ cup) or 55 grams shredded sharp American-style cheddar cheese

1 tablespoon or 15 milliliters Worcestershire sauce

½ teaspoon table salt

Up to ½ teaspoon ground black pepper

1 cup all-purpose flour or 120 grams plain flour

4 large eggs

¼ cup or 60 milliliters whole or low-fat milk

3 cups or 150 grams Italian-seasoned panko bread crumbs

Nonstick spray

Master the Method

Buy the thinnest, most flexible nonstick-safe spatula, particularly if you're working with a drawer-style air fryer. There's not much space in that drawer so it can be tricky to get the spatula underneath items in the basket.

RAISE THE BAR

After you arrange the rings in the machine, dust them with mild paprika for a little color.

Or dust them with a very small amount of ground cumin for some flavor.

1. With the basket in the machine or the tray set at the center level in a toaster-oven-style model, heat an air fryer to 400°F or 200°C on the air fryer setting.

2. Slice the root end off the onion, then peel it. Slice it into ½-inch or 1-centimeter thick rings. Separate these into individual rings and choose 12 rings that are 2 to 3 inches or 5 to 8 centimeters in diameter. (The meat mixture won't hold together in large rings and small rings are a waste of effort). Seal the remaining pieces of onion in a plastic bag and freeze them for a soup or stew down the road. Ⓐ

3. Crumble the ground beef into a medium bowl. Stir in the cheese, Worcestershire sauce, salt, and pepper to taste until uniform. Ⓑ

4. Lay the onion rings in a single layer on your cutting board or work surface. Fill the center of each ring with the ground beef mixture, packing it into the open space so that it's flush with the sides of the ring (although the coarsely ground meat and grated cheese will never yield a fully flat surface). Ⓒ

5. Pour the flour into a shallow soup plate, small pie plate, or a medium food storage container. Whisk the eggs and milk in a second shallow soup plate, small pie plate, or medium food storage container until no bits of egg white are visible. Finally, pour the bread crumbs into a third shallow soup plate, small pie plate, or medium food storage container. Set one of the filled rings in the flour and turn it to coat all sides, even the perimeter of the onion itself. Transfer to the egg mixture and coat well on all sides. Ⓓ

6. Transfer to the bread crumbs and coat well on all sides. Set aside and repeat the three-dip process with the remaining filled rings. Generously coat *both sides* of the rings with nonstick spray. Ⓔ

7. Set the filled rings in a single layer without touching in the heated machine. Work in batches if necessary. Air-fry for 8 minutes, *turning once with nonstick-safe tongs halfway through the cooking process*, until the coating is lightly browned and crunchy. Transfer the rings to a wire rack and cool for a few minutes before serving warm. Ⓕ

Meatball Lollipops

Here's an easy version of kofta, the Middle Eastern ground meat mixture that is often grilled on cinnamon sticks. The cinnamon imparts a delicate but savory flavor to the beef mixture as it cooks, particularly in the air fryer as the meat renders some of its "juices" onto the sticks.

We use fattier ground beef for this recipe because there are no bread crumbs or egg in the ground beef mixture. Leaner ground beef will toughen with this technique. Granted, fattier meat will make more of a mess in the machine and cause a bigger cleanup. Life is all about trade-offs, no?

Don't be tempted to turn the lollipops when they're in the machine. They're fragile before they're set. The tips of the cinnamon sticks may singe a bit, but you're not going to eat them.

1½ pounds moderately fatty ground beef or 680 grams moderately fatty beef mince (80% to 85% lean)

½ packed cup or 30 grams stemmed fresh parsley leaves, minced

1 medium single-lobed shallot, peeled and minced

3 medium garlic cloves, peeled and minced (about 1 tablespoon)

1 teaspoon ground coriander

1 teaspoon ground cumin

½ teaspoon ground dried ginger

½ teaspoon table salt

Twelve 3- to 4-inch or 8- to 10-centimeter cinnamon sticks

Master the Method

If you use your hands to mix together ingredients that include ground meat of any sort (or even ground fish), rub your fingernails with a sponge when you wash your hands to get rid of any bits stuck underneath.

1. With the basket in the machine or the tray set at the center level in a toaster-oven-style model, heat an air fryer to 400°F or 200°C on the air fryer setting.

2. Crumble the ground beef into a large bowl. Add the parsley, shallot, garlic, coriander, cumin, ginger, and salt. **A**

3. Stir well to combine, then form the mixture into 12 golf-ball-sized balls. **B**

4. Push a cinnamon stick through each of the meatballs. Compact the ground beef mixture to a torpedo shape at the stick's end. **C**

5. Set the meatballs on their cinnamon sticks in the heated machine in a single layer without touching. Alternating directions will help you fit more, but work in batches as necessary. **D**

6. Air-fry *undisturbed* for 14 minutes, or until the meatballs are well browned and sizzling. Use nonstick-safe tongs to transfer the meatballs on their sticks to a wire rack. (Cleanup is easier if you put paper towels or even wax paper underneath the wire rack to catch the drips.) Cool for a few minutes before serving warm. **E**

RAISE THE BAR

Serve the meatballs with tzatziki. You can often find it near or at the supermarket deli counter—or make your own: Peel a small cucumber, then halve it lengthwise. Use a spoon to scrape out the seeds and their pulp. Shred the cucumber through the large holes of a box grater into a medium bowl. Stir in 1 cup or 225 grams plain yogurt (whole-milk or low-fat, but not Greek), 1 peeled and minced medium garlic clove (about 1 teaspoon), 1 teaspoon dried dill, ½ teaspoon table salt, and ground black pepper to taste.

Swedish Meatballs

We made a change here from the more standard Swedish meatball, both for health and flavor. In most cases, Swedish meatballs are made from a mix of ground beef and pork (aka beef and pork mince). But there are two problems: 1) ground pork is increasingly hard to find in run-of-the-mill supermarkets. And 2) ground pork turns the meatballs into a greasy mess in the air fryer since the exteriors of the meatballs aren't first browned or seared (to help retain rendered fat). So ground turkey to the rescue!

And the best part? Ground turkey has a milder flavor that lets all the spices come through. If you can find ground white meat turkey (or just ground turkey breast, without the skin and cartilage), the texture of these meatballs will be even better.

1 small yellow or white onion, peeled

1 pound lean ground beef or 450 grams lean beef mince (at least 90% lean)

1 pound ground turkey or 450 grams turkey mince, preferably ground turkey breast

½ cup or 25 grams plain panko bread crumbs or plain gluten-free panko bread crumbs

¼ cup or 4 grams dried parsley leaves

1 large egg

1½ teaspoons table salt

1 teaspoon ground sage

1 teaspoon ground allspice

½ teaspoon celery seeds

¼ teaspoon ground nutmeg

¼ teaspoon ground black pepper

Olive oil, for greasing your hands

Master the Method

Ground turkey or turkey mince is often *not* labeled "white" or "dark" at your local supermarket (but is almost always labeled so at larger, high-end supermarkets). If in doubt, ask the butcher. Or simply pick up a turkey breast cutlet and ask to have it ground for you.

1. With the basket in the machine or the tray set at the center level in a toaster-oven-style model, heat an air fryer to 400°F or 200°C on the air fryer setting.

2. Grate the onion through the large holes of a box grater into a large bowl. **A**

3. Crumble in the ground beef and turkey. Add the bread crumbs, parsley, egg, salt, sage, allspice, celery seeds, nutmeg, and black pepper. Stir well to combine. Your clean hands work best, especially since you're about to get them dirty anyway. **B**

4. Pour a little oil into your palms and rub it around. Form about ¼ cup or 60 grams of the meat mixture into a ball. Set it aside and continue to make about 15 more balls, oiling your hands as necessary so the mixture doesn't stick. **C**

5. Set the meatballs in the heated machine in an even layer without being squashed together, even if they're very close together. Work in batches as necessary. **D**

6. Air-fry for 12 minutes, *turning the balls twice with nonstick-safe tongs*, or until an instant-read meat thermometer inserted into one ball registers 165°F or 75°C. **E**

7. Use clean tongs to transfer the meatballs to a wire rack. Cool for a few minutes before serving warm. **F**

RAISE THE BAR

To make a cream gravy for these meatballs, pour the pan drippings from the cooking tray or the bottom of the basket into a large saucepan. Stir in 2 cups or 500 milliliters beef broth, 3 tablespoons or 30 grams all-purpose flour, 1 teaspoon table salt, ½ teaspoon ground allspice, ¼ teaspoon ground nutmeg, and ground black pepper to taste (not too much). Set the saucepan over medium-low heat and stir until the mixture comes to a bubble and thickens. Stir in ½ cup or 125 milliliters heavy or double cream and pour over the meatballs—or toss them into the saucepan with the sauce.

Old-School Meatloaf

This recipe may be the best use *ever* of canned fried onions. They are mixed into a classic meatloaf for better flavor, making a cross between onion soup and 1970s comfort food.

Here's a surprise: We include ground turkey in our meatloaf mix, rather than all ground beef or a 50/50 mix of ground beef and pork. While a meatloaf made from only ground beef might get tough in an air fryer, the ground turkey keeps it from becoming a brick.

1 pound lean ground beef or 450 grams lean beef mince (at least 90% lean)

1 pound ground turkey or 450 grams turkey mince, preferably white meat turkey

1 packed cup or 115 grams canned fried onions (about two-thirds of a 6-ounce or 170-gram package)

½ cup or 25 grams plain panko bread crumbs

½ cup or 125 milliliters whole, low-fat, or fat-free milk

3 tablespoons or 45 milliliters bottled steak sauce

1 large egg

1 teaspoon dried thyme

1 teaspoon garlic powder

1 teaspoon table salt

At least ½ teaspoon ground black pepper (we like much more)

Master the Method

Whenever you remove heavy items from a drawer-style air fryer, it's always best to pull the drawer fully out of the machine to have the most room for leverage.

1. With the basket in the machine or the tray set at the lower third level in a toaster-oven-style model, heat an air fryer to 350°F or 180°C on the air fryer setting.

2. Crumble the ground beef and ground turkey into a large bowl. Add the fried onions, bread crumbs, milk, steak sauce, egg, thyme, garlic powder, salt, and ground black pepper. Ⓐ

3. Stir well to combine. Gather this mixture together and dump it onto a cutting board. Form it into a rectangular loaf with a flat bottom that's 8 inches or 20 centimeters long, 4½ inches or 11 centimeters wide, and 2 inches or 5 centimeters thick. Smooth the top fairly flat. (The problem with the more traditional oval shape in an air fryer? The ends burn.) Ⓑ

4. Use a sturdy but nonstick-safe spatula (and maybe your clean hand or a second nonstick-safe spatula in the other hand for balance) to transfer the meatloaf to the heated machine. Ⓒ

5. Air-fry undisturbed for 45 minutes or until an instant-read meat thermometer inserted into the center of the loaf registers 165°F or 75°C. Ⓓ

6. Use a sturdy, clean, nonstick-safe spatula to transfer the meatloaf to a *clean* cutting board. Cool for about 5 minutes. Carve the meatloaf into 1-inch or 2½-centimeter thick slices and serve warm. Ⓔ

RAISE THE BAR

To give the meatloaf a glaze, brush it with barbecue sauce, ketchup, or chutney of any sort for the last 5 minutes of cooking.

This meatloaf makes terrific sandwiches the next day. Slice it warm, then store those slices under plastic wrap in the fridge. Need we add that meatloaf sandwiches should be made on white bread with mayonnaise as the condiment? Don't make us come to your house and take away the ketchup.

Healthier Bone-in Pork Chops

Modern pork is so lean that we felt free to add some oil to the seasoning mixture and gussy it up with all sorts of flavors. In fact, because boneless pork loin chops are so lean, we found that bone-in pork chops work best in a simple, healthy preparation like this one. Let's face it: The bone adds tons of flavor to the chops as they cook.

3 tablespoons or 45 milliliters olive oil

1 tablespoon or 6 grams finely grated orange zest

Up to 3 medium garlic cloves, peeled and minced (up to 1 tablespoon)

2 teaspoons dried oregano

1 teaspoon ground cumin

1 teaspoon table salt

½ teaspoon ground black pepper (or even more!)

Four 10-ounce or 285-gram *bone-in* loin or rib pork chops, each about ¾ inch or 2 centimeters thick

Master the Method

If you don't have a citrus zester, grate the orange zest with the small holes of a box grater. Don't press the orange against the holes but zip it along them, just to remove the brightly colored zest.

RAISE THE BAR

Substitute 1½ teaspoons jerk or Cajun dried spice blend for the oregano *and* cumin.

To make a Brussels sprout slaw to go alongside these pork chops, mix 2 cups or 220 grams shredded Brussels sprouts, ½ cup or 55 grams slivered almonds, and ¼ cup or 40 grams dried cranberries in a medium bowl. Add 3 tablespoons or 45 milliliters olive oil, 1 tablespoon or 20 grams honey, 1 tablespoon or 15 grams Dijon mustard, ½ teaspoon table salt, and ¼ teaspoon garlic powder. Toss well to coat.

1. With the basket in the machine or the tray set at the center level in a toaster-oven-style model, heat an air fryer to 375°F or 190°C on the air fryer setting.

2. Use a fork to stir the oil, zest, garlic, oregano, cumin, salt, and pepper in a small bowl until well combined. Ⓐ

3. Rub this mixture all over the pork chops—both sides, even around the edges. (Your clean hands work best, although you can use a pastry brush or even the fork from the last step.) Ⓑ

4. Set the pork chops in a single layer without touching in the heated machine. Work in batches as necessary. Ⓒ

5. Air-fry for 10 minutes, then use clean nonstick-safe tongs to turn the pork chops over. Ⓓ

6. Continue air-frying for about 10 more minutes, or until well browned and sizzling. Use clean tongs to transfer the pork chops to a wire rack or a serving platter. Cool for a few minutes before serving warm. Ⓔ

A

B

C

D

E

Crunchy-Cheesy Pork Loin Chops

Pork loin chops—rounds cut from a pork loin—are so lean that they need a quite thick coating to protect them in an air fryer. The chops release very little fat, so a thinner coating won't easily adhere to the meat as the chops cook. So for the best success, we double-dip the chops in eggs and bread crumbs to make a spectacularly crunchy (and thick) coating.

Watch the chops carefully as they cook—check on them a few times. We like them very crunchy, so we're always looking for dark brown spots. You might prefer them a little less crunchy. Take the internal temperature fairly often, maybe two or three times, so you always know where you are in the cooking process. But keep in mind that the temperature rises exponentially faster as the meat cooks. So if the internal temperature is, say, 75°F or 24°C, the cut is not "halfway there"—it's closer to two-thirds of the way to 145°F or 63°C. By the way, those two internal temperatures are now the USDA standard for pork cuts (but not ground pork) and yield pink pork. Head for 165°F or 75°C if you want no speck of pink in the meat.

4 large eggs

1¼ cups or 65 grams Italian-seasoned panko bread crumbs or Italian-seasoned gluten-free panko bread crumbs

1 ounce (½ cup) or 30 grams finely grated Parmigiano-Reggiano

At least ½ teaspoon ground black pepper (we prefer lots more)

Four 6- to 8-ounce or 170- to 225-gram *boneless center-cut* pork loin chops (each *at least* ½ inch or 1¼ centimeters thick)

Olive oil spray

Lemon wedges, for garnishing

Master the Method

If you use pre-ground Parmesan cheese as part of a coating for a protein or vegetable in an air fryer, watch the food carefully as it cooks. The pre-ground stuff loses moisture as it sits on the shelf at the store and can burn quickly. If you notice deeply browned bits on the coating, reduce the heat by 25°F or 15°C and turn the food more often to keep it from burning.

RAISE THE BAR

Dollop the pork chops with pesto or tapenade (particularly a *green* olive tapenade).

1. With the basket in the machine or the tray set at the center level in a toaster-oven-style model, heat an air fryer to 400°F or 200°C on the air fryer setting.

2. Beat or whisk the eggs in a shallow soup plate, small pie plate, or medium food storage container until no bits of egg white are floating in the mix. Mix the bread crumbs, cheese, and pepper into a second shallow soup plate, small pie plate, or medium food storage container until uniform. Ⓐ

3. Dip one pork chop into the egg mixture and turn it to coat it on both sides, even around the edge. Set it in the bread crumb mixture and turn to coat well. Ⓑ

4. Dip that same pork chop back into the eggs, repeating the coating process. Then dip it into the bread crumb mixture and again coat it well on all sides. Set aside and continue this dipping process (egg, bread crumbs, egg, bread crumbs) with the remaining three pork chops. Ⓒ

5. Coat the pork chops *on both sides* with olive oil spray. Ⓓ

6. Set the chops in a single layer without touching in the heated machine. Work in batches as necessary. Air-fry for 6 minutes, then gently flip the chops over with clean nonstick-safe tongs. Ⓔ

7. Continue air-frying for about 5 minutes, or until an instant-read meat thermometer inserted into the center of one pork chop registers 145°F or 63°C. Use clean nonstick-safe tongs to transfer the chops to a wire rack. Cool for a few minutes, then squeeze a little lemon juice over the chops and serve warm. Ⓕ

French-Onion-Soup Pork Loin Chops

We crafted this recipe so that the pork chops are like a cross between crunchy air-fried chops and French onion soup. The trick is the combination of onion soup mix and thyme in the coating—and then, of course, the cheese over the chops for their last few minutes in the machine.

There's no added salt in the coating because onion soup mix already contains lots. Pass more at the table for those who like an even saltier meal.

1¾ cups or 90 grams plain panko bread crumbs or plain gluten-free panko bread crumbs

One 1-ounce or 28-gram envelope of onion soup mix

1 teaspoon dried thyme

1 teaspoon mild paprika

1 teaspoon granulated white sugar

4 large eggs

Four 6- to 8-ounce or 170- to 225-gram *boneless center-cut* pork loin chops (each *at least* ½ inch or 1¼ centimeters thick)

Eight 1-ounce or 30-gram slices of Swiss cheese

Master the Method

Air fryers eat salt. For one thing, an exterior coating that includes salt liquefies with, say, a pork chop's juices and runs into the bottom of the drawer or cooking tray, not sticking around near the chop as it might in a skillet. For another, many crunchy coatings seem less salty because the crisp texture makes you salivate more and so lose more salt as you swallow each bite. So no matter what you might anticipate, the coatings or crusts often need more. Always have more at the table.

1. With the basket in the machine or the tray set at the center level in a toaster-oven-style model, heat an air fryer to 375°F or 190°C on the air fryer setting.

2. Pulse the bread crumbs, onion soup mix, thyme, paprika, and sugar in a food processor until well combined but not powdery. **A**

3. Pour this ground mixture into a shallow soup plate, small pie plate, or medium food storage container. Beat or whisk the eggs in a second shallow soup plate, small pie plate, or medium food storage container until no bits of egg white are floating in the mix. **B**

4. Dip one pork chop in the eggs, turning it to coat on all sides, even the edges. Transfer it to the bread crumb mixture and press gently, turning repeatedly, to coat both sides and the edges. **C**

5. Repeat this two-dip process with *the same* pork chop: eggs, then bread crumb mixture. Set aside and continue the same four-dip process with the remaining pork chops (egg, bread crumb mixture, egg, bread crumb mixture). Generously coat *both sides* of the chops with nonstick spray. **D**

6. Set the chops in a single layer without touching in the heated machine. Work in batches as necessary. Air-fry for 6 minutes. Gently flip the chops over with clean nonstick-safe tongs. Continue air-frying for 3 minutes, then lay two slices of cheese on top of each chop. **E**

7. Continue air-frying for 3 more minutes, or until the cheese has melted, is bubbling, and maybe even a little browned. Use clean nonstick-safe tongs to transfer the chops cheese side up to a wire rack. Cool for a few minutes before serving warm. **F**

RAISE THE BAR

Make a kidney bean salad to go with these chops: Mix 1 cup or 180 grams drained and rinsed canned red kidney beans, 1 shredded medium carrot, 1 finely chopped tomato, 3 thinly sliced radishes, 1 thinly sliced medium scallion, and ¼ cup or 40 grams crumbled feta in a medium bowl. Add 3 tablespoons or 45 milliliters olive oil, 2 tablespoons or 30 milliliters lemon juice, 1 teaspoon dried oregano, ½ teaspoon table salt, and ¼ teaspoon garlic powder. Toss well.

Healthier Pork Tenderloin and Butternut Squash Dinner

Here's another complete meal from an air fryer, using a pork tenderloin and purchased butternut squash cubes. But there's a complication: You may need to cut store-bought butternut squash cubes into smaller, 2-inch or 5-centimeter pieces (although, of course, they'll all be irregularly shaped, curved, and maybe indented because of the shape of the vegetable).

If you'd like to use a whole squash, buy one that's about 1¾ pounds or 800 grams. Stem and peel it, then cut it in half widthwise and scoop out the seeds. Cut the squash into 2-inch or 5-centimeter irregular pieces.

1¼ pounds or 575 grams purchased peeled and seeded butternut squash pieces, each about 2 inches or 5 centimeters

2 small red onions, peeled and each cut into 6 wedges

1½ tablespoons or 25 milliliters olive oil

1 teaspoon table salt

½ teaspoon ground sage

½ teaspoon dried thyme

No more than ¼ teaspoon ground black pepper (in this case, less is more)

One 1¼-pound or 575-gram pork tenderloin, cut in half widthwise

Nonstick spray

¼ teaspoon dried oregano

¼ teaspoon mild paprika

¼ teaspoon garlic powder

Master the Method

Dried spices need refreshing, too. If yours are more than 1 year old, consider replacing them with a new batch. Paprika is particularly prone to turning into nothing more than a red coloring agent.

RAISE THE BAR

Consider using winter squash beyond the butternut standard, particularly blue Hubbard, red kuri, (savory!) kabocha, or (very savory!) buttercup squash.

1. With the basket in the machine or the tray set at the center level in a toaster-oven-style model, heat an air fryer to 400°F or 200°C on the air fryer setting.

2. Put the squash pieces and onion wedges in a large bowl. Add the oil, ½ teaspoon salt, the sage, thyme, and black pepper. Toss well to coat evenly and thoroughly. Ⓐ

3. Pour and scrape the contents of the bowl into the heated machine. Air-fry for 6 minutes. Ⓑ

4. Before you begin air-frying again, lightly coat the pork tenderloin pieces with nonstick spray. Sprinkle the meat evenly with the oregano, paprika, garlic, and remaining ½ teaspoon salt. Ⓒ

5. Place the tenderloin pieces on top of the vegetables with at least 1 inch or 2½ centimeters space between each. Ⓓ

6. Air-fry for 10 minutes, then toss the vegetables and turn the pieces of pork over with clean tongs. Ⓔ

7. Continue air-frying for about 12 more minutes, until the vegetables are tender and browned and an instant-read meat thermometer inserted into the center of the thickest piece of pork registers 145°F or 63°C (the interior of the pork will still be pink but safe). Use nonstick-safe tongs to transfer the pork and vegetables to a serving platter. Cool for about 5 minutes before slicing the pork into rounds to serve with the vegetables. Ⓕ

Coconut-Crusted Pork Tenderloin

Pork and coconut are a traditional Caribbean or Polynesian combo: Two sweet ingredients with decidedly savory undertones combine for a sophisticated flavor. This recipe asks you to butterfly a pork tenderloin so you can get more crunchy crust on every speck of meat. We offer you instructions on how to do this task, as well as a photo of the process. But if you want to make your life much easier, pick up a pork tenderloin at the supermarket and ask the butcher to halve it widthwise, then butterfly both pieces for you.

Don't use sweetened flaked coconut. Look for unsweetened desiccated coconut in the health-food or gluten-free aisle of most supermarkets.

One 1¼-pound or 575-gram pork tenderloin

2 tablespoons or 30 milliliters regular or reduced-sodium soy sauce, or gluten-free tamari

1 tablespoon or 15 milliliters mirin

1 tablespoon or 15 grams light brown sugar

2 teaspoons or 8 grams minced ginger

1 cup or 85 grams *unsweetened* shredded or desiccated coconut

½ cup or 25 grams plain panko bread crumbs or plain gluten-free panko bread crumbs

Nonstick or coconut oil spray

Master the Method

Spray any nonstick or oil sprays close to foods. The farther away you spray, the bigger the mess you make.

RAISE THE BAR

Make an easy peanut and vegetable salad to go with the pork: In a large bowl, combine 1 stemmed, seeded, and diced medium red bell pepper with 2 grated medium carrots, 2 thinly sliced medium celery stalks, 2 thinly sliced medium scallions, and ¼ cup or 35 grams salted shelled peanuts. Add 2 tablespoons or 30 milliliters toasted sesame oil, 2 tablespoons or 30 milliliters regular or reduced-sodium soy sauce, 1 tablespoon or 15 milliliters lemon juice, 1 tablespoon or 20 grams honey, and up to 2 teaspoons or 8 grams minced ginger. Toss well to serve.

1. With the basket in the machine or the tray set at the center level in a toaster-oven-style model, heat an air fryer to 350°F or 180°C on the air fryer setting.

2. Halve the pork tenderloin widthwise, then cut each half lengthwise without cutting through it, to be able to open it like a book with its spine. **A**

3. Whisk the soy sauce, mirin, brown sugar, and ginger in a small bowl until the brown sugar dissolves. Spread this mixture over all sides of the butterflied tenderloin pieces. **B**

4. Whisk the coconut and bread crumbs in a shallow soup plate, small pie plate, or medium food storage container. Use nonstick-safe tongs to set one tenderloin piece into this mixture, pressing the meat gently but firmly and turning it to coat on all sides, even the edges. Set aside and coat the second piece in a similar way. **C**

5. Generously coat *all sides* of the tenderloin with nonstick spray. **D**

6. Set the pieces of tenderloin in a single layer without touching in the heated machine. Work in batches as necessary. Air-fry for 8 minutes (or 7 minutes in a smaller, drawer-style model), then *gently* flip the pork pieces with *clean* nonstick-safe tongs. **E**

7. Continue air-frying for about 7 more minutes, or until the crust is lightly browned and an instant-read meat thermometer inserted into the thickest section of one piece of pork registers 145°F or 63°C (for pork that's still a bit pink inside); or air-fry for about 9 minutes for 165°F or 75°C (for pork that is well-done). Use clean nonstick-safe tongs to transfer the pork to a wire rack. Cool for a few minutes before slicing to serve. **F**

Salt-and-Pepper Baby Back Ribs

These simple pork ribs have just a salt-and-pepper rub, so the meat is not covered up with a sweet glaze. To be honest, we find super sweet glazes too much for modern pork as they cover up the savory, tasty flavor of leaner meat. So we opt for preparations like this one: simpler, more straightforward, and a better meal all around.

Better yet, the ends of the bones will even get a little charred as the ribs cook—which then means more flavor per bite!

One 3-pound or 1⅓-kilogram rack of pork baby back ribs

1 tablespoon table or kosher salt

1 tablespoon ground black pepper

½ teaspoon onion powder

¼ teaspoon garlic powder

Master the Method

Not only should you clean the interior of an air fryer after every use, you should also clean the exterior. Greasy fingerprints on the digital panel can eventually compromise its effectiveness.

RAISE THE BAR

Serve the ribs with an easy version of Alabama white sauce: Whisk 1 cup or 225 grams mayonnaise of any sort, ¼ cup or 60 milliliters distilled white vinegar, 2 peeled and minced medium garlic cloves (about 2 teaspoons), 1 teaspoon or 5 grams Dijon mustard, ½ teaspoon table salt, and lots and lots of fresh ground black pepper (go nuts!).

1. With the basket in the machine or the tray set at the center level in a toaster-oven-style model, heat an air fryer to 375°F or 190°C on the air fryer setting.

2. Use a paring knife to pick at and loosen the silky membrane that covers the rack's underside. Grab the nicked up bit with a paper towel and peel off the membrane. **A**

3. Use a chef's knife (or any knife larger than a paring knife) to slice the rack into three even sections. **B**

4. Mix the salt, pepper, onion powder, and garlic powder in a small bowl until uniform. Sprinkle evenly over both sides (meat and bone) of the rib sections. **C**

5. Arrange the three sections in the heated machine so that air can circulate around them. In smaller machines, they can overlap but should be set higgledy-piggledy, certainly not evenly stacked on top of each other. Work in batches as necessary. **D**

6. Air-fry for 15 minutes. Use clean nonstick-safe tongs to rearrange the pieces to expose more sections as the ribs continue to cook. **E**

7. Continue air-frying for about 15 more minutes, until well browned and sizzling. Use clean tongs to transfer the rib sections to a clean cutting board. Cool for a few minutes before slicing between the bones into individual ribs. Serve warm. **F**

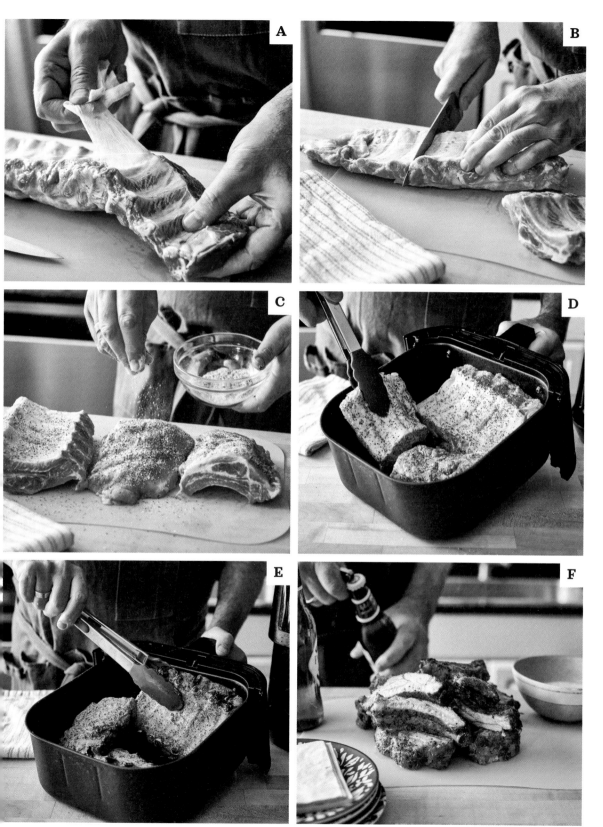

Chinese Take-Out Baby Back Ribs

We cut these ribs into individual one-bone pieces so that every speck of the meat can get as crunchy as possible in the air fryer. There's a little sugar in the spice mix, although not enough to turn them sticky-sweet. The brown sugar is mostly to get caramelization evenly over every bit of meat.

The pork will dry out a bit with this technique, so it's best to serve the ribs with a dipping sauce. We suggest our favorites below and in the Raise the Bar.

One 3-pound or 1⅓-kilogram rack of pork baby back ribs

1 tablespoon or 13 grams light brown sugar

1 tablespoon mild paprika

1 tablespoon table salt

½ tablespoon ground white pepper

½ tablespoon garlic powder

½ teaspoon five-spice powder (see Raise the Bar, page 132)

Purchased duck sauce or a sweet-and-sour sauce like Saucy Susan, for dipping

Master the Method

When you stack items or dump them into the machine in a random way—say, these ribs, or French fries, or even air-fried parsnips—make sure they're not piled up high and too close to the fan and/or heating element. The closer they are to it, the more likely they'll burn.

RAISE THE BAR

Skip the duck sauce and dip the ribs in Chinese hot mustard.

Or a 1:1:1 mix of soy sauce, Worcestershire sauce, and unseasoned rice vinegar.

1. With the basket in the machine or the tray set at the center level in a toaster-oven-style model, heat an air fryer to 350°F or 180°C on the air fryer setting.

2. Use a paring knife to pick at and loosen the silky membrane that covers the rib rack's underside. Grab the nicked up bit with a paper towel and peel the membrane off the rack. (See photo A for Salt-and-Pepper Baby Back Ribs on page 183 to show you how to do this.) Slice the rack into individual ribs. Ⓐ

3. Mix the brown sugar, paprika, salt, white pepper, garlic powder, and five-spice powder in a small bowl. Sprinkle over the pork ribs, gently rubbing it in. Ⓑ

4. Pile the ribs into the heated machine like a bunch of small twigs dumped on the ground—that is, with lots of space between them as they lie this way and that. Work in batches as necessary. Ⓒ

5. Air-fry for 10 minutes. Rearrange the ribs by tossing the basket or moving them around with nonstick-safe tongs. Ⓓ

6. Continue air-frying for another 10 minutes. *Again*, rearrange the ribs, making sure that any bits covered up to this point are now exposed to the air currents. Continue air-frying for about another 10 minutes, or until the ribs are well browned and sizzling, with the meat pulling back a bit from the bones. Use clean tongs to transfer the ribs to a wire rack. Cool for a few minutes before serving warm with duck sauce or sweet-and-sour sauce for dipping. Ⓔ

Sticky-Garlicky Country-Style Pork Ribs

A pork lover's delight, country-style pork ribs are super meaty cuts, sometimes with a bit of bone in each "rib," but certainly not the traditional "finger" of bone in usual pork racks. They can even be boneless, as we call for here. Curiously, country-style pork ribs don't come from the rib section of the pig. They're cut from the shoulder area near the loin. Some butcher shops even call them "pork shoulder ribs." They take exceptionally well to an air fryer because there's so much protective fat around the meat.

Of all the pork recipes in this book, this one is the sweetest because the cut is fatty and so can stand up to a heavy glaze. But we can't put a sugary glaze on the country-style ribs from the start because they need a long cook and the sugar would burn before the meat is done. To solve those problems, we give the meat a spice rub, then glaze them with store-bought barbecue sauce for the last few minutes.

1½ tablespoons mild paprika

2 teaspoons garlic powder

1 teaspoon onion powder

1 teaspoon table or kosher salt

1 teaspoon ground black pepper

½ teaspoon celery seeds

½ teaspoon dried thyme

½ teaspoon ground allspice

½ teaspoon ground cumin

Four 8-ounce or 225-gram boneless country-style pork ribs

Nonstick spray

½ cup or 125 milliliters bottled barbecue sauce, preferably a plain barbecue sauce

Master the Method

Although thin cuts of meat are best if you take them out of the fridge for 10 to 15 minutes before putting in the machine, thick cuts like these country-style ribs cook more evenly when they're right out of the refrigerator. The cold meat heats more slowly, so the fat doesn't instantly melt and run off.

RAISE THE BAR

Serve with air-fried Brussels sprouts (see page 225) or parsnips (see page 226). Make the vegetables first, then keep them on a wire rack until the ribs are ready. Recrisp the vegetables in a 350°F or 180°C air fryer for 2 to 3 minutes.

1. With the basket in the machine or the tray set at the center level in a toaster-oven-style model, heat an air fryer to 375°F or 190°C on the air fryer setting.

2. Mix the paprika, garlic powder, onion powder, salt, black pepper, celery seeds, thyme, allspice, and cumin in a small bowl until uniform. Ⓐ

3. Sprinkle and rub the paprika mixture over all sides of the country-style ribs. Ⓑ

4. Coat them generously *on all sides* with nonstick spray. Ⓒ

5. Set them in a single layer without touching in the heated machine. Work in batches as necessary. Air-fry for 14 minutes. Flip the ribs over with nonstick-safe tongs. Ⓓ

6. Brush about half of the barbecue sauce over the top of each rib. Ⓔ

7. Continue air-frying for 5 more minutes, then flip the ribs over again. Brush the other sides with the remaining barbecue sauce. Continue air-frying for about 4 more minutes, or until the glaze has caramelized and even started to turn crunchy at the edges. Use clean tongs to transfer the ribs to a wire rack. Cool for a few minutes before serving hot. Ⓕ

Char Siu

Is there anything better than char siu, that roast pork familiar from Chinese stir-fries and dumpling fillings? Hardly! Sweet, aromatic, and very porky—in other words, simply the best.

Admittedly, we can't make traditional Chinese char siu in an air fryer. But we can get very close with pork shoulder "steaks" and a flavorful rub. We use a boneless pork shoulder roast that you must cut into "steaks." (You'll never find packaged pork shoulder steaks.) To save a step, ask the butcher to cut a small piece of pork shoulder into the right-sized steaks for this recipe.

Two important notes: Do not used a "bagged" pork shoulder, which is really a bunch of trimmings held together by netting. And you *must* start this recipe at least 2 hours in advance, if not the day before, to let the marinade soak into the meat.

1½ pounds or 680 grams boneless pork shoulder

1 medium garlic clove, peeled and minced (about 1 teaspoon)

2 tablespoons or 30 grams hoisin sauce (see headnote to Classic Chicken Egg Rolls, page 48)

2 teaspoons or 10 milliliters regular or reduced-sodium soy sauce

2 teaspoons or 10 milliliters dry sherry or Shaoxing (a rice wine) or unsweetened apple juice

1½ teaspoons or 10 grams molasses

1½ teaspoons table salt

½ teaspoon five-spice powder (see Raise the Bar, page 132)

¼ teaspoon ground white pepper

½ teaspoon toasted sesame oil

1 tablespoon or 20 grams honey

2 teaspoons or 3 milliliters water

2 drops of red food coloring, optional

Master the Method

Sticky marinades prove difficult in an air fryer. They cause meat or fish to stick to the cooking tray or basket, even if it's a nonstick surface. Use a nonstick-safe spatula or tongs to get under almost everything in the basket or tray to *loosen* the food *before* flipping it.

1. Set the pork shoulder on a cutting board and slice into three or four 1-inch or 2½-centimeter thick "steaks." Ⓐ

2. Whisk the garlic, hoisin sauce, soy sauce, sherry or its substitutes, molasses, salt, five-spice powder, white pepper, and sesame oil in a large bowl until uniform. Ⓑ

3. Add the pork "steaks" to the bowl and toss well to coat them on all sides. Cover and refrigerate for at least 2 hours or up to 24 hours, rearranging the meat occasionally to make sure it's all coated in the garlic mixture. Ⓒ

4. With the basket in the machine or the tray set at the center level in a toaster-oven-style model, heat an air fryer to 350°F or 180°C on the air fryer setting.

5. Put the "steaks" in a single layer in the heated machine. They can touch in spots but should not overlap; there should be little spaces between them where air can flow. Work in batches as necessary. Ⓓ

6. Air-fry for 10 minutes. Meanwhile, whisk the honey, water, and red coloring, if using, in a small bowl. Flip the steaks over with nonstick-safe tongs. Continue air-frying for 5 minutes, then brush about half of the honey mixture over the top of the steaks. Ⓔ

7. Flip the steaks over again and brush them with the remaining honey mixture. Continue air-frying for about 7 more minutes, or until the glaze has caramelized and is dark, even a little burned at the edges. Use clean tongs to transfer the "steaks" to a cutting board. Cool for a few minutes before slicing them into strips and small chunks to serve warm. Ⓕ

RAISE THE BAR

Serve the chunks of pork with cooked white long-grain rice, pickled ginger, and steamed baby bok choy, maybe drizzled with some more soy sauce.

Or take it over the top and search out haiga-mai rice at Korean grocery stores like H-Mart. The rice has no bran but still the germ, giving it a more intense flavor, sort of like a lighter version of brown rice.

Cheese-Stuffed Sausage Balls

These easy pork meatballs are stuffed with mozzarella for a cheesy bit of goodness in each bite. Can you use spicy Italian sausage instead of mild? Of course!

Repeatedly wet your hands to form the balls or else the sticky pork will make a mess. We find the easiest way to get the job done with minimal fuss is to bring the cutting board near the sink, with the water running slowly, to form the balls. That way, you don't have to turn the faucet on and off with porky hands.

Form the balls *before* you stick the little piece of cheese inside because there's really no way to form the sticky mixture around a piece of cheese.

1 pound or 450 grams loose or bulk sweet Italian sausage meat or sweet Italian sausages with any casings removed

1 large egg

¼ cup or 30 grams Italian-seasoned dried bread crumbs or Italian-seasoned gluten-free dried bread crumbs

2 tablespoons or 20 grams golden raisins or sultanas, chopped

2 tablespoons or 15 grams pine nuts, chopped

½ teaspoon fennel seeds

½ teaspoon red pepper flakes

2 sticks of mozzarella string cheese or Cheestrings, each cut crosswise into 6 equal pieces

Master the Method

Most cooking trays and racks can go in the dishwasher. (Check your instruction manual.) But never put the drawer from a drawer-style model in the dishwasher, even if the manufacturer says you can. We've found the alignment tracks can warp after repeatedly getting wet and heat-dried.

RAISE THE BAR

Serve the meatballs over cooked and drained spaghetti and top with lots of warmed marinara sauce. Add a simple tossed salad, if you'd like. To make your own marinara sauce, see page 38.

1. With the basket in the machine or the tray set at the center level in a toaster-oven-style model, heat an air fryer to 375°F or 190°C on the air fryer setting.

2. Crumble the sausage meat into a large bowl. Add the egg, bread crumbs, raisins, pine nuts, fennel seeds, and red pepper flakes. **A**

3. Mix until well combined and uniform. Using clean but *wet* hands, form the sausage mixture into 12 even balls. *Repeatedly* wet your hands as you form the balls to keep the mixture from sticking. **B**

4. Push a piece of string cheese into a ball, closing the mixture back around the piece of cheese. Repeat with the remaining pieces of cheese and the sausage balls. And remember to wet your hands even now as you work with the meatballs. Wet hands lead to sealed meatballs that won't leak. **C**

5. Set the balls in a single layer without touching in the heated machine. Work in batches as necessary. **D**

6. Air-fry for 5 minutes, then flip the balls over with clean nonstick-safe tongs. **E**

7. Continue air-frying for 10 more minutes, turning one more time, until well browned and sizzling. Use clean tongs to transfer the balls to a wire rack. Cool for a few minutes before serving warm. **F**

5

FISH & SHELLFISH

Fish and shellfish seem to be made for crunch. Witness the tourists at a beach shack or dockside restaurant. Hardly anybody orders the pan-sautéed snapper or shrimp. Sure, those vacation meals are a calorie splurge. At home, you probably want healthier fare. But you can get crunch without all the grease out of an air fryer! Even better, cleanup is much easier without a filthy, oily skillet to deal with when you're ready to just stream a movie or sit back with a novel.

Every recipe in this chapter was tested with both fresh and frozen fillets, shrimp, and scallops. We could rarely tell a difference. By the time we gave the cut a salty or spicy marinade, or a crunchy crumb coating, we didn't know which was which. The only recipe where we noticed a difference is the super healthy one for Herbed Salmon Dinner with Asparagus Spears (page 200). Because the preparation is so simple, we noticed that fresh salmon was far better than previously frozen.

Otherwise, stock up on frozen fish and shellfish when you see sales. A bag (or two!) of peeled and deveined shrimp or cod fillets in the freezer means there's an easy dinner in the offing.

For both shellfish and fish fillets individually frozen in packets, quickly thaw them in a bowl of cool water on the counter in about 30 minutes. (Don't unwrap the fillets until they're thawed.) Dinner's minutes away, a healthy weeknight meal that makes you feel as if you're still on vacation.

Beer-Batter Fish Fillets

Crispy fish fillets are no longer a splurge with an air fryer! But truth be told, traditional beer batters prove difficult in the machine. The swirling heat can strip the batter off a fillet. And a wet batter won't puff, because it's vibrating in the air currents when it should be firming up (as it would in a deep fryer).

The solution for cod (and other thick fish) fillets is to use a standard beer batter, then *also* coat the battered fillets in a bread crumb mixture. That crumb mixture will 1) add lots of flavor, with herbs and such, 2) hold the batter in place, and 3) offer more crunch per bite.

1½ cups all-purpose flour or 180 grams plain flour

¾ cup or 185 milliliters amber or light-colored beer, preferably a Pilsner or a lager

1 large egg

2 tablespoons or 15 grams cornstarch

1 teaspoon baking powder

½ cup or 80 grams yellow cornmeal

½ cup or 60 grams Italian-seasoned dried bread crumbs

2 teaspoons dried thyme

2 teaspoons mild paprika

2 teaspoons onion powder

1 teaspoon table salt

Four 6- to 8-ounce or 170- to 225-gram skinned cod fillets or thick white-fleshed skinned fillets such as tilapia, snapper, or bass (thawed if frozen)

Nonstick spray

Master the Method
To tell if a fish fillet is cooked through, insert a flatware knife into the thickest part, hold it in place for about 5 seconds, then remove it and set its flat (not sharp!) side against your lips. The metal should feel warm, not hot, but certainly not cool.

1. With the basket in the machine or the tray set at the center level in a toaster-oven-style model, heat an air fryer to 400°F or 200°C on the air fryer setting.

2. Whisk 1 cup or 120 grams of the flour, the beer, egg, cornstarch, and baking powder in a shallow soup plate, shallow food storage container, or small pie plate until uniform. Ⓐ

3. Mix the remaining ½ cup or 60 grams of flour, the cornmeal, bread crumbs, thyme, paprika, onion powder, and salt in a second shallow soup plate, food storage container, or pie plate until uniform. Ⓑ

4. Set a cod fillet in the beer mixture and turn it several times to coat evenly and well. Transfer it straight to the bread crumb mixture and turn it several times, pressing gently, to get a solid even coating on the fish without any wet spots. Set the fillet aside on a cutting board and continue dipping and coating the remaining fillets. Ⓒ

5. Generously coat the fillets *on all sides* with nonstick spray. Ⓓ

6. Set them in a single layer without touching in the heated machine. Air-fry for 4 minutes. Flip the fillets with a nonstick-safe spatula. Ⓔ

7. Continue air-frying for about 4 more minutes, until the fillets are browned, crunchy, and cooked through. Thicker fillets will take the full time; thinner, maybe only 2 minutes. Use that spatula to transfer the fillets to a wire rack. Cool for a couple of minutes before serving hot. Ⓕ

RAISE THE BAR

For homemade tartar sauce, whisk all of the following in a large bowl: 1 cup or 225 grams mayonnaise of any sort; 1½ tablespoons or 25 milliliters lemon juice; 1 tablespoon or 15 grams pickle relish; 1 tablespoon packed and minced fresh dill fronds; 1 tablespoon packed and minced fresh parsley leaves; 1 teaspoon minced, drained, and rinsed capers; ½ teaspoon granulated white sugar; and ½ teaspoon table salt. Store any leftovers, covered, in the fridge for up to 4 days.

Crumb-Coated Fish Fillets

Bread crumbs give fish fillets a bit more texture but no less crunch than a batter coating (as for the fillets on page 194). However, crumb coatings don't stick well to fish fillets without a little help. Here, we slather the fillets in olive oil for a more even crumb coating. The oil also adds a pleasant, aromatic flavor.

    Take care: That crumb coating is fragile before it firms up. Be careful when you turn the fillets even while spraying them. Your clean fingers might be the best tool. And don't be tempted to play with them or check under them in the machine before they've cooked for at least 6 minutes.

Four 6- to 8-ounce or 170- to 225-gram skinned cod fillets or thick white-fleshed skinned fillets such as tilapia, snapper, or bass (thawed if frozen)

1½ tablespoons or 25 milliliters olive oil

1½ cups or 170 grams plain dried bread crumbs

1 teaspoon dried thyme

1 teaspoon ground sage

1 teaspoon mild paprika

1 teaspoon onion powder

1 teaspoon table salt

½ teaspoon garlic powder

½ teaspoon ground black pepper

Nonstick spray

Master the Method

Dried bread crumbs don't last forever. Keep them in a cool, dark pantry for no more than 4 months; or store them in the freezer in a sealed plastic bag for up to 1 year. Thaw to room temperature before use.

RAISE THE BAR

Omit the thyme, sage, paprika, onion powder, and garlic powder. Substitute 2 tablespoons dried Cajun seasoning blend or Old Bay seasoning. Check the label of the blend to see if it contains salt. If it does, omit the salt as well.

Use a garlic-flavored nonstick spray.

Or coat the fish fillets with a toasted nut oil or even melted butter, rather than olive oil.

1. With the basket in the machine or the tray set at the center level in a toaster-oven-style model, heat an air fryer to 400°F or 200°C on the air fryer setting.

2. Set the fillets on a cutting board and use your clean hands to rub them all over with the olive oil. (If you're squeamish, use a pastry brush.) Ⓐ

3. Mix the bread crumbs, thyme, sage, paprika, onion powder, salt, garlic powder, and black pepper in a shallow soup plate, shallow food storage container, or small pie plate. Ⓑ

4. Dip one oiled fillet into the bread crumb mixture, turning several times and pressing gently to coat with a fairly thick layer, even along the "sides." Set aside and continue coating the remaining fillets. Ⓒ

5. Generously coat the fillets *on all sides* with nonstick spray. Ⓓ

6. Set them in a single layer without touching the heated machine. Air-fry *undisturbed* for 8 minutes, or until browned, crunchy, and cooked through. Transfer the fillets to a wire rack. Cool for a couple of minutes before serving hot. Ⓔ

A

B

C

D

E

Teriyaki and Sesame Salmon Fillets

These fillets are dinner-party worthy, if only because they're so beautiful on the plates. (Plus, they couldn't be easier.) We've even served them as a weekend brunch for house guests with toasted bagels and a carrot slaw.

Sesame seeds go rancid quickly, usually within a month, even in a cool, dark pantry. Store them in a sealed bottle or container in the freezer for up to one year. (You can use them directly from the freezer for this recipe.) And make sure you sniff any you buy. They do sit on store shelves a while and go, well, wonky. Always get a full refund for inferior purchases.

Four 4- to 6-ounce or 115- to 170-gram skin-on salmon fillets

Nonstick spray

½ cup or 125 milliliters regular or reduced-sodium soy sauce

¼ packed cup or 50 grams light brown sugar

2 tablespoons or 30 milliliters unseasoned rice vinegar

3 medium garlic cloves, peeled and minced (about 1 tablespoon)

1 tablespoon or 15 milliliters toasted sesame oil

1 teaspoon ground dried ginger

½ cup or 70 grams sesame seeds, preferably a blend of white and black seeds

Master the Method

Fish skin is difficult in an air fryer. It sticks to the cooking surface, no doubt. The skin needs a generous coating of fat or just nonstick spray. Even so, don't beat yourself up if you leave some behind.

RAISE THE BAR

Serve these fillets with cooked and drained soba noodles, as well as lots of bottled pickled sushi ginger, maybe some purchased seaweed salad, and even chunky kimchi.

1. With the basket in the machine or the tray set at the center level in a toaster-oven-style model, heat an air fryer to 400°F or 200°C on the air fryer setting.

2. Lay the fillets skin side up on a cutting board and generously coat *the skins only* with nonstick spray. Ⓐ

3. Whisk the soy sauce, brown sugar, vinegar, garlic, sesame oil, and ginger in a shallow soup plate, shallow food storage container, or small pie plate until the brown sugar dissolves and the mixture is uniform. Ⓑ

4. Dip one fillet *skin side up* into the soy-sauce mixture. Let it rest there for a few seconds, just to pick up as much flavor as possible. Transfer it *skin side down* to a cutting board and continue dipping and transferring the remaining fillets. Ⓒ

5. Sprinkle the flesh of each fillet with an even coating of about a quarter of the sesame seeds. Ⓓ

6. Lightly coat *the seeded tops* of the fillets with nonstick spray. Set them *skin side down* in the air fryer. Air-fry *undisturbed* for 8 minutes, or until cooked through and lightly browned at the edges. Use a nonstick-safe spatula *and* a rubber spatula for balance to transfer the fillets skin side down to serving plates. Cool for a couple of minutes before serving. Ⓔ

A

B

C

D

E

Herbed Salmon Dinner with Asparagus Spears

It's so easy to make a meal in an air fryer with salmon fillets and asparagus. The only problem is that you can't make more than two fillets, given that space is at a premium in the machine.

In fact, the space is even more at a premium in toaster-oven-style machines. If you have two cooking trays, use one for the salmon fillets and the other for the asparagus. Also, swap those trays top to bottom when you rearrange the spears and add the compound butter to the salmon fillets.

2 tablespoons or 30 grams butter, softened to room temperature

1 medium garlic clove, peeled and minced (about 1 teaspoon)

1 teaspoon stemmed fresh thyme leaves, minced

Two 6-ounce or 170-gram skin-on salmon fillets

½ teaspoon table salt

Ground black pepper, to taste

Olive oil spray

6 ounces or 170 grams pencil-thin asparagus spears, any dried ends cut off

Master the Method

If you're making multiple batches of a fish or shellfish dish, we don't recommend putting the first batch in a low oven to keep it warm. Instead, put oven-safe dinner plates in a 175°F or 80°C oven for about 20 minutes before you prepare the meal. Put individual servings onto these (hot!) plates and leave them at room temperature before making another batch. Just remember that the plates are hot if you've got kids at the table.

RAISE THE BAR

Double the compound butter and save the remaining half for the asparagus spears after they come out of the machine hot.

We can use fresh herbs here because of the quick cooking time. Swap out the thyme in the butter for minced fresh oregano leaves, minced fresh parsley leaves, or minced fresh tarragon leaves.

1. With the basket in the machine or the tray set at the center level in a toaster-oven-style model, heat an air fryer to 400°F or 200°C on the air fryer setting.

2. Use a fork to mash the butter, garlic, and thyme in a small bowl until uniform to make a compound (or flavored) butter. **A**

3. Season the fillets with the salt and pepper. Coat them *on both sides* with nonstick spray. Give a particularly generous coating to the skin side. **B**

4. Lightly coat the asparagus spears with nonstick spray. **C**

5. Set the fillets skin side down in one half of the basket or cooking tray. Pile the asparagus spears in the remaining space, overlapping the spears as necessary. **D**

6. Air-fry for 5 minutes. Use nonstick-safe tongs to rearrange the asparagus spears. Dot half the compound butter over each salmon fillet. **E**

7. Continue air-frying for about 3 minutes, or until the salmon is cooked through and even beginning to brown at the thinnest spots. Divide the fillets and asparagus spears between two serving plates and serve hot. **F**

Good Ol' Fried Shrimp

Who doesn't love fried shrimp? Here's a recipe for a homemade version that's a little spicy, a bit aromatic, and very crunchy (which is *the point*, right?).

Why do we insist on a mixture of bread crumbs, flour, *and* cornmeal? Wouldn't one or two be enough? Actually, no. They each contribute to the final crunch: The bread crumbs for tooth, the cornmeal for just a little pop, and the flour to help it all adhere in the heat.

2 large egg whites

2 tablespoons or 30 milliliters water

1 cup or 115 grams plain dried bread crumbs

¼ cup or 35 grams yellow cornmeal

¼ cup all-purpose flour or 30 grams plain flour

2 teaspoons table salt

1 teaspoon ground sage

½ teaspoon celery seeds

½ teaspoon mild paprika

¼ teaspoon cayenne

1 pound or 450 grams peeled and deveined *large* shrimp (18 to 20 shrimp)

Nonstick spray

Master the Method

If you want to use gluten-free flour in a recipe, here's a rule-of-thumb: If the flour (or its substitute) is to go *under* beaten eggs or a liquid coating, you're free to use almost any gluten-free flour substitute. But if the flour is to go *over* the liquid ingredients or be the main coating in and of itself, unfortunately most gluten-free substitutes won't work with these recipes—*unless* the bulk of the substitute is made with almond flour and includes no xanthan gum.

1. With the basket in the machine or the tray set at the center level in a toaster-oven-style model, heat an air fryer to 400°F or 200°C on the air fryer setting.

2. Whisk the egg whites and water in a shallow soup plate, shallow food storage container, or small pie plate until foamy and well combined. **A**

3. Mix the bread crumbs, cornmeal, flour, salt, sage, celery seeds, paprika, and cayenne in a second shallow soup plate, shallow food storage container, or small pie plate until uniform. **B**

4. Dip one shrimp in the egg white mixture, turning it several times to coat well. Lift it up and let any excess run off. Set it in the bread crumb mixture and turn several times, pressing gently to give it an even, light coating. Set aside on a clean cutting board and continue dipping and coating the remaining shrimp. **C**

5. Lightly coat the shrimp *on all sides* with nonstick spray. **D**

6. Set the shrimp in a single layer without touching in the heated machine. Air-fry for 4 minutes. Flip the shrimp over with nonstick-safe tongs. **E**

7. Continue air-frying for about 3 more minutes, or until browned, crunchy, and cooked through. Use those tongs to transfer the shrimp to a wire rack. Cool for a couple of minutes before serving warm. **F**

RAISE THE BAR

Make an easy cocktail sauce by stirring all of the following in a medium bowl: 1 cup or 235 grams sweet red chili sauce (such as Heinz Chili Sauce), 1 tablespoon or 15 grams prepared white horseradish, 2 teaspoons or 10 milliliters Worcestershire sauce, 2 teaspoons or 10 milliliters lemon juice, and several dashes of a hot red pepper sauce (such as Tabasco sauce).

Scampi-Style Shrimp Dinner with Green Beans

Here's a one-step prep for an easy dinner right out of the air fryer. You can even make a light, lemony sauce right in the machine just before the shrimp and green beans are served.

Large shrimp work a bit better than smaller ones because their extra heft allows them to cook more evenly in the intense heat. Admittedly, bigger shrimp can be pricey. Stock up on bags of frozen large shrimp when you see them on sale. And look for already peeled and deveined frozen shrimp, making this supper an even easier meal.

1½ pounds or 680 grams peeled and deveined *large* shrimp (27 to 30 shrimp)

1½ pounds or 680 grams green beans, trimmed

½ cup or 125 milliliters olive oil

Up to 9 medium garlic cloves, peeled and minced (up to 3 tablespoons)

1½ teaspoons dried oregano

1 teaspoon fennel seeds

Up to 1 teaspoon red pepper flakes

½ teaspoon table salt

2 tablespoons or 30 milliliters lemon juice

RAISE THE BAR

Add up to 2 tablespoons or 30 grams butter with the lemon juice to the juices remaining in the machine.

Drizzle the servings with some fine finishing extra virgin olive oil, along with the sauce from the machine.

If you want to go all out, spoon the shrimp and green beans over buttery mashed potatoes.

1. With the basket in the machine or the tray set at the center level in a toaster-oven-style model, heat an air fryer to 400°F or 200°C on the air fryer setting.

2. Toss the shrimp, green beans, olive oil, garlic, oregano, fennel seeds, red pepper flakes, and salt in a large bowl until the shrimp and green beans are glistening and coated in the garlic and spices. Ⓐ

3. Pour and scrape the contents of the bowl willy-nilly into the heated machine. Do not pack the items together, but scrape out every drop and spice speck from the bowl. Air-fry for 3 minutes. Toss all the ingredients in the machine with nonstick-safe tongs. Ⓑ

4. Continue air-frying for about 4 more minutes, or until the shrimp are pink and firm while the green beans are still crisp-tender. Spoon the shrimp and green beans onto a serving platter or serving plates. Ⓒ

5. If the basket-style machine has a cooking tray, use nonstick-safe tongs to remove it. If the toaster-oven-style-oven machine has a mesh cooking rack, use those tongs to remove it. (Either is hot!) Pour the lemon juice into the juices in the basket or the cooking tray. Ⓓ

6. To serve, stir the sauce well and spoon over the shrimp and beans on the platter or plates. (Remember that the drawer or the cooking tray is hot!) Serve warm. Ⓔ

A

B

C

D

E

Island Shrimp Kebabs

With a dried jerk rub and some canned pineapple, you can make these easy skewers in a snap, either for dinner or just nibbles on the patio some evening. There's no need to soak the skewers because the cooking time is so quick.

To thread shrimp onto skewers, run the sharp point through the thick part of the shrimp, then bend the thin end of the tail over and run it through with the skewer as well, thereby holding the shrimp onto the skewer in two places.

For the reason that larger shrimp work better in an air fryer, see the headnote to Scampi-Style Shrimp Dinner on page 204.

1 pound or 450 grams peeled and deveined *large* shrimp (18 to 20 shrimp)

1 tablespoon or 15 milliliters olive oil

1 tablespoon or 15 milliliters apple cider vinegar

1 tablespoon or 5 grams dried jerk seasoning spice rub

1 teaspoon granulated white sugar

12 drained canned pineapple chunks, packed in juice or water

1 large red bell pepper, cored, seeded, and cut into 1-inch or 2½-centimeter squares

Six 6-inch or 15-centimeter bamboo skewers

Master the Method

Granulated white sugar helps make spice-based coatings crunchy in an air fryer. Consider adding even as little as ¼ teaspoon to any spice rub for a better overall finish to a dish.

1. With the basket in the machine or the tray set at the center level in a toaster-oven-style model, heat an air fryer to 400°F or 200°C on the air fryer setting.

2. Toss the shrimp, olive oil, vinegar, jerk rub, and sugar in a large bowl until the shrimp are glistening and well coated. Ⓐ

3. Alternate threading the shrimp, pineapple chunks, and bell pepper squares on the skewers. (See the headnote for more information on skewering shrimp.) Ⓑ

4. Place the skewers in a single layer without touching in the heated machine. Work in batches as necessary. Ⓒ

5. Air-fry for 4 minutes. Turn the skewers over with nonstick-safe tongs (and maybe a flatware fork in the other hand for balance). Ⓓ

6. Continue air-frying for 2 to 3 more minutes, or until the shrimp are pink and firm—and maybe with a touch of brown at the edges. Transfer the skewers to a platter or serving plates and cool for a couple of minutes before serving warm. Ⓔ

RAISE THE BAR

Brush the skewers with bottled Asian-style peanut sauce or dressing during their last minute of air-frying.

Use fresh pineapple cubes (about 1 inch or 2½ centimeters each) instead of canned.

Serve the skewers over cooked white or brown rice.

Mix a little minced peeled fresh ginger into that rice before you plate it.

Or serve the skewers over a plate of cooked and drained soba noodles, dressed with a little soy sauce, unseasoned rice vinegar, and toasted sesame oil.

A

B

C

D

E

Shrimp Dumpling and Broccoli Dinner

Frozen shrimp dumplings can be hard to track down outside of Asian supermarkets and large high-end supermarkets. But they make an easy, full dinner from an air fryer.

Look for half-moon dumplings with fairly thin wrappers (*not* the paper-thin rice wrappers as on *har gow*—that is, the pale, translucent dumplings often served for dim sum). The dumplings might be called "pot stickers," but make sure you're not buying open-at-the-top shumai.

We also tested this recipe with frozen pork dumplings and it worked with the exact same timing.

One 1½-pound or 680-gram bag of frozen shrimp dumplings (*do not thaw*)

Nonstick spray

12 ounces or 340 grams medium broccoli florets (about 4 cups)

2 tablespoons or 30 milliliters regular or reduced-sodium soy sauce

2 teaspoons or 10 grams peanut butter of any sort

1 teaspoon granulated white sugar

1 teaspoon or 5 milliliters toasted sesame oil

1 teaspoon or 5 milliliters apple cider vinegar

Several dashes of hot red pepper sauce, such as Tabasco sauce or Texas Pete

Master the Method

Although a rubber spatula is the usual go-to when it comes to tossing things in sauces and such, two wooden spoons (one in each hand) work almost as well.

RAISE THE BAR

Swap in Chinese broccoli for the more standard florets, trimming off the dried stems and cutting the Chinese broccoli into 2-inch or 5-centimeter pieces (it's otherwise all edible: leaves, flowers, stems).

Use chili crisp (a hot, spicy Asian condiment) as a dip for the sauced dumplings.

1. With the basket in the machine or the tray set at the center level in a toaster-oven-style model, heat an air fryer to 400°F or 200°C on the air fryer setting.

2. Put the dumplings in a large bowl and coat well with nonstick spray, tossing and respraying several times until they're all shiny and coated. **A**

3. Pour the dumplings willy-nilly into the heated machine. Do not pack them down into layers. **B**

4. Air-fry for 3 minutes. Meanwhile, put the broccoli florets in that same large bowl and coat them well with nonstick spray, using that same toss-and-respray technique. **C**

5. Pour the broccoli florets into the machine and toss them well with the dumplings. Air-fry for 3 minutes. *Again*, toss well. **D**

6. *Continue* air-frying for 3 more minutes. Toss well one more time and *continue* air-frying for 3 *final* minutes, or until the dumplings are crispy at the edges but just starting to brown. (The dumplings have been in the machine for 12 minutes with four tossings.) **E**

7. Whisk the soy sauce, peanut butter, sugar, sesame oil, vinegar, and hot red pepper sauce in that same large bowl until smooth. Pour the hot dumplings and broccoli into the bowl and toss well until everything is well coated. **F**

A

B

C

D

E

F

Super Crunchy Scallops

You'll have a hard time believing these tender and flavorful scallops didn't come out of a deep fryer. They're just that irresistible.

Scallops are often doped with chemicals to preserve their moisture content. That excess liquid can ooze out and turn any crust soggy. Instead, look for "dry packed" scallops. Also, reject any scallops with a feathery white surface (a sign of freezer burn), brown edges or spots (a sign of age), or a rainbow-hued sheen (a sign of contamination).

1 cup all-purpose flour or 120 grams plain flour

2 tablespoons or 13 grams cornstarch

2 tablespoons or 10 grams Old Bay seasoning

1 tablespoon mild paprika

1 teaspoon baking powder

1 large egg

¾ cup or 185 milliliters light-colored beer, preferably a pilsner or a lager

1½ cups or 130 grams purchased corn flake crumbs

12 large sea scallops (about ¾ pound or 340 grams in total)

Nonstick spray

Master the Method

Get your hands dirty when you're coating foods in liquid or dry-ingredient mixtures! Your fingers are more dexterous than tongs. Just make sure your hands are clean before you start dredging and coating.

RAISE THE BAR

Serve these with a creamy cole slaw: In a large bowl, toss a 10-ounce or 285-gram bag of shredded cabbage with ½ cup or 55 grams mayonnaise of any sort, 2 tablespoons or 30 milliliters lemon juice, 1 tablespoon or 15 grams Dijon mustard, 1 tablespoon or 15 milliliters Worcestershire sauce, ½ teaspoon table salt, and ½ teaspoon ground black pepper. To go over the top, omit the salt and add 2 tablespoons or 30 grams jarred pickle relish or *up to* 2 tablespoons or 30 grams jarred jalapeño relish.

1. With the basket in the machine or the tray set at the center level in a toaster-oven-style model, heat an air fryer to 400°F or 200°C on the air fryer setting.

2. Whisk the flour, cornstarch, Old Bay seasoning, paprika, and baking powder in a large bowl until uniform. Add the egg and beer; whisk until smooth. **A**

3. Set the flour mixture aside for 15 minutes so the flour's gluten relaxes a bit and the dry ingredients better absorb the wet ones. Meanwhile, spread the corn flakes into a shallow soup plate, shallow food storage container, or small pie plate. **B**

4. Pour the scallops into the wet batter and fold *gently* to coat them thoroughly. **C**

5. Use nonstick-safe tongs to pick out a scallop from the batter, let some of the excess drip off, then set the scallop in the corn flake crumbs. Press and turn a few times to coat evenly and thoroughly on both sides and around the perimeter. Set aside on a cutting board and continue this process with the remaining scallops. **D**

6. Generously coat the scallops *on all sides* with nonstick spray. **E**

7. Set the scallops in a single layer without touching in the heated machine. Air-fry for 4 minutes. Then turn the scallops with clean nonstick-safe tongs. *Continue* air-frying for about 4 more minutes, or until the coating is well browned and noticeably crispy. Transfer the scallops to a wire rack and cool for a few minutes before serving warm. **F**

Bacony Crab Cakes

Crab cakes are easy in an air fryer, partly because there's no skillet of grease to clean up afterwards. The cakes are more tender but also more fragile than those fried in oil—which means you must take extra care when removing them from the machine.

There's no need to buy jumbo lump crabmeat. In fact, you could (and maybe should) use backfin meat, which is far more economical (if stronger tasting). The best crabmeat is sold in pasteurized containers (rather than shelf-stable cans) in the refrigerator case near the fish counter.

Four thin U.S.-style bacon slices

¾ pound or 340 grams lump crabmeat (see the headnote for more information)

½ cup or 25 grams *Italian-seasoned* panko bread crumbs or Italian-seasoned gluten-free panko bread crumbs

6 tablespoons or 85 grams regular or low-fat mayonnaise (do not use fat-free)

One 4-ounce or 110-gram jar of diced pimientos, drained (about ½ cup)

½ teaspoon dried dill

½ teaspoon dried thyme

½ teaspoon garlic powder

½ teaspoon mild paprika

½ teaspoon table salt

Ground black pepper, to taste

2 cups or 100 grams *plain* panko bread crumbs or gluten-free plain panko bread crumbs

Nonstick spray

Master the Method

To make cleanup easier, lay paper towels underneath the wire rack to catch crumbs or drips. Make sure the paper towels are flat to allow good air circulation under the rack.

1. With the basket in the machine or the tray set at the center level in a toaster-oven-style model, heat an air fryer to 350°F or 180°C on the air fryer setting.

2. When the machine is hot, add the bacon and air-fry *undisturbed* for 5 minutes, or until browned and crisp. Transfer to a wire rack with nonstick-safe tongs. Cool for 5 minutes, then chop into fine bits. **A**

3. Raise the heat in the air fryer to 400°F or 200°C.

4. Stir the crabmeat, *seasoned* panko bread crumbs, mayonnaise, pimientos, dill, thyme, garlic powder, paprika, salt, pepper, and the chopped bacon in a medium bowl until well combined. Work gently so as not to break the crab into threads. **B**

5. Spread the *plain* panko bread crumbs on a large serving plate or pie plate. Use your clean hands to divide the crab mixture into six equal balls. Flatten into 4-inch or 10-centimeter diameter patties with your hands, then set them one by one into the panko bread crumbs. Gently press and turn the patties to coat them on all sides, even around the perimeter. **C**

6. Lightly coat the patties *on both sides* with nonstick spray. **D**

7. Set them in a single layer without touching in the heated machine. Air-fry *undisturbed* for 10 minutes, or until lightly browned and crisp. Use a nonstick-safe spatula to transfer the fragile(!) patties to a wire rack. Cool for a couple of minutes before serving warm. **E**

RAISE THE BAR

Although French fries are the go-to side, we prefer these light crab cakes with a vinegary cole slaw (sometimes called "health salad" at the delicatessen).

For a condiment, consider a spicy German mustard or sweet red chili sauce.

If you want to make homemade sweet red chili sauce, we've got a recipe on our YouTube channel, *Cooking With Bruce & Mark*.

Fish-Stick Fish Cakes

The simplest way to make fish cakes is to use frozen fish sticks. Once thawed, they're already seasoned and have all the breading necessary to become tender and moist in an air fryer.

If you buy prechopped celery as a convenience, you'll need to mince about ⅓ cup or 45 grams into smaller bits for the best texture.

Note: There's no salt in this recipe. Fish sticks are loaded with it. There's also no added oil or even nonstick spray. There's plenty of fat in the breading on the fish sticks as well as in the mayo.

One 11.4-ounce or 325-gram box of fish sticks, thawed

½ cup or 55 grams regular or low-fat mayonnaise (do not use fat-fat)

One 4-ounce or 110-gram jar of diced pimientos, drained (about ½ cup)

1 medium celery stalk, *minced*

¼ teaspoon dried dill

¼ teaspoon celery seeds

¼ teaspoon onion powder

Master the Method

To mince long vegetables like celery, cut the vegetable lengthwise into long, thin strips (about ¼ inch or ½ centimeter thick). If the vegetable is round, like a carrot, first slice it into quarters lengthwise, then slice these quarters into thinner strips. Now gather these strips together and slice them widthwise into ¼-inch or ½-centimeter pieces.

RAISE THE BAR

These cakes are great on slider buns with tartar sauce (for a recipe, see Raise the Bar, page 194) and perhaps some chopped, crunchy iceberg lettuce.

Or change it up and serve them with mayonnaise and kimchi on slider buns.

Don't like kimchi? Try a combo of pickled jalapeño rings and sweet pickle relish.

1. With the basket in the machine or the tray set at the center level in a toaster-oven-style model, heat an air fryer to 400°F or 200°C on the air fryer setting.

2. Crumble the thawed fish sticks into a large bowl. Ⓐ

3. Add the mayonnaise, pimientos, celery, dill, celery seeds, and onion powder. Mix until well combined, taking care not to turn the fish sticks into mush. Ⓑ

4. Form the fish mixture into eight patties, each about 2½ inches or 6 centimeters in diameter. Ⓒ

5. Set the patties in a single layer without touching in the heated machine. Ⓓ

6. Air-fry *undisturbed* for 13 minutes, or until crisp and brown. Transfer the fish patties to a wire rack with a nonstick-safe spatula and cool for a few minutes before serving warm. Ⓔ

Crumbed Salmon Patties

These tasty salmon patties are more like burger patties, *not* the more traditional salmon croquettes often made with canned salmon. Burger-like patties work so much better in an air fryer. This is because the more standard croquettes are usually rounded, so they don't cook as evenly in an air fryer as they do in an inch or so of oil in a skillet. Essentially, we've flattened the salmon mixture into patties and fixed the problem. Even better, the patties are more suitable with burger buns.

1 small single-lobe shallot, peeled

1 *mini* red or yellow bell pepper

1 small celery stalk

One 15-ounce or 425-gram can of pink salmon, drained

1 large egg

2 tablespoons or 30 grams regular or low-fat mayonnaise (do not use fat-free)

1 tablespoon or 15 grams pickle relish

1 teaspoon or 5 milliliters Worcestershire sauce

½ teaspoon dried thyme

¼ teaspoon cayenne

1½ cups or 75 grams Italian-seasoned panko bread crumbs

Nonstick spray

Master the Method

Try not to press flattened fish patties into bread crumbs with your fingertips. You'll make indentations across the surface which will lead to uneven cooking. Instead, use the length of your fingers or even use the flat part of your palm to press the patty gently into the bread crumbs.

RAISE THE BAR

Serve the patties on toasted brioche buns with deli mustard, a thin slice of red onion, and a splash of unseasoned rice vinegar.

1. With the basket in the machine or the tray set at the center level in a toaster-oven-style model, heat an air fryer to 400°F or 200°C on the air fryer setting.

2. Mince the shallot, bell pepper, and celery on a cutting board. Ⓐ

3. Transfer the vegetables to a large bowl. Crumble the salmon into the bowl, picking off any skin or bones that adhere to or are stuck inside the meat. Add the egg, mayonnaise, pickle relish, Worcestershire sauce, thyme, and cayenne. Stir gently but well until uniform. Ⓑ

4. Spread the bread crumbs on a large plate or pie plate. Divide the salmon mixture into four even balls and form into patties, each about 3 inches or 8 centimeters in diameter. Set a patty into the bread crumbs and press gently to coat it, turning it several times to coat all sides, including the perimeter. Set aside and repeat with the remaining patties. Ⓒ

5. Lightly coat the patties *on both sides* with nonstick spray. Set them in a single layer without touching in the heated machine. Air-fry for 6 minutes. Flip them over with a nonstick-safe spatula (and perhaps a rubber spatula in the other hand for balance). Ⓓ

6. Continue air-frying for about 4 more minutes, or until the patties are browned and cooked through. Use that spatula to transfer the croquettes to a wire rack and cool for a few minutes before serving warm. Ⓔ

Tuna Noodle Patties

We've taken the flavors of tuna noodle casserole—even the noodles!—and turned them into patties for an easy meal that's one part comfort food, one part air fryer magic.

The right noodles for this recipe are "fine" egg noodles that look like broken-up dried angel-hair pasta, not the more standard egg noodles you'd use for mac-and-cheese. You can often find these "fine" egg noodles in the kosher food section of supermarkets.

1 rounded cup or 40 grams dried *fine* egg noodles (see the headnote for more information)

Boiling water, as needed

Two 5-ounce or 140-gram cans of tuna packed in olive oil, preferably yellowfin tuna, drained

2 tablespoons or 30 grams regular or low-fat mayonnaise (do not use fat-free)

1 teaspoon onion powder

1 teaspoon table salt

½ teaspoon celery seeds

Ground black pepper, to taste

1½ cups or 170 grams Italian-seasoned dried bread crumbs

Nonstick spray

4 ounces (1 cup) or 115 grams shredded Swiss cheese

Master the Method

Air fryers create quite a bit of heat: 400°F or 200°C? That's a hot oven! If you store a machine out on the counter, make sure you pull it out from underneath the overhead cupboard before you turn it on. It can warp the wood above it and ruin under-counter lighting.

RAISE THE BAR

Sprinkle the cheese with mild paprika, hot paprika, or even cayenne after you place it on top of the patties.

1. Put the noodles in a heat-safe medium bowl and cover with boiling water. Set aside for 10 minutes, stirring after about 5 minutes. **A**

2. Drain the noodles in a colander set in the sink. Put them back in the bowl and cool for 5 minutes. Add the tuna, mayonnaise, onion powder, salt, celery seed, and pepper. Stir gently but well until uniform, taking care not to turn the tuna into mush. **B**

3. With the basket in the machine or the tray set at the center level in a toaster-oven-style model, heat an air fryer to 400°F or 200°C on the air fryer setting.

4. Spread the bread crumbs on a large plate or pie plate. Divide the tuna mixture into four equal balls. Flatten these to patties about 3 inches or 8 centimeters in diameter. Set one patty in the bread crumbs, then press gently, turn it over, press again, and roll it in the bread crumbs, all to get an even coating across all of its exposed surfaces. Repeat to coat all the patties. **C**

5. Lightly coat the patties *on both sides* with nonstick spray, then set them in the heated machine with a little space between them. Air-fry for 6 minutes, then flip them over using a nonstick-safe spatula (and perhaps a rubber spatula in the other hand for balance). **D**

6. Continue air-frying for 2 minutes, then top each patty with a quarter of the shredded cheese. **E**

7. Air-fry for 2 more minutes, or until the cheese has melted and is even browned a bit. Use that spatula to transfer the patties to a wire rack. Cool for a couple of minutes before serving warm. **F**

Crispy Seafood-Stuffed Shells

Here's a fantastic seafood meal to impress your friends (or even your in-laws). Cooked pasta shells are stuffed with a cheesy seafood mixture, then breaded, fried, and topped with warmed marinara sauce. And maybe some more cheese? Sure, why not?

This recipe calls for jumbo pasta shells, not large ones. They're always labeled "jumbo," and most brands show them stuffed (rather than just sauced) right on the box.

8 ounces or 225 grams backfin or claw crabmeat (don't waste jumbo lump crabmeat for this recipe), picked over for shell and cartilage

8 ounces or 225 grams purchased *cooked* peeled and deveined cocktail shrimp, finely chopped

2 medium scallions, trimmed and very thinly sliced

¼ cup or 55 grams regular or low-fat mayonnaise (do not use fat-free)

¼ cup or 55 grams regular or low-fat ricotta (do not use fat-free)

1 tablespoon or 15 grams Dijon mustard

½ teaspoon Old Bay seasoning

¼ teaspoon table salt

16 jumbo pasta shells, cooked in boiling water according to the package instructions, drained, rinsed under cold water, and blotted dry

2 large egg whites

3 tablespoons or 45 milliliters water

1 cup or 115 grams Italian-seasoned bread crumbs (do not use panko bread crumbs)

Olive oil spray

1½ cups or 375 grams jarred plain marinara sauce, warmed

Finely grated Parmigiano-Reggiano, for garnishing, optional

Master the Method

In most cases, fat-free dairy ingredients won't work in an air fryer. The intense heat causes the stabilizers in the ingredients to break and create a runny mess with curdled bits.

1. With the basket in the machine or the tray set at the center level in a toaster-oven-style model, heat an air fryer to 400°F or 200°C on the air fryer setting.

2. Put the crabmeat, shrimp, scallions, mayonnaise, ricotta, mustard, Old Bay, and salt in a medium bowl. Ⓐ

3. Fold the ingredients gently to create a uniform mixture. Spoon a scant 2 tablespoons or about 40 grams of the crab mixture into each of the cooked shells. The shells' edges will naturally flop over a little onto the filling. Ⓑ

4. Whisk the egg whites and water in a shallow soup plate, shallow food storage container, or small pie plate until uniform. Spread the bread crumbs in a second shallow soup plate, shallow food storage container, or small pie plate. Ⓒ

5. Dip a filled shell into the egg white mixture and turn it to coat well on all sides. (Because of the odd shape of these shells, tongs won't work; you must work with your clean hands.) Pick it up, let any excess drip off, and gently press the edges together to cover the filling. Set the shell in the bread crumbs. Turn, pressing gently to coat well on all sides. Set aside and coat the remaining 15 shells. Ⓓ

6. Generously coat the shells *on all sides* with olive oil spray. Set them in the heated machine in a single layer, touching as little as possible. Work in batches as necessary. Ⓔ

7. Air-fry *undisturbed* for 8 minutes, or until brown and crunchy. Use a nonstick-safe spatula (and perhaps a rubber spatula in the other hand for balance) to transfer the shells to serving plates or a serving platter. Spoon the warmed marinara over the crispy shells and finish with a sprinkle of finely grated Parmigiano-Reggiano (if desired) before serving. Ⓕ

RAISE THE BAR

Skip the marinara and Parmigiano-Reggiano. Spoon pesto over the cooked shells. To make your own, put all of the following in a food processor *in this order*: 2 packed cups or 55 grams fresh basil leaves; 2 tablespoons or 15 grams unsalted shelled walnuts or pine nuts; 1 peeled and minced medium garlic clove (about 1 teaspoon); ⅓ cup or 80 milliliters olive oil; ⅓ cup or 20 grams finely grated Parmigiano-Reggiano; ½ teaspoon table salt; and ground black pepper to taste (not too much). Cover and process until fairly smooth, stopping the machine at least once to scrape down the inside of the canister.

A

B

C

D

E

F

6

VEGETABLE SIDES & MAIN COURSES

If we got into air-frying because of bites and nibbles, we stuck with it for side dishes. In fact, the second air fryer we bought was a small one we could keep out on the counter for crispy Brussels sprouts, curried cauliflower florets, and frozen onion rings. What's more, these crispy vegetables and sides could get made with way less fat, and so could be way healthier. What's not to like?

This chapter includes a large chart that gives the basic timings for a bevy of common vegetables found in supermarkets. None of these really needs a full recipe, other than a notion of temperature and time.

Still, you should pay careful attention to vegetables in the air fryer. With the time spent in transit and on the shelves, vegetables lose moisture. Less internal moisture means a quicker burn in the air fryer. Don't be tempted to leave vegetables to themselves. Keep an eye on what's happening in the machine.

The rest of this chapter is taken up with full recipes for vegetable sides and mains, like a pretty fine version of Broccoli Cheese Casserole (page 246). There are recipes for from-scratch French fries (page 228) and onion rings (page 230), as well as a few elaborate vegetarian (or even vegan) main courses, such as Eggplant Parmesan (page 250) and Crispy Sweet-and-Sour Tofu (page 254).

All in all, an air fryer on the counter, even a smaller one like ours, means you can have quick, healthy vegetables in no time. What's better than warmed, olive-oiled broccoli or green beans over purchased hummus for lunch? All you need is a few whole-grain crackers and you're good to go.

A Chart for Air-Frying Common Vegetables

The chart on the following pages was developed for the vegetables we most often find in our supermarkets. It'll help you get a side dish on the table without much fuss. These are the four central steps:

1. Preparing (or "prepping" in chef lingo) the vegetable in some way. This most often involves trimming off stems or woody ends, slicing the vegetable into smaller pieces, and/or peeling and taking the seeds out of hard winter squash.

2. Spraying the vegetable with nonstick or olive oil spray. Both will work. Most vegetables need a coating of fat to protect them from the intense air currents. Make sure to coat all sides.

3. Tossing (that is, flipping, turning, or moving around) the vegetable pieces in some way. We have gotten comfortable enough to do this by sliding out the basket drawer and quickly moving it up and away from us, the way a chef does with a skillet at the stove, thereby flipping and rearranging everything inside. You might want to use nonstick-safe tongs for your first few tries. If you want to get good at this cheffy technique, practice with still-frozen French fries in the basket. However, in a toaster-oven-style machine, you *must* use tongs because you can't touch the hot cooking basket.

4. Cooking the vegetables long enough that they're either tender or browned (or both). Our timings are suggestions: They're based on our machines, the moisture content of the vegetables we tested, and the exact size of our trimmed pieces. Your results may vary. Follow the visual cues for the proper doneness.

VEGETABLE	AMOUNT	PREP	SPRAY	TEMP	TIME	TURN, TOSS, OR FLIP	UNTIL
Artichoke hearts, either fresh or thawed frozen (not whole artichokes, which tend to burn at their leaves' edges)	1½ pounds or 680 grams	Quartered (and squeezed dry if thawed frozen)	Generously	400°F or 200°C	16 min	Twice	Well browned and noticeably crisp
Asparagus spears, fresh and pencil thin (or shaved to pencil thin)	1½ pounds or 680 grams	Any woody bottoms removed, the spears then trimmed to the length that allows them to lie flat if on top of each other in the machine	Generously	400°F or 200°C	10 min	Twice	Crisp-tender, plus spots of browning at the crowns
"Baby" carrots (that is, those trimmed to thumb-size and sold in bags), fresh	2 pounds or 900 grams	Whole	Lightly	400°F or 200°C	30 min	Every 5 min	Crisp-tender and lightly browned in spots
Beets, fresh	2 pounds or 900 grams	Trimmed of leaves and roots, the beets peeled and cut into 1-inch or 2½-centimeter cubes	Generously	400°F or 200°C	20 min	Quite often, at least 3 times	Fork-tender yet crispy brown at the edges
Bell peppers of any color, fresh (do not use frozen halves or strips)	6 small or medium	Stemmed, halved, and seeded	Lightly	400°F or 200°C	12 min	Fairly often, at least 2 times	Skins blistered in spots and peppers themselves crisp-tender
Broccoli florets, fresh (frozen florets burn, and fresh broccoli *stems* require much longer cooking)	2¼ pounds or 1 kilogram	1½-inch or 4-centimeter pieces	Lightly	375°F or 190°C	12 min	Twice	Crisp-tender but lightly browned at the edges
Brussels sprouts, medium (about 2 inches or 5 centimeters each)	1½ pounds or 680 grams	Stemmed, trimmed of any brown leaves, and halved through stem	Generously	400°F or 200°C	12 min	Quite often, at least 3 times	Crisp-tender at the stems and crispy brown at the edges of the leaves
Cabbage, green, whole	1 medium (about 2 pounds or 900 grams)	Outer leaves with brown spots removed, the head cut into ¾-inch or 2-centimeter thick "steaks" (cook each separately)	Generously	375°F or 190°C	10 min	After 5 min	Lightly browned and fork-tender

VEGETABLE	AMOUNT	PREP	SPRAY	TEMP	TIME	TURN, TOSS, OR FLIP	UNTIL
Cabbage, **red**, whole	1 small (about 1¼ pounds or 575 grams)	Halved, cored, and roughly chopped	Generously	375°F or 190°C	8 min	Every 2 min	Browned at the edges of the leaves but still crisp-tender
Cauliflower florets, fresh (do not use frozen)	1½ pounds or 680 grams	1-inch pieces	Lightly	375°F or 190°C	14 min	Fairly often, at least 2 times	Crisp-tender with even, light browning across the florets
Celeriac	1 large (about 1½ pounds or 680 grams)	Trimmed of any hairy roots, peeled, and cut into 1½-inch or 4-centimeter uneven chunks	Lightly	375°F or 190°C	20 min	Every 7 min	Fork-tender inside and well browned in spots (even with crispy edges)
Corn on the cob, fresh or thawed frozen	4 ears	Husks and silks removed (if necessary), ears cut into 4-inch or 10-centimeter long pieces	Lightly	400° or 200°C	14 min	Every 5 min	Fairly evenly golden brown with a few darker spots
Fennel	2 large bulbs (8 to 10 ounces or 225 to 285 grams each)	Stems and fronds removed, each bulb cut into 6 even wedges through the stem	Generously	375°F or 190°C	18 min	Every 6 min	Fork-tender, well browned in spots, and decidedly fragrant
Green beans, fresh (do not use thin haricots verts or frozen green beans)	1½ pounds or 680 grams	Tips removed (as well as any stems, if desired)	Generously	400°F or 200°C	10 min	Every 3 min	Blistered but crisp-tender
Mushrooms, white or brown button, whole, small to medium	1½ pounds or 680 grams	Wiped clean, stemmed, and trimmed to remove squishy bits (but otherwise whole caps)	Lightly	400°F or 200°C	10 min	Every 3 min	Lightly browned in spots and decidedly shriveled but not dried at the edges
Parsnips, medium (no more than 2½ inches or 6½ centimeters wide at the bottom)	2 pounds or 900 grams	Peeled, then sliced into 3-inch or 8-centimeter long and ½-inch or 1-centimeter wide "fries"	Generously	375°F or 190°C	25 min	Quite often, at least 3 times	Well and evenly browned and crispy at the edges
Potatoes, whole small (no more than 1½ inches or 4 centimeters in diameter), yellow, red purple, or white	3 pounds or 1350 grams	Rinsed to remove grime but otherwise whole	Lightly	400°F or 200°F	25 min (red and purple potatoes may take more time)	Every 5 min	Crunchy on the outside, fork-tender on the inside, and evenly browned

VEGETABLE	AMOUNT	PREP	SPRAY	TEMP	TIME	TURN, TOSS, OR FLIP	UNTIL
Potatoes, russet or baking	Four 8-ounce or 225-gram potatoes	Rinsed to remove grime, *not dried*, left whole, but wrapped in aluminum foil	No	375°F or 190°C	45 min	Once after 25 min	Tender when pierced with a fork
Radicchio, whole	Up to five 6-ounce or 170-gram heads	Cut into quarters through the stem	Generously	375°F or 190°C	4 min	After 2 min	Leaf ends are charred (watch because this happens quickly)
Rutabaga, large whole	About 2 pounds or 900 grams	Peeled and cut into 4-inch or 10-centimeter long and ¾-inch or 2-centimeter thick wedges like steak fries	Generously	375°F or 190°C	20 min	Every 5 min	Well-browned in spots and crisp-tender
Snow peas, fresh (do not use frozen)	1 pound or 450 grams	Stemmed	Generously	400°F or 200°C	7 min	Twice	Slightly shriveled and even brown in spots but crisp-tender
Sugar snap peas, fresh (do not use frozen)	1 pound or 450 grams	Stemmed and destringed (zip the stem along the inner curve of the pea to remove the fibrous "string")	Generously	400°F or 200°C	9 min	Every 3 min	Slightly shriveled in spots but still crisp
Sweet potatoes, whole	Two 12-ounce or 340-gram each sweet potatoes	Rinsed for grime, not dried, left whole, but each poked in six spots with a fork	No	350°F or 180°C	45 min	Once after 25 min	Tender inside with decidedly crispy skin
Winter squash, fresh (such as acorn, butternut, buttercup, kabocha, or red kuri)	2½ pounds or 1150 grams total weight (1 large, or 2 medium, or several small)	Peeled, halved, seeded, and cubed into 2-inch or 5-centimeter irregular chunks	Generously	400°F or 200°C	22 min	Quite often, at least 4 times	Centers are soft but with crispy brown edges
Zucchini	Two 6- to 7-ounce or 170- to 200-gram zucchini	Sliced into ½-inch or 1-centimeter thick rounds	Lightly	375°F or 190°C	18 min	Quite often, at least every 3 min (zucchini burns quickly)	Lightly browned at the edges and soft at the centers

Hand-Cut French Fries

The trick to homemade French fries from an air fryer is to do them in batches. Yes, we know: Every advertisement for the machine shows a basket brimming with fries. But fresh potato fries won't work in big batches because there's not enough air circulation around (and, more importantly, through) a big pile in the machine. (By the way, we do have a great recipe for from-frozen fries in *The Instant Air Fryer Bible*.)

The cut potatoes must be soaked in water to get rid of some of the starch that will turn even smaller batches of the fries soggy. And the fries must be cooked twice. The first time, they can't overlap or even touch. The second time, they can all be poured into the machine at once to recrisp. They've already dried out, so they're really just heating up and getting one last finishing blast of hot air.

Here's one plus: You can make these fries through step 6 up to 2 hours in advance, leave them out at room temperature, then recrisp them in one go when you're ready to serve them.

Four 8- to 9-ounce or 225- to 255-gram russet or baking potatoes (do not use yellow potatoes, white potatoes, red-skinned potatoes, or any other variety—and do not peel for the best texture)

Nonstick or olive oil spray

Table or kosher salt, to taste

Master the Method

You can keep adding time to almost all air fryer models. Check the manufacturer's instructions to find out how. Just remember: You don't have to wait for the machine to count down to zilch to then add more minutes.

RAISE THE BAR

Sure, almost everybody in North America loves ketchup with fries. But what about barbecue sauce, chili crisp, sweet red chili sauce, mayonnaise (hello, Belgium!), or honey mustard? Or a 50/50 mix of chili crisp and mayonnaise. Or a 50/50 mix of minced kimchi and mayonnaise?

For Poutine, follow the recipe on page 252 starting at step 5 (since you've already made the fries).

1. Slice the potatoes *lengthwise* into ½-inch or 1-centimeter thick ovals. Ⓐ

2. Slice the ovals into ½-inch or 1-centimeter thick sticks. Ⓑ

3. Place the sticks in a large bowl, cover with cool tap water, and set aside at room temperature for 1 hour. Ⓒ

4. With the basket in the machine or the tray set at the center level in a toaster-oven-style model, heat an air fryer to 400°F or 200°C on the air fryer setting.

5. Scoop out enough potato sticks from the water that they'll make an even layer in your machine with the tiniest bit of space between each stick. Blot these sticks dry with paper towels, then lightly coat the sticks *on all sides* with spray. Keep the remaining sticks in the water. Ⓓ

6. Put the dried sticks in the air fryer in a random way, not stacked on each other evenly but at various diagonals with lots of air space among the pieces. Air-fry for 16 minutes, *turning with nonstick-safe tongs at the halfway point*, until the fries are crunchy and brown. Pour these fries onto a wire rack and add another blotted and sprayed small batch to the machine, air-frying and turning these in the same way, then repeating this process until you've air-fried them all. Ⓔ

7. Once all the sticks have been air-fried, return them in a big batch to the machine and air-fry for 5 to 7 minutes, *tossing every minute*, until browned and crisp. Pour the fries back onto the wire rack and season with salt (to taste) while hot. Ⓕ

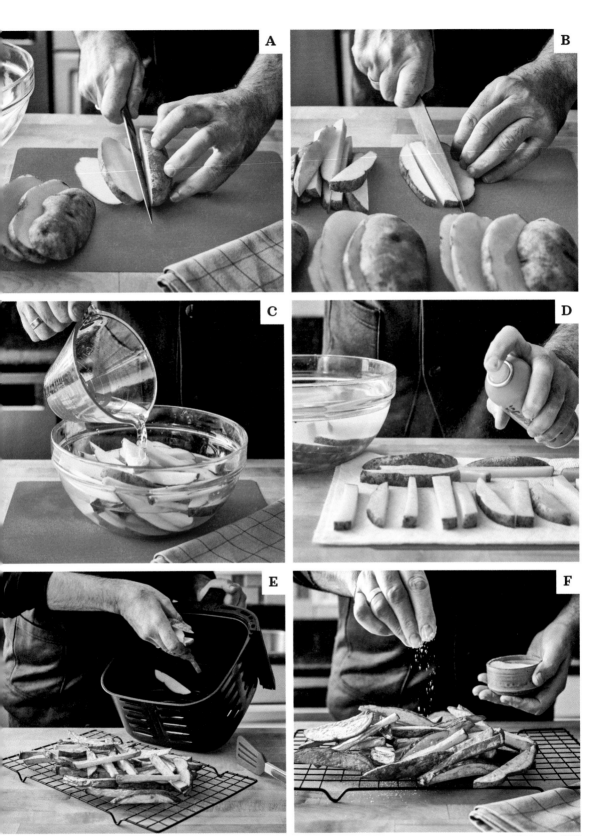

Crumb-Coated Onion Rings

Yep, we have a great recipe for from-frozen onion rings in *The Instant Air Fryer Bible*. However, this recipe is for *homemade* onion rings.

As we've said (repeatedly!), wet batters prove a problem in the machine. They tend to get blown around, turn waggly, or just come unstuck in the fast air currents. Crumb coatings work better, and the one for these onion rings is a doozy! It's made from purchased croutons. You can create any flavor profile you like, from simple oil-and-salt versions to much more complicated flavor combos, based on the croutons you choose.

2 medium (7- to 8-ounce or 200- to 225-gram) white or yellow onions, peeled

4 cups (about one-and-a-half 5-ounce or 140-gram bags) croutons of any flavor

1 cup all-purpose flour or 120 grams plain flour

3 large eggs

2 tablespoons or 30 grams regular or low-fat sour cream (do not use fat-free)

Nonstick spray

Master the Method

Unfortunately, we don't recommend storing your air fryer in an appliance garage. Unless the machine is kept scrupulously clean, it will stink up the small, enclosed space. Leave the machine out on the counter. You'll use it enough. Otherwise, leave it on a pantry or cupboard shelf with plenty of air flow around it.

RAISE THE BAR

Salad dressings are the best dips for onion rings: ranch, blue cheese, creamy Italian, even Russian dressing.

Recrisp any onion rings that have gotten soggy in a 350°F or 180°C machine for 2 to 3 minutes.

1. With the basket in the machine or the tray set at the center level in a toaster-oven-style model, heat an air fryer to 375°F or 190°C on the air fryer setting.

2. Slice the onions into ¾-inch or 2-centimeter thick rings. Separate the rings, then choose the 24 largest. (Reserve the remainder for another use—maybe chopped and in a sealed bag in the freezer for the next time you need chopped onions for any soup, stew, or braise.) Ⓐ

3. Pour the croutons into a food processor, cover, and pulse until fine crumbs: not ground and powdery, but with the texture of very coarse sand. Pour those ground croutons into a shallow soup plate, small pie plate, or food storage container. Ⓑ

4. Pour the flour into a second shallow soup plate, small pie plate, or food storage container. Finally, whisk the eggs and sour cream in a third shallow soup plate, small pie plate, or food storage container until homogenous. Ⓒ

5. Set up the bowls in this order: flour, egg mixture, ground croutons. Dip one onion ring into the flour and turn to coat well. Transfer it in the egg mixture and again turn to coat well, perhaps spooning some of the egg into the ring's interior. Transfer the ring to the ground croutons and press gently to get an even coating on both sides, as well as the interior *and* exterior of the ring. Scooping the crumbs over the ring with a spoon works best. Set aside and continue dipping the remaining rings with this three-step process: flour, eggs, ground croutons. Ⓓ

6. Generously coat *both sides* of the rings with nonstick spray. Ⓔ

7. Set as many rings as you can to form one layer with only minimal touching in the heated machine. Smaller rings can go inside larger ones so long as they don't fully touch. Work in batches as necessary. Air-fry *undisturbed* for about 9 minutes, or until well browned, quite aromatic, and noticeably crunchy. Use nonstick-safe tongs to transfer the onion rings to a wire rack and continue air-frying more as needed. Cool for a few minutes before serving. Ⓕ

A

B

C

D

E

F

Potato Pancakes

For potato pancakes, Yukon Golds offer the right balance of moisture and starch, a sort of middle ground between waxier red-skinned potatoes and starchy baking potatoes. For the best results, the shredded potatoes and onions *must* be squeezed dry to remove excess moisture. Otherwise, the pancakes will never get crisp—which is the whole point of their existence, right?

Although the caraway seeds could perhaps be optional, we find they add a great, savory flavor to the crisp little disks, the better to pair them with any roasted meat or even just ketchup.

If you'd like to make this recipe for Passover, substitute matzo meal for the bread crumbs and give the pancakes an extra minute or two in the machine to get crisp.

1¼ pounds or 570 grams Yukon Gold potatoes, peeled

1 small yellow or white onion, peeled

½ cup or 25 grams plain panko bread crumbs

2 large eggs

1 teaspoon table salt

½ teaspoon caraway seeds

½ teaspoon ground black pepper

Nonstick spray

Master the Method

Box graters get dull over time. Replace yours if it's over three years old. A sharp box grater will get the job done much more quickly. Just be careful of the skin on your knuckles. Invest in a cut-proof glove for the best safety precaution.

RAISE THE BAR

Use these potato pancakes for an elegant starter. Top each with a little sour cream or crème fraîche, then with a spoonful of whitefish salad (from the deli) or a small slice of smoked salmon.

Better yet, top all that with a pickled jalapeño ring.

1. With the basket in the machine or the tray set at the center level in a toaster-oven-style model, heat an air fryer to 400°F or 200°C on the air fryer setting.

2. Grate the potatoes through the large holes of a box grater into a large bowl. Grate the onion over the potatoes as well. Ⓐ

3. Stir the mixture a bit, then pick up a handful and squeeze it over a bowl or the sink to remove as much moisture as possible. Set the handful aside and continue squeezing the remainder by handfuls to remove as much moisture as possible. Ⓑ

4. Return all the squeezed potato and onion to the bowl. Stir in the bread crumbs, eggs, salt, caraway seeds, and pepper until uniform. Ⓒ

5. Form about ¼ cup or 90 grams of this mixture into a disk about 2½ inches or 6½ centimeters in diameter. Set aside and continue making the remainder of these disks. Ⓓ

6. Generously coat both sides of the disks with nonstick spray. Set them in a single layer without touching in the heated machine. Work in batches as necessary. Air-fry for 10 minutes, then flip the potato pancakes over with a nonstick-safe spatula (and perhaps a rubber spatula in the other hand for balance). Ⓔ

7. Continue air-frying for about 10 more minutes, or until well-browned and sizzling. Transfer the potato pancakes to a wire rack with that same spatula. Cool for a few minutes before serving warm. Ⓕ

Crispy Artichoke Hearts

Artichoke hearts are often deep-fried as a side dish, but we can get just as much crunch from them out of an air fryer with a few tricks: 1) the hearts must be canned, not fresh, because they have to have a small jump on the softening process to work in an air fryer; 2) they must *not* be marinated artichoke hearts; 3) they must be halved and drained a bit; and 4) they should be sifted with flour, rather than tossed in it, to keep them intact *and* give them a thinner, more delicate coating.

There are usually six artichoke hearts per can, although some cans have only five because one is larger. No worries: Go with what you have from two cans.

Two 14-ounce or 400-gram cans of whole artichoke hearts packed in water, drained

2 tablespoons all-purpose flour or 15 grams plain flour

Table, kosher, or flaked sea salt, to taste

Olive oil spray

Master the Method

Excess moisture is the enemy of air-frying. For better texture, you must remove it from vegetables like artichoke hearts and zucchini by squeezing them dry in some recipes or setting them on paper towels to drain, as in this one.

RAISE THE BAR

Serve the hearts with a creamy dressing as a dip, like creamy Italian, ranch, or even blue cheese.

Or drizzle them with a syrupy, aged balsamic vinegar just before serving.

1. With the basket in the machine or the tray set at the center level in a toaster-oven-style model, heat an air fryer to 400°F or 200°C on the air fryer setting.

2. Slice the artichoke hearts in half through their stems, then set them cut side down on paper towels to drain for 10 minutes. Do not press, squeeze, or flatten them. Ⓐ

3. Turn the halved artichoke hearts over (that is, cut side up). Put the flour in a fine-mesh sieve or flour sifter. Gently sift the flour over the hearts, turning the hearts this way and that to get the flour all over them. Ⓑ

4. Lightly coat all sides of the hearts with olive oil spray. Ⓒ

5. Set the coated hearts in a single layer without touching in the heated machine. Work in batches as necessary. Air-fry for 8 minutes, then use nonstick-safe tongs to turn the artichoke hearts over. Ⓓ

6. Continue air-frying for about 8 more minutes, or until browned and crispy at the edges (or even a minute or two more for almost blackened edges). Use clean tongs to transfer the hearts to a wire rack. Sprinkle the hearts with salt to taste. Cool for at least a few minutes before serving warm or at room temperature. Ⓔ

Roasted Fennel with Red Onion and Cheese

Although this recipe creates a rather attractive side dish, perfect for any roast or just about anything off the grill, even fish fillets, we also like it as a vegetarian main course, particularly with a baguette that we've heated in the oven until it's crackling crisp.

The fennel takes a little longer than the onion in the machine, so the vegetables need to be added in stages for a successful dish.

2 large fennel bulbs

2 tablespoons or 30 milliliters olive oil

1 teaspoon table salt

½ teaspoon ground black pepper

1 large red onion

3 medium garlic cloves, peeled and minced (about 1 tablespoon)

1 tablespoon finely grated orange zest

½ teaspoon red pepper flakes

1 tablespoon balsamic vinegar

¼ cup (½ ounce or 15 grams) grated Parmigiano-Reggiano

Master the Method

For your safety, you must let your air fryer cool before you can clean it. Even wiping out rendered grease from a hot machine can be dangerous.

RAISE THE BAR

Substitute shredded mozzarella or even crumbled Gorgonzola for the Parmigiano-Reggiano.

Or use one of those cheeses *with* the Parmigiano-Reggiano.

1. With the basket in the machine or the tray set at the center level in a toaster-oven-style model, heat an air fryer to 400°F or 200°C on the air fryer setting.

2. Trim the stalks, any fronds, and the root end from the fennel bulb. (Those stalks and fronds can be frozen in a sealed plastic bag for a soup or stew down the road.) Set one bulb root side down on your cutting board and slice the bulb lengthwise in half, stalk end to root end. Set the halves cut side down on the cutting board and slice them widthwise (or the short way) into 1-inch or 2½-centimeter thick sections. Set aside and repeat with the second fennel bulb. Ⓐ

3. Put the fennel pieces, 1 tablespoon or 15 milliliters oil, ½ teaspoon salt, and ¼ teaspoon black pepper in a large bowl. Toss well until the pieces are glistening and well seasoned. Pour them into the heated machine in a random and not layered arrangement. Ⓑ

4. Air-fry for 5 minutes. Meanwhile, peel the onion, then slice off the root end so the onion will stand up on your cutting board. Slice it top to bottom in half, then set the halves cut side down on your cutting board and slice them into 1-inch or 2½-centimeter thick pieces. Put these in the bowl the fennel was in. Add the garlic, orange zest, red pepper flakes, the remaining 1 tablespoon or 15 milliliters oil, remaining ½ teaspoon salt, and remaining ¼ teaspoon black pepper. Toss well. Ⓒ

5. Pour this mixture into the machine with the fennel and toss well. Air-fry for 7 minutes, then toss well. Ⓓ

6. Continue air-frying for 8 minutes, *tossing once after 4 minutes*, until lightly browned and even crispy at the edges. Pour the vegetables from the machine into a serving bowl. Drizzle with the vinegar and sprinkle the cheese on top. Ⓔ

Mixed Roots

Although we have various root vegetables in our basic vegetables chart on page 224, we love this mix of carrots, potatoes, and parsnips as a more substantial side dish. It's even great for brunch along with poached eggs.

We made this mix its own recipe because the different veggies take different amounts of time. In other words, you'll need to stagger their entrance into the machine for the best results.

8 ounces or 225 grams "baby" carrots (that is, bagged, small carrot pieces, usually made for children, not purchased carrot matchsticks)

2 tablespoons or 30 milliliters olive oil

¾ teaspoon table salt

¾ teaspoon ground black pepper

12 ounces or 340 grams small red-skinned or yellow potatoes, each 1 to 1½ inches or 2½ to 4 centimeters in diameter

1 pound or 450 grams medium parsnips, peeled and cut into rounds about as thick as the baby carrots (however, larger-in-diameter rounds must be sliced into two half-moons)

½ teaspoon garlic powder

¼ teaspoon ground rosemary, optional

Master the Method

Root vegetables lose a lot of moisture as they sit on store shelves. In any recipe, if they're getting browned before they've softened, reduce the temperature by 25°F or 15°C and toss them more often.

RAISE THE BAR

Add up to ½ teaspoon cayenne with the spice mixture on the parsnips.

Serve the roots with Healthier Herb-Marinated Chicken Breasts (page 112) or Strip Steaks with Garlic Butter (page 148).

1. With the basket in the machine or the tray set at the center level in a toaster-oven-style model, heat an air fryer to 400°F or 200°C on the air fryer setting.

2. Toss the carrots, 2 teaspoons or 10 milliliters olive oil, ¼ teaspoon salt, and ¼ teaspoon ground black pepper in a large bowl until the carrots are glistening and well seasoned. Pour the carrots in a random fashion into the heated machine. Ⓐ

3. Air-fry for 5 minutes. Meanwhile, toss the potatoes in the same bowl with 2 teaspoons or 10 milliliters oil, ¼ teaspoon salt, and ¼ teaspoon ground black pepper until the potatoes are glistening and well seasoned. After the carrots have cooked for 5 minutes, toss them in the machine to rearrange them and pour in the potatoes in a random fashion. Ⓑ

4. Air-fry for another 5 minutes. Meanwhile, toss the parsnips in the same bowl with the garlic powder, ground rosemary (if using), remaining 2 teaspoons or 10 milliliters oil, remaining ¼ teaspoon salt, and remaining ¼ teaspoon ground black pepper. After the carrots and potatoes have cooked for their 5 minutes, rearrange the carrots and potatoes, then pour in the parsnips in a random way. Scrape every drop and speck from the bowl over the vegetables. Ⓒ

5. Air-fry for 20 more minutes, *tossing every 5 minutes*, or until the vegetables are crunchy yet tender and lightly browned. Ⓓ

6. Pour the vegetables into a serving bowl and cool for a few minutes before serving warm. Ⓔ

Zucchini Fritters

Zucchini are loaded with moisture, even more so than potatoes. Although we squeezed the grated potatoes and onions for Potato Pancakes (page 232), we have to go the extra mile with zucchini fritters. We have to salt the zucchini, set the threads aside to let the salt work, and *then* squeeze the vegetable dry. Smaller handfuls are always better than larger. In this way, the fritters will have the best texture: soft and tender without being soggy. Plus, there'll be a better chance for a little crust to form on each fritter.

Leftovers can be stored on a plate under plastic wrap in the fridge for up to 3 days, then recrisped in a 350°F or 180°C air fryer for 2 to 3 minutes.

---

2 medium zucchini (about 1¼ pounds or 570 grams total weight)

1½ teaspoons table salt

6 tablespoons or 45 grams Italian-seasoned dried bread crumbs

6 tablespoons (¾ ounce or 20 grams) finely grated Parmigiano-Reggiano

½ teaspoon ground black pepper

1 large egg

Olive oil spray

Master the Method

Air fryers seem to eat ground black pepper. It almost disappears from some dishes. If you like black pepper, have more at the ready when a dish is finished.

RAISE THE BAR

Swap in finely grated Gruyère or a very aged, hard Gouda for the Parmigiano-Reggiano.

Top the fritters with sweet chutney and sriracha. Add some chopped roasted cashews to really go over the top.

1. With the basket in the machine or the tray set at the center level in a toaster-oven-style model, heat an air fryer to 375°F or 190°C on the air fryer setting.

2. Grate the zucchini through the large holes of a box grater into a large bowl. Then toss it with the salt and set aside for 10 minutes. Ⓐ

3. After 10 minutes, pick up a handful of the zucchini and squeeze it dry over a bowl or the sink. Repeated with remaining handfuls of the zucchini. Ⓑ

4. Put all the zucchini back in the bowl. Stir in the bread crumbs, cheese, and black pepper. Add the egg and stir well until evenly coated and uniform. Ⓒ

5. Use about ⅓ cup or 85 grams of the zucchini mixture to form a patty about 3 inches or 7½ centimeters in diameter. Set aside and continue to make about seven more patties. Ⓓ

6. Generously coat *both sides* of each patty with olive oil spray. Ⓔ

7. Set the patties in one layer without touching in the heated machine. Work in batches as necessary. Air-fry for 7 minutes. Flip the patties over with a nonstick-safe spatula. Continue air-frying for about 3 more minutes, or until well browned and firm. Use that spatula to transfer the patties to a wire rack to cool for a few minutes before serving warm. Ⓕ

Cauliflower Patties

Frozen cauliflower is too wet after it thaws to make decent vegetable patties. And riced cauliflower is too dry. The only way to hit the right amount of moisture to make tender cauliflower patties is to use fresh florets and microwave them for a bit so that some of that internal moisture comes out and even evaporates off the surface of the florets as they cool. The results are worth the effort: tender little disks of cauliflower and cheese, a great side for roasted chicken or turkey.

If you want to go all out for a vegetarian main course, spread a little hummus on a plate, top with one or two of these patties, and pile a lightly dressed chopped salad of bell peppers, celery, cucumbers, and cherry tomatoes over everything.

12 ounces or 340 grams *small* cauliflower florets (large ones should be cut into 1-inch or 2½-centimeter pieces—about 4 cups in all)

2 large eggs

3 ounces (¾ cup) or 85 grams shredded sharp American-style cheddar cheese

¼ cup or 40 grams Italian-seasoned panko bread crumbs, or Italian-seasoned gluten-free panko bread crumbs

Olive oil spray

Master the Method

The stickier the food, the more it should be sprayed or coated in some way to keep it from sticking even to the nonstick surface of the machine.

RAISE THE BAR

Drizzle the patties with ranch dressing.

Or dot them with honey mustard.

1. Put the florets in a large, microwave-safe bowl. Microwave uncovered on high for 3 minutes. Set aside to cool for 15 minutes. **Ⓐ**

2. Pour the florets into the canister of a large food processor. Add the eggs, cheese, and bread crumbs. Cover and pulse until a coarse paste forms, stopping the machine at least once to scrape down the inside of the canister. **Ⓑ**

3. With the basket in the machine or the tray set at the center level in a toaster-oven-style model, heat an air fryer to 400°F or 200°C on the air fryer setting.

4. Scrape down and remove the blade from the food processor. Scoop up a rounded ¼ cup or 75 grams of the cauliflower mixture and form it into a ball in your clean hands. Set it on a clean cutting board and press gently to flatten slightly. Set aside and make seven more disks with the remaining cauliflower mixture. **Ⓒ**

5. Generously coat the disks *on both sides* with olive oil spray. **Ⓓ**

6. Set the disks in a single layer without touching in the heated machine. Work in batches as necessary. Air-fry for 10 minutes, then flip the disks with a nonstick-safe spatula. **Ⓔ**

7. Continue air-frying for about 5 more minutes, or until golden brown and firm. Use that same spatula to transfer the disks to a wire rack. Cool for a few minutes before serving warm. **Ⓕ**

Asparagus Bundles

Here's a pretty side dish for a holiday meal: thin asparagus spears wrapped in puff pastry, which forms a crunchy "belt" around the spears.

The asparagus spears must be no thicker than a no. 2 pencil. Fatter ones should be trimmed down to the proper size with a vegetable peeler. All those trimmed parts are indeed edible. You can save them for up to 1 year in a sealed plastic bag in the freezer for soups or stews. Or you can steam them and use them as a green garnish over the meat or dressing at a holiday meal.

One sheet (half of a 14¼-ounce or 400-gram box) of frozen puff pastry, thawed

24 *pencil-thin* asparagus spears, any woody ends trimmed off

2 tablespoons or 30 grams butter, melted and cooled for a few minutes

1 teaspoon table salt

1 large egg, well beaten in a small bowl

RAISE THE BAR

Sprinkle the egged puff pastry with poppy or caraway seeds before baking.

Wrap a piece of prosciutto around the bundles before you wrap them with the puff pastry.

Drizzle the exposed bits of the asparagus with purchased Caesar dressing as a garnish.

1. With the basket in the machine or the tray set at the center level in a toaster-oven-style model, heat an air fryer to 375°F or 190°C on the air fryer setting.

2. Unfold the puff pastry sheet on a dry cutting board. Cut it into thirds lengthwise, then in half widthwise to make six rectangles. Set aside. Ⓐ

3. Lay the asparagus spears in a layer on a cutting board. Cut off any woody ends, but make sure all the spears are the same length. Brush the butter evenly over them. Sprinkle them with the salt. Ⓑ

4. Wipe off your cutting board. Set a puff pastry rectangle on the cutting board. Set four asparagus spears widthwise in the middle of the rectangle. Ⓒ

5. Wrap the puff pastry around the spears, then pinch it to seal along the seam. Set it aside, seam side down, and continue making five more asparagus bundles. Ⓓ

6. Brush the tops of the puff pastry with the beaten egg. Ⓔ

7. Set the bundles seam side down in a single layer with at least ½ inch or 1 centimeter between them in the heated machine (the puff pastry will expand a bit as it cooks). Work in batches as necessary. Air-fry for 8 minutes, *then turn* the bundles over with nonstick-safe tongs. Air-fry for about 6 more minutes, or until golden brown (be careful that they don't burn—check often). Use tongs to transfer the bundles to a wire rack to cool for a few minutes before serving warm. Ⓕ

Broccoli Cheese Casserole

We've chosen to use frozen broccoli florets for this casserole favorite because they save us the step of blanching the florets before they go into the baking dish. There's no real difference between fresh and frozen broccoli in the dish's final texture because the florets are cooked in the cheese sauce for the last step.

Although this dish would be a perfect side on a holiday table, we'll admit to making it for an easy vegetarian lunch many a day after a morning garden cleanup or a long walk down a quiet New England road with our dogs.

1 pound or 450 grams frozen *small* (or sometimes labeled "petit") broccoli florets, thawed

2 tablespoons or 30 grams butter, cut into small bits

1½ cups or 375 milliliters whole, low-fat, or fat-free milk

2 tablespoons all-purpose flour or 15 grams plain flour

½ teaspoon table salt

¼ teaspoon garlic powder

¼ teaspoon onion powder

¼ teaspoon ground black pepper

4 ounces (1 cup) or 115 grams shredded sharp American-style cheddar cheese

Master the Method

There's a wide disparity in the depth of the basket on drawer- and basket-style machines. In some, foods are much closer to the fan and heating element at the top. Other baskets or drawers are deeper. These variables affect the cooking times. Deeper drawers may require an extra couple of minutes for proper doneness.

RAISE THE BAR

Stir a drained 4-ounce or 115-gram jar of diced pimientos into the dish with the broccoli florets in step 2.

Sprinkle up to ½ cup or 25 grams Italian-seasoned panko bread crumbs on top of the cheese in step 5.

1. With the basket in the machine or the tray set at the center level in a toaster-oven-style model, heat an air fryer to 350°F or 180°C on the air fryer setting.

2. Pour the broccoli florets every which way into an air-fryer-safe 7-cup, 8 x 6 x 2-inch or 20 x 15 x 5-centimeter rectangular pan. Top them with the butter bits. Ⓐ

3. Set the pan in the heated machine and air-fry for 5 minutes. Meanwhile, whisk the milk, flour, salt, garlic powder, onion powder, and pepper in a 2-cup or 500-milliliter microwave-safe measuring vessel or high-sided container until the flour has dissolved. Microwave on high for 1 minute, then whisk again. Continue microwaving on high in 15-seconds increments, whisking after each, until the mixture is bubbling and begins to thicken. Let it come to a bubble once more in a 15-second increment, then whisk in ½ cup (2 ounces or 60 grams) of the shredded cheese until smooth. Ⓑ

4. Remove the (hot!) baking pan from the air fryer. Pour the cheese sauce evenly over the florets. Ⓒ

5. Sprinkle with the remaining ½ cup or 55 grams of cheese. Ⓓ

6. Return the pan to the machine and air-fry for about 7 minutes, or until the cheese has melted and the sauce is bubbling. Transfer the (hot!) baking dish to a wire rack and cool for a few minutes before serving up with a big spoon. Ⓔ

Fried Spaghetti Bars

There are plenty of online recipes for deep-fried spaghetti balls. Problem is, the balls are hard to shape *and* (worse yet) flatten considerably in an air fryer.

So we recrafted this internet favorite for the air fryer by making mini loaves of cooked angel-hair pasta, jarred marinara, and other ingredients. Stick to angel-hair pasta; others are too thick to be successful in this recipe.

8 ounces or 225 grams dried angel-hair pasta, cooked and drained according to the package instructions

¾ cup or 190 grams jarred plain marinara sauce or plain red pasta sauce

½ cup or 125 grams whole-milk or low-fat ricotta (do not use fat-free)

½ cup or 55 grams Italian-seasoned dried bread crumbs

2 ounces (½ cup) or 55 grams shredded mozzarella

1 large egg

2 cups or 100 grams plain panko bread crumbs

Olive oil spray

Master the Method

As a rule of thumb, undercook pasta that is going into a casserole in the air fryer. The pasta will cook more in the machine.

RAISE THE BAR

Grate Parmigiano-Reggiano or an aged Asiago over the still-warm rectangles.

Warm more of the jarred marinara sauce and serve it as a dip.

Or serve with warmed jarred Alfredo sauce as a dip.

1. Mix the cooked pasta, marinara sauce, ricotta, seasoned dried bread crumbs, mozzarella, and egg in a large bowl until even and well combined. Two flatware forks works best to start, then your clean hands work better as you get going. Just take care not to mix it into a mush. Spread this mixture into an 8-inch or 20-centimeter square baking pan, cover, and refrigerate for at least 30 minutes or up to 12 hours. **A**

2. Use a nonstick-safe knife to slice the pasta mixture into eight even rectangles. Use a narrow, nonstick-safe spatula to transfer them to a cutting board. **B**

3. With the basket in the machine or the tray set at the center level in a toaster-oven-style model, heat an air fryer to 375°F or 190°C on the air fryer setting.

4. Pour the plain panko bread crumbs into a shallow soup plate, small pie plate, or medium food storage container. Set one of the rectangles in the bread crumbs, press gently, and turn repeatedly to coat well and evenly. Set aside and continue coating the remaining rectangles. **C**

5. Generously coat the rectangles *on all sides* with olive oil spray. **D**

6. Set the rectangles in a single layer without touching in the heated machine. Air-fry for 10 minutes, then flip them over with nonstick-safe tongs. **E**

7. Continue air-frying for about 6 more minutes, or until golden brown and noticeably crunchy. Use those tongs to transfer the rectangles to a wire rack. Cool for at least 5 minutes before serving warm or at room temperature. **F**

Eggplant Parmesan

Nothing says "worth the effort" like eggplant parm. And nothing is better than an eggplant parm made in an air fryer: lighter, more flavorful, not loaded with oil—and crisper, too, since the coating sets firm in the machine without all the excess oil from deep-frying.

Since we're going all out for this vegetarian main course, we might as well make a homemade tomato sauce, too, because we can reduce it to a thick, rich consistency.

The eggplant slices go through a three-bowl dipping process to get coated, then get air-fried until they're almost cooked through. The finished dish then consists of stacks of these slices, layered with sauce and cheese.

1 tablespoon or 15 milliliters olive oil

2 medium garlic cloves, peeled and minced (about 2 teaspoons)

½ teaspoon fennel seeds

½ teaspoon dried oregano

¼ teaspoon ground rosemary

¼ teaspoon red pepper flakes

¼ teaspoon table salt

One 28-ounce or 800-gram can of crushed tomatoes

1 cup all-purpose flour or 120 grams plain flour

5 large eggs

2 cups or 225 grams Italian-seasoned dried bread crumbs

Two 12-ounce or 340-gram medium eggplants, stemmed, peeled, and cut into ¾- to 1-inch or 2- to 2½-centimeter thick rounds (8 slices per eggplant)

Olive oil spray

1 ounce (½ cup) or 30 grams finely grated Parmigiano-Reggiano

4 ounces (1 cup) or 115 grams grated semi-firm mozzarella

1. Begin by making the sauce. Heat the oil in a medium saucepan over medium heat for 1 or 2 minutes. Add the garlic, fennel seeds, oregano, rosemary, red pepper flakes, and salt. Stir constantly for 20 seconds, or until aromatic. Pour in the crushed tomatoes and bring to a simmer. Reduce the heat to low and simmer slowly for 20 minutes, or until the overall volume is reduced to about half. Ⓐ

2. With the basket in the machine or the tray set at the center level in a toaster-oven-style model, heat an air fryer to 375°F or 190°C on the air fryer setting.

3. Pour the flour into a shallow soup plate, small pie plate, or medium food storage container. Whisk or beat the eggs in a second shallow soup plate, small pie plate, or medium food storage container until no bits of egg white float in the mix. Finally, pour the bread crumbs into a third shallow soup plate, small pie plate, or medium food storage container. Ⓑ

4. Set an eggplant slice in the flour and turn it to evenly coat it. Transfer it to the eggs and again turn it to coat evenly it. Pick it up, let the excess egg run back into its container, and set the slice in the bread crumbs. Press gently and turn a few times to coat it well, even along the side. Set the slice aside and dip the remaining slices in the same manner: flour, egg, bread crumbs. Ⓒ

5. Generously coat the slices with olive oil spray on both sides. Set the coated slices in a single layer without touching in the heated machine. Work in batches as necessary. Air-fry undisturbed for 8 minutes, or until golden brown. Transfer the slices to a wire rack with a nonstick-safe spatula. Maintain the air fryer's heat. Ⓓ

6. To build the stacks, set one coated eggplant slice on a clean cutting board. Spread 1 heaping tablespoon or 20 milliliters of tomato sauce over it, then sprinkle 1 tablespoon or a little less than 4 grams of finely grated Parmigiano-Reggiano evenly over the tomato sauce. Set a second, similarly sized eggplant slice on top, then spread another 1 heaping tablespoon or 20 milliliters of tomato sauce on top, and top with 2 tablespoons or a little less than 15 grams shredded mozzarella. Set aside and continue to make seven more stacks. Ⓔ

7. Use a nonstick-safe spatula to place the stacks without touching in the heated machine. Work in batches as necessary. Air-fry for 3 minutes, or until the cheese is melty and lightly browned. Use that spatula to transfer the stacks to a serving platter or plates and cool for a couple of minutes before serving hot. Ⓕ

RAISE THE BAR

Add 1 or 2 tinned anchovy fillets, minced, to the tomato sauce with the garlic and spices.

Poutine

To make great poutine in an air fryer, the fries have to be *super* crispy. To that end, we call for frozen shoestring fries, the better to get crunch in every bite.

Cheese curds are the go-to standard for this favorite, but you might have a hard time tracking them down outside of Canada and the Upper Midwest of the U.S. Luckily, you can easily substitute mozzarella string cheese sticks. Use 4 ounces or 115 grams and slice the unwrapped sticks into ½-inch or 1-centimeter sections.

1½ pounds or 680 grams frozen shoestring potato fries (*do not thaw*)

Nonstick spray

½ teaspoon dried thyme

½ teaspoon garlic powder

½ teaspoon onion powder

½ teaspoon table salt

½ teaspoon ground black pepper

¾ cup or 185 milliliters vegetable broth

1 tablespoon or 7 grams cornstarch

½ teaspoon mild paprika

½ teaspoon celery seeds

½ teaspoon ground sage

4 ounces or 115 grams (about 1 cup) small cheese curds

Master the Method

Nothing can go inside an air fryer that isn't broiler-safe. There are also sorts of TikTok videos of plates and mugs in an air fryer. Just don't. The pottery can break. It will also get absurdly hot.

RAISE THE BAR

For a more traditional flavor, use beef broth.

Although not traditional, try a squiggle of sriracha over the top.

Really up the game by adding a layer of browned ground beef. You'll need about ½ pound of lean ground beef or 225 grams of lean beef mince, crumbled into a skillet with a little oil and cooked over medium heat with lots of stirring until well browned. Pour this ground beef over the fries before the gravy and curds.

1. With the basket in the machine or the tray set at the center level in a toaster-oven-style model, heat an air fryer to 400°F or 200°C on the air fryer setting.

2. Put the fries in a large bowl. Spray them well with nonstick spray and toss. Sprinkle them with the dried thyme, garlic powder, onion powder, salt, and pepper. Ⓐ

3. Spray well *again* and toss *repeatedly* until the fries are coated and shiny. Pour the fries every which way into the heated machine. Do not pack them in. Air-fry for 10 minutes, then toss well. Ⓑ

4. Continue air-frying for about 15 more minutes, or until well browned and very crisp. Pour the fries onto a large platter. Ⓒ

5. Whisk the broth, cornstarch, paprika, celery seeds, and sage in a medium microwave-safe bowl or measuring vessel. Microwave the broth mixture on high for 30 seconds, then whisk well. Continue microwaving on high for about 20 seconds, or until bubbling. Whisk well, then do that again: Microwave on high just until it's bubbling. Whisk yet again. Ⓓ

6. Pour this gravy over the fries and top with the cheese curds to serve. Ⓔ

Crispy Sweet-and-Sour Tofu

Making crispy tofu is super easy in an air fryer because you don't have to dirty a huge saucepan or skillet of oil on the stove. The best results are to be had with extra-firm tofu. Soft or silken tofu proves too fragile.

The sauce here is a simple microwaved mix, a delicious pairing for the crunchy tofu pieces. Have cooked long-grain white rice on the side to soak up every drop of the sauce.

One 12-ounce or 340-gram box of extra-firm tofu

6 paper towels

½ cup plus 2 tablespoons or 70 grams cornstarch

Nonstick spray

1 cup or 250 milliliters pineapple juice

⅓ packed cup or 70 grams light brown sugar

⅓ cup or 80 milliliters unseasoned rice vinegar

1 tablespoon or 15 milliliters regular or reduced-sodium soy sauce

1 or 2 drops red food coloring, optional

2 tablespoons or 20 grams chopped *roasted* unsalted shelled peanuts

1 medium scallion, trimmed and thinly sliced

RAISE THE BAR

A squiggle of sriracha over the top wouldn't be a bad thing.

And/or some toasted sesame oil.

And/or maybe a very slight drizzle of fish sauce.

And/or the squeeze of a lemon wedge.

1. Remove the tofu block from its packaging as directed on the box. Set the block on top of three paper towels, then set three paper towels on top of the block. Set aside for 5 minutes to pull out some of the moisture. Remove and discard the paper towels. Slice the block in half lengthwise, then slice each of the halves widthwise to create four even sections. Ⓐ

2. Separate these sections and cut each of them in half widthwise. Ⓑ

3. With the basket in the machine or the tray set at the center level in a toaster-oven-style model, heat an air fryer to 400°F or 200°C on the air fryer setting.

4. Put ½ cup or 55 grams of the cornstarch in a large bowl. Set a piece of tofu in the cornstarch and turn it to coat it on all sides, even around the edges. Transfer it to a cutting board and continue coating the remaining pieces of tofu in the same way. Lightly coat them on all sides with nonstick spray. Ⓒ

5. Set the pieces in a single layer without touching in the heated machine. Work in batches as necessary. Air-fry for 15 minutes, then gently flip the pieces over with a nonstick-safe spatula. Ⓓ

6. Air-fry for 5 more minutes. Meanwhile, whisk the pineapple juice, brown sugar, vinegar, the remaining 2 tablespoons or 15 grams cornstarch, soy sauce, and red food coloring, if using, in a 2-cup or 500-milliliter microwave-safe measuring vessel or high-sided container until the brown sugar dissolves. Microwave on high for 1 minute, stopping to whisk the mixture when it begins to bubble. Continue microwaving until it has bubbled and you've whisked it back down three times in total. Ⓔ

7. Pour the sauce into a serving bowl. Transfer the hot tofu pieces to the sauce in the bowl. Garnish it all with the peanuts and scallion before serving hot. Ⓕ

7
DESSERTS & SWEETS

For a lot of people, making desserts in an air fryer is a shock. But why not? You're working with a powerful countertop convection oven. If brownies come out with a better crumb in a convection oven, they do the same in an air fryer—and maybe even more so, since we can set the top of fudgy brownies without any of that yucky stickiness on the exterior (see page 266).

But there are a couple things to note. In *drawer-style machines*, the heat doesn't come from the bottom of the machine, so the bottom of a cake won't be as brown as it would be from a conventional oven. No worries: It'll set. But it may have a paler bottom than you're used to.

For another thing, a *toaster-oven-style machine* often offers heat from two directions. Using one of these machines is like baking with *both* the heating and broiling elements in your oven. Although the fan spins fast enough that the machine's heat isn't quite as relentless as that of your oven's broiler, it is nonetheless a substantial amount of heat close to the top of a cake. Make sure the rack with the cooking tray is set in the center of the machine. By the way, none of these recipes asks you to cook directly on the solid cooking tray in a toaster-oven-style machine. They were designed to use the cooking tray along with the air-frying basket (and sometimes a standard baking pan set in that basket).

Baking takes patience but the rewards . . . well, are worth it. The Peach Dumplings (page 272) have become a standard in our house. We hope they'll be the same in yours.

Stuffed Baked Apples

Because of the depth of many machines, a whole apple is impossible in an air fryer. The fruit is just too tall and gets too close to the heating element, causing the top to burn before the apple softens. To fix that problem, we split apples in half, then stuff the centers with a crumble that gets absurdly crunchy. We will often prepare a full batch of four apple halves just for the two of us. We've got to have something left over for breakfast, right?

½ cup all-purpose flour or 60 grams plain flour, or a gluten-free flour substitute

½ cup or 45 grams rolled oats (do not use quick-cooking or steel-cut oats)

3 packed tablespoons or 40 grams light brown sugar

3 tablespoons or 15 grams sliced almonds

2 tablespoons or 30 milliliters vegetable or canola oil

1 tablespoon or 15 milliliters maple syrup (the real thing, please)

½ teaspoon ground cinnamon

¼ teaspoon table salt

2 large juicy apples, preferably Honey Crisps or Galas

1 tablespoon or 15 grams butter, cut into 4 pieces

1 teaspoon granulated white sugar

Master the Method

If you go to a store to buy an air fryer, notice which display models sit level on a flat surface. There are definitely inferior models on the market now that air friers have become so popular.

RAISE THE BAR

Serve the apple halves with a drizzle of caramel sauce, dollops of sweetened whipped cream, vanilla ice cream, or even salted caramel ice cream.

1. With the basket in the machine or the tray set at the center level in a toaster-oven-style model, heat an air fryer to 325°F or 165°C on the air fryer setting.

2. Stir the flour, oats, brown sugar, almonds, oil, maple syrup, cinnamon, and salt in a medium bowl until a bit pasty, like cookie dough. Ⓐ

3. Slice each apple in half through its "equator" (that is, not through its stem). Use a melon baller or a small spoon (preferably, a serrated grapefruit spoon) to scrape out the seeds and core from each half, leaving an indentation about 1½ inches or 4 centimeters in diameter in each. Ⓑ

4. Divide the oat mixture between those indentations, mounding the filling as necessary. Ⓒ

5. Press 1 small bit of butter into the filling in each half. Sprinkle the top of the filling in each half with ¼ teaspoon granulated white sugar. Ⓓ

6. Set the halves filling side up without touching in the heated machine. Work in batches as necessary. Air-fry *undisturbed* for 25 minutes, or until the filling has browned and the apples have noticeably softened. Use a nonstick-safe spatula (and perhaps a rubber spatula in the other hand for balance) to transfer the apple halves to a wire rack or serving plates. Cool for at least 5 minutes before serving warm or at room temperature. Ⓔ

Strawberry Shortcakes

No, you can't make an entire strawberry shortcake in an air fryer. But you can make some pretty fine biscuits that become the base for the dessert.

The biscuits will get noticeably crunchy in the machine, the better to pair with soft whipped cream. You'll want big flatware tablespoons and a fork when you serve the shortcakes.

18 large ripe strawberries, hulled and thinly sliced

¼ cup plus 2 tablespoons or 75 grams granulated white sugar

2½ cups or 295 grams powdered biscuit mix, such as Bisquick

½ cup or 125 milliliters whole, low-fat, or fat-free milk

4 tablespoons (½ stick) or 60 grams butter, melted and cooled for a few minutes

1 cup or 250 milliliters heavy or whipping cream

2 tablespoons or 15 grams confectioners' sugar

½ teaspoon vanilla extract

Master the Method

Analog or digital? With an air fryer, it's your choice. Some have dials; some, touchpads. Buy your preference.

RAISE THE BAR

Add a handful of fresh blueberries to the whipped cream before spooning it on the shortcakes.

Before air-frying, sprinkle each biscuit with ¼ teaspoon granulated white sugar to create a sugary glaze.

Add up to 1 tablespoon or 15 milliliters Amaretto, Kahlúa, Bailey's Irish Cream, or Cointreau to the whipped cream with the vanilla.

1. Mix the sliced strawberries and 2 tablespoons or 25 grams white sugar in a bowl until the strawberry slices are evenly coated. Set the strawberries aside at room temperature to macerate while you make the biscuits. **A**

2. With the basket in the machine or the tray set at the center level in a toaster-oven-style model, heat an air fryer to 325°F or 165°C on the air fryer setting.

3. Stir the biscuit mix, milk, melted butter, and remaining ¼ cup or 50 grams sugar in a large bowl to make a soft dough. **B**

4. Divide the dough into six even portions. Gently pat the portions into six 2½- to 3-inch or 6½- to 7½-centimeter diameter disks. **C**

5. Set the disks in a single layer in the heated machine with at least 1 inch or 2½ centimeters between them. Work in batches as necessary. Air-fry *undisturbed* for 15 minutes, or until risen, golden brown, and firm to the touch. Use a nonstick-safe spatula to transfer the biscuits to a wire rack. Cool for at least 15 minutes or to room temperature. **D**

6. Pour the cream into a large bowl. Use an electric mixer at high speed to beat the cream until foamy. Add the confectioners' sugar and vanilla. Continue beating at high speed to make soft peaks, scraping down the inside of the bowl occasionally with a rubber spatula. **E**

7. Build the strawberry shortcakes. Slice each biscuit into two disks. Set the bottom disk on a plate. Top with about a sixth of the strawberries, then about a sixth of the whipped cream. Set the top disk on the stack and continue making more shortcakes, using the same approximate amounts of strawberries and whipped cream. Serve at once. **F**

Blueberry Crisp

An air fryer seems the perfect vehicle for a crisp because the topping can get impossibly crunchy as the fruit bubbles underneath.

However, a crisp *must* be a two-step process in the machine because the topping will get crunchy (and even burned) long before the fruit filling has cooked enough to get that irresistible almost-jammy consistency. So fruit first, then topping, for the best success.

3 cups or 450 grams fresh or thawed frozen blueberries

½ cup or 100 grams granulated white sugar

½ cup plus 2½ tablespoons all-purpose flour or 80 grams plain flour

2 tablespoons or 30 grams butter, cut into small bits, plus 2 tablespoons or 30 grams butter, melted and cooled for a few minutes

Aluminum foil

½ cup or 45 grams rolled oats (do not use quick-cooking or steel-cut oats)

2 packed tablespoons or 25 grams light brown sugar

2 tablespoons or 30 milliliters maple syrup (the real thing, please)

½ teaspoon ground cinnamon

½ teaspoon table salt

Master the Method

As a general rule, the footprint of toaster-oven-style air fryers is larger than that of drawer-style models. If space is at a premium in your kitchen, consider a drawer-style model.

RAISE THE BAR

Reduce the blueberries to 2 cups or 300 grams and add 1 cup or 125 grams fresh raspberries or blackberries.

Add up to ½ teaspoon finely grated orange zest to the blueberry mixture before air-frying.

1. With the basket in the machine or the tray set at the center level in a toaster-oven-style model, heat an air fryer to 400°F or 200°C on the air fryer setting.

2. Mix the blueberries, white sugar, and 2½ tablespoons or 20 grams flour in a large bowl. Ⓐ

3. Pour the blueberry mixture into an air-fryer-safe, 7-cup, 8 x 6 x 2-inch or 20 x 15 x 5-centimeter rectangular baking pan. (Reserve the bowl as it is for step 4.) Dot the blueberry mixture with the cut-up butter. Ⓑ

4. Cover the baking dish with aluminum foil, set it in the heated machine, and air-fry for 20 minutes. Meanwhile, stir the oats, brown sugar, maple syrup, cinnamon, salt, remaining ½ cup or 60 grams flour, and the melted butter in the same bowl that had the blueberry mixture to make a crumbly topping. Ⓒ

5. After the baking dish has been in the air fryer for 20 minutes, remove the (hot!) foil from the (hot!) baking dish. Stir the blueberry mixture. Crumble the topping evenly over the blueberries. Ⓓ

6. Reduce the machine's temperature to 350°F or 180°C. Continue air-frying uncovered for about 10 minutes, or until the topping is set and definitely crunchy. Use oven mitts to transfer the baking dish to a wire rack. Cool for at least 5 minutes before serving warm or at room temperature. Ⓔ

Vanilla Pound Cake

A dense (even chewy) but still tender pound cake out of the air fryer? Yep! The top of the cake sets so quickly in the supercharged convection currents that this pound cake is even a little denser than one out of the oven. In other words, a slice is better as a platform for ice cream!

Notice that both the butter and the eggs *must* be at room temperature. If not, you won't get the proper rise and crumb. Set both the butter and the eggs out on the counter for about 1 hour before you make the batter.

1¼ cups all-purpose flour or 150 grams plain flour

1 teaspoon baking powder

¼ teaspoon table salt

12 tablespoons (1½ sticks or 170 grams) butter, *softened to room temperature*

¾ cup or 150 grams granulated white sugar

3 large eggs, *at room temperature*

2 tablespoons or 30 milliliters whole or low-fat milk, or heavy cream

1 teaspoon vanilla extract

Baking spray

Aluminum foil

Master the Method

Some air fryer models have see-through windows. A nice feature! But like an oven window, these windows get dirty. They must be repeatedly cleaned to use them properly.

1. With the basket in the machine or the tray set at the center level in a toaster-oven-style model, heat an air fryer to 325°F or 165°C on the air fryer setting.

2. Whisk the flour, baking powder, and salt in a medium bowl until uniform. **A**

3. Use an electric mixer at medium speed to beat the softened butter and sugar in a large bowl, stopping the mixer to occasionally scrape down the inside of the bowl, until light and fluffy. **B**

4. Beat in the eggs one at a time, scraping down the interior of the bowl after each egg. **C**

5. Beat in the milk or cream and the vanilla. Stop, scrape down, and remove the mixer blades. Use a rubber spatula to fold in the flour mixture just until fully moistened, not until smooth. **D**

6. Lightly coat the inside of an air-fryer-safe, 7-cup, 8 x 6 x 2-inch or 20 x 15 x 5-centimeter rectangular baking pan with baking spray. Pour, scrape, and spread the batter evenly in the pan. **E**

7. Air-fry *undisturbed* for 20 minutes. Cover the (hot!) pan with aluminum foil. Continue air-frying for about 20 more minutes, or until a toothpick or cake tester inserted into the center of the cake comes out clean. Transfer the (hot!) pan to a wire rack with oven mitts and uncover it. Cool for at least 10 minutes or to room temperature before serving. **F**

RAISE THE BAR

Once cooled to room temperature, dust the cake with confectioners' sugar.

To make a chocolate frosting, beat 8 tablespoons (1 stick or 115 grams) butter, softened to room temperature, and ¼ cup or 20 grams unsweetened cocoa powder in a medium bowl with an electric mixer at medium speed until light and airy. Beat in about 2½ cups or 260 grams confectioners' sugar in ½-cup or 52-gram increments to make a smooth icing. (Depending on the butter's moisture content, you may need more confectioners' sugar.) Beat in 1 tablespoon or 15 milliliters whole milk or heavy cream and 1 teaspoon or 5 milliliters vanilla extract until smooth. If the frosting is too thick, beat in a little more milk or cream. Spread the frosting evenly over the room-temperature cake.

Brownies

Why make brownies in an air fryer? Because it's as if you made them in a supercharged convection oven that gives you a crunchy top with a dense, chewy center. This recipe makes *fudgy* brownies, almost as sticky as toffee at the center of the pan.

6 tablespoons or 85 grams butter, cut up into small pieces

6 ounces or 170 grams semisweet chocolate chips

½ cup or 100 grams granulated white sugar

½ packed cup or 105 grams light brown sugar

2 large eggs, at room temperature

1 tablespoon or 15 milliliters vanilla extract

½ cup all-purpose flour or 60 grams plain flour

¼ cup or 20 grams unsweetened cocoa powder

½ teaspoon table salt

Baking spray

Master the Method

As a general rule, look for an air fryer with more metal than plastic. Metal retains heat more efficiently. Metal is also more durable.

RAISE THE BAR

Add up to ½ cup or 55 grams chopped unsalted shelled pecans or walnuts with the flour.

Make brownie sundaes: Top the brownies with a scoop of vanilla ice cream, a drizzle of caramel sauce, and sweetened whipped cream.

1. Put the butter pieces and chocolate chips in a large, microwave-safe bowl. Microwave on high for 1 minute, then stir well. Microwave on high for about another 30 seconds, until about three-quarters melted. Remove the bowl and stir until the chocolate and butter have melted and become uniform. Cool for 5 minutes. Ⓐ

2. With the basket in the machine or the tray set at the center level in a toaster-oven-style model, heat an air fryer to 300°F or 150°C on the air fryer setting.

3. Whisk the white sugar and brown sugar into the chocolate mixture. Then whisk in the eggs and vanilla until smooth. Ⓑ

4. Add the flour, cocoa powder, and salt. Whisk just until the flour is thoroughly moistened. Ⓒ

5. Generously coat the inside of an air-fryer-safe, 7-cup, 8 x 6 x 2-inch or 20 x 15 x 5-centimeter rectangular pan with baking spray. Pour and scrape all of the chocolate batter evenly into the pan. Ⓓ

6. Set the pan in the heated machine and air-fry *undisturbed* for about 50 minutes, maybe 55 minutes, until a toothpick or cake tester inserted into the center of the cake comes out with a few moist crumbs attached. Transfer the (hot!) pan to a wire rack with oven mitts. Cool for at least 20 minutes before unmolding and cutting into eight brownies to serve (preferably) warm or at room temperature. Ⓔ

Banana Bread Cake

Why do we call this a "cake" and not just "banana bread"? Because it's lighter than the traditional sweet bread, with a crumb a bit more like a sponge cake. A more traditional dense, heavy banana bread just won't bake properly in an air fryer, but we love this lighter option for an afternoon snack or an on-the-go breakfast. We cut the number of bananas to one and lightened the batter considerably for success in an air fryer. Look for a very dark, extra ripe banana on the sale rack in your supermarket's produce section.

1 very ripe large banana, peeled

½ cup or 100 grams granulated white sugar

½ cup or 125 milliliters regular or low-fat cultured buttermilk (do not use fat-free buttermilk)

¼ cup or 60 milliliters canola or a neutral-flavored vegetable oil

1 large egg, *at room temperature*

½ teaspoon vanilla extract

1 cup all-purpose flour or 120 grams plain flour

½ teaspoon baking powder

½ teaspoon baking soda

½ teaspoon table salt

¼ teaspoon ground cinnamon

Baking spray

Aluminum foil

Confectioners' sugar, for dusting

Master the Method
Air fryers come with lots of features. Do you need all of those on high-end machines? Don't pay for features you don't want.

RAISE THE BAR

After the batter has been made in the food processor, scrape down and remove the blade. Fold in ½ cup or 55 grams chopped unsalted shelled pecans or walnuts.

And/or fold in up to ¼ cup or 45 grams semisweet chocolate chips.

1. Put the banana, white sugar, buttermilk, egg, and vanilla in a food processor. Cover and process until smooth. Turn off the machine and scrape down the inside of the canister. Add the flour, baking powder, baking soda, salt, and cinnamon. Cover and pulse just until all the flour has been moistened, stopping the machine at least once to scrape down the inside of the canister. **Ⓐ**

2. With the basket in the machine or the tray set at the center level in a toaster-oven-style model, heat an air fryer to 325°F or 165°C on the air fryer setting.

3. Lightly coat the inside of an air-fryer-safe 7-inch or 18-centimeter round springform pan with baking spray. **Ⓑ**

4. Pour and scrape all of the batter into the prepared pan. **Ⓒ**

5. Smooth the top of the batter. Set the pan in the heated machine and air-fry for 15 minutes. Then reduce the temperature to 300°F or 150°C and continue air-frying for 5 more minutes. Cover the top of the (hot!) pan with aluminum foil.

6. Continue air-frying for about 12 more minutes, or until a toothpick or cake tester inserted into the cake comes out *clean*. Transfer the (hot!) pan to a wire rack with oven mitts. Uncover and cool for at least 20 minutes before removing the collar. Dust with confectioners' sugar and cut into eight wedges to serve. **Ⓔ**

Rugelach-Style Rolled Cookies

Hardly traditional, these rugelach are nonetheless easy, made from a purchased refrigerator pie crust and jam (with some chopped nuts).

No, the cookies are not as flaky as the standards. But they're oozing with jam . . . and intensely satisfying. Best of all, you can make several batches and store them between wax paper in a sealed container in the freezer for up to 4 months.

Must you use the jam and nuts we suggest? Of course not! Consider raspberry, blueberry, or blackberry jam. (*Always* jam, *never* preserves or jelly.) And consider chopped slivered almonds or finely chopped unsalted shelled walnuts or hazelnuts.

Parchment paper

One crust from a 14.1-ounce or 400-gram two-crust box of refrigerator pie crusts, at room temperature

½ cup or 170 grams apricot jam (do not use preserves or jelly)

½ cup or 55 grams finely chopped unsalted shelled pecans

½ teaspoon ground cinnamon

1 large egg, well beaten in a small bowl

Master the Method

Measurements in baking recipes are often crucial to success. So a ruler is as important a baking tool as a spatula!

RAISE THE BAR

To make a glaze for the cooled cookies, whisk lemon juice in 1-teaspoon or 5-milliliter increments into ½ cup or 55 grams of confectioners' sugar until the mixture can be drizzled but hold its shape. Use the tines of a flatware fork to dip into this glaze and drizzle in squiggles across the cookies.

1. Cut a piece of parchment paper to line the basket or tray in your model of air fryer. Set it aside. With the basket in the machine or the tray set at the center level in a toaster-oven-style model, heat an air fryer to 375°F or 190°C on the air fryer setting.

2. Unroll the pie crust and cut off 1 inch or 2½ centimeters from two "sides" of the circle, thereby giving it two straight, parallel edges. Ⓐ

3. Tear each cut-off section in half. Moisten the edges of these piece and place them moistened side down on the two curved sides of the circle of dough, creating a (sort of) rectangle. Ⓑ

4. Use a rolling pin to roll the dough to a 12 x 7-inch or 30 x 18-centimeter rectangle. Spread the jam evenly over the rectangle, then sprinkle evenly with the pecans and cinnamon. Ⓒ

5. Roll up the dough into a log starting at one of the long sides. Cut the dough log into 1-inch or 2½-centimeter pieces. Ⓓ

6. Set the pieces on their dough "rims" on a cutting board. Brush the tops with the beaten egg. Ⓔ

7. Set the cut piece of parchment in the cooking basket or tray. Set the cookies in one layer without touching in the heated machine. Air-fry *undisturbed* for 8 minutes, or until brown and firm at the sides. Transfer them to a wire rack with a nonstick-safe tongs. Cool for at least 10 minutes or to room temperature before serving. Ⓕ

Peach Dumplings

With canned peach slices and purchased puff pastry dough, you can make crave-worthy dumplings, sort of like an upscale version of the old-school turnovers.

Watch carefully as these air-fry. They can start to turn too dark in spots. If so, turn them more often and reduce the machine's temperature to 350°F or 180°C.

3 tablespoons or 16 grams sliced almonds

3 packed tablespoons or 40 grams light brown sugar

½ teaspoon ground cinnamon

Half of a 17¼-ounce or 495-gram box of frozen puff pastry (that is, 1 sheet), thawed

All-purpose flour, as needed

8 canned peach slices packed in syrup, patted dry with paper towels

1 large egg, well beaten in a small bowl

Master the Method

If you like to geek out with your appliances, look for new air fryer models that have connectivity, letting you control them from your smart phone.

RAISE THE BAR

Open up these dumplings while they're warm and top them with vanilla, salted caramel, or butter pecan ice cream.

1. With the basket in the machine or the tray set at the center level in a toaster-oven-style model, heat an air fryer to 375°F or 190°C on the air fryer setting.

2. Stir the almonds, sugar, and cinnamon in a small bowl until uniform. Ⓐ

3. Unfold the piece of thawed puff pastry. Lightly dust a large dry cutting board or work surface with all-purpose flour. Lightly flour a rolling pin and roll the puff pastry into a 12-inch or 30-centimeter square. Cut this square into four 6-inch or 15-centimeter squares. Place two peach slices in the center of each of the squares and sprinkle each with a quarter of the almond mixture. Ⓑ

4. Brush the exposed edges of the pieces of dough with beaten egg. Starting with one of the squares, fold two opposing sides to come up over the slices without meeting in the middle. Starting at one of the unfolded side, roll up the dough to enclose the slices. Repeat with the remaining three squares. Ⓒ

5. Set the rolls seam side down. Brush the tops with any of the remaining egg. Ⓓ

6. Set the rolls in a single layer with at least 1 inch or 2½ centimeters between them in the heated machine. Work in batches as necessary. Air-fry for 10 minutes, then gently turn the dumplings over with nonstick-safe tongs. Ⓔ

7. Continue air-frying for about 3 more minutes, or until the dumplings are golden brown and crisp. Use nonstick-safe tongs to transfer the dumplings to a wire rack and cool for about 5 minutes before serving warm. Ⓕ

Chocolate Chip Wonton Cookies

A wonton wrapper provides a crunchy shell over purchased cookie dough for some of the most imaginative and decadently crunchy "cookies" we've ever had. If you don't like chocolate, use refrigerator sugar cookie dough instead.

12 wonton wrappers

4 ounces (½ cup) or 115 grams refrigerator chocolate chip cookie dough

1 large egg, well beaten in a small bowl

Nonstick spray

1 tablespoon or 12 grams granulated white sugar

½ teaspoon ground cinnamon

Master the Method

All air fryers come with a warranty. Use it! Ask for a replacement if your machine breaks under warranty.

RAISE THE BAR

Glaze the wonton cookies once they've cooled to room temperature: Stir ½ cup or 55 grams confectioners' sugar, 1 tablespoon or 15 milliliters water, and a drop or two of vanilla extract in a small bowl until you have a glaze that can be drizzled off the tines of a fork. Add more water in 1-teaspoon increments to get the right consistency. Drizzle over the wonton cookies.

1. With the basket in the machine or the tray set at the center level in a toaster-oven-style model, heat an air fryer to 375°F or 190°C on the air fryer setting.

2. Lay a wonton wrapper with a corner facing you on a clean dry work surface or cutting board. Place a rounded teaspoon of cookie dough in the middle of the wrapper and use your clean fingers to flatten the dough just slightly. **A**

3. Dip a finger or two in the beaten egg and brush it on the exposed bit of the wrapper. Fold the point nearest you over to meet the farthest point to make a triangle. Press to seal all around. Then continue making 11 more of the filled wontons. **B**

4. Generously coat the wonton cookies *on both sides* with nonstick spray. Mix the white sugar and cinnamon in a small bowl. Sprinkle one side of each cookie with the cinnamon sugar. **C**

5. Set the cookies sugared side up in a single layer in the heated machine. They can touch a bit but the thick centers should not overlap. Work in batches as necessary. Air-fry for 3 minutes, then turn the wrappers over with nonstick-safe tongs. **D**

6. Continue air-frying for 1 more minute, or until the cookies are golden brown and noticeably crunchy at the edges. Transfer the wontons sugared side up to a wire rack and cool for at least 10 minutes or to room temperature. **E**

Crispy Ricotta Rolls

These elegant cheese-filled dessert rolls are made with phyllo dough, which is most often sold frozen in supermarkets. Thaw it overnight in the fridge, then take out as many sheets as you need (and a few spares, in case of torn bits). Now reseal the box (just close the end and wrap it all in plastic wrap) to refreeze for another use.

Set the thawed phyllo sheets under a clean kitchen towel on a scrupulously dry work surface to keep them from drying out as you make the rolls.

They must be drizzled with honey while they're still warm so the honey is absorbed. The rolls will still return to a crunchy state (seemingly miraculously).

¾ cup or 190 grams whole-milk ricotta (do not use low-fat or fat-free)

3 tablespoons or 40 grams granulated white sugar

1 teaspoon finely grated lemon zest

½ teaspoon vanilla extract

⅛ teaspoon grated nutmeg, optional

12 sheets of phyllo dough (thawed if frozen)

Nonstick spray

½ cup or 170 grams honey

Master the Method

Remember that almost all air-fryer models come with preset times for various features. You must adjust the timing to fit any recipe. We suggest adding extra minutes, just to give yourself leeway.

RAISE THE BAR

Add up to ¼ cup or 25 grams chopped unsalted shelled pistachios to the ricotta filling.

Up the game dramatically by using a dark honey, like oak or pine tree honey.

1. With the basket in the machine or the tray set at the center level in a toaster-oven-style model, heat an air fryer to 375°F or 190°C on the air fryer setting.

2. Stir the ricotta, sugar, lemon zest, vanilla, and nutmeg, if using, in a medium bowl until uniform. Ⓐ

3. Set a sheet of phyllo dough on a dry work surface or cutting board with a short end of the sheet facing you. Lightly coat the sheet with nonstick spray. Set a second one on top and again lightly coat with nonstick spray. Ⓑ

4. Form about 2 tablespoons or 60 grams of the ricotta mixture into a 3-inch or 8-centimeter log and set it on the phyllo sheets' short end nearest you. Ⓒ

5. Roll the dough for two rotations, starting at the end nearest you. Then fold the long sides over the log. The long sides should not overlap or even touch. Ⓓ

6. Roll closed and coat generously with nonstick spray on all sides. Set aside and make five more rolls, following the method in steps 3 through 6. Ⓔ

7. Set the rolls seam side down in one layer without touching in the heated machine. Air-fry for 6 minutes. *Gently* turn the rolls over with nonstick-safe tongs. Continue air-frying for about 4 more minutes, or until golden brown and noticeably crunchy. Use those tongs to transfer the rolls to a wire rack. Cool for just a couple of minutes, then set the rolls in a serving dish. Drizzle the honey over them. Serve at once or at room temperature. Ⓕ

A B C D E F

Blueberry Cheesecake Burritos

There's been an internet craze recently for deep-fried cheesecake slices. We can't go quite that far with an air fryer, but we can get pretty close. Here's our version, with a flour tortilla standing in for a batter that coats a slice of cheesecake and turns into a crust in a deep-fat fryer.

Look in the freezer section for frozen, 3- to 4-ounce or 85- to 115-gram, single slices of plain cheesecake. Or buy a whole, frozen, 17-ounce or 480-gram cheesecake, divide it into fourths, and use one of those quarters.

If you don't like canned blueberry pie filling, try purchased cherry pie filling.

2 large burrito-size flour tortillas

1 frozen 3- to 4-ounce or 85- to 115-gram slice of plain cheesecake, thawed

¼ cup or 70 grams blueberry pie filling

Nonstick spray

Master the Method

As a general rule, smaller air fryers cook more quickly than larger ones. Think about it: less space, less air to heat up and get moving. Watch items in small air fryers. If you notice yours cooks quickly, shave 25°F or 15°C off the stated temperature in any recipe.

RAISE THE BAR

Use a slice of frozen chocolate cheesecake and top with purchased strawberry pie filling.

1. With the basket in the machine or the tray set at the center level in a toaster-oven-style model, heat an air fryer to 375°F or 190°C on the air fryer setting.

2. Set a tortilla on a dry work surface or cutting board. Cut the slice of cheesecake in half lengthwise. Set one half in the center of the tortilla and smear it like cream cheese (crust and all) across the tortilla, leaving a 2-inch or 5-centimeter border on 2 "sides" of the circle and 1-inch or 2½-centimeter border on the other two "sides." Ⓐ

3. Spread 2 tablespoons or 35 grams of the blueberry pie filling on top of smeared cheesecake. Ⓑ

4. Fold the opposing 1-inch or 2½-centimeter "sides" of the tortilla over the cheesecake (the sides will not meet). Then roll the tortilla closed, like a burrito, starting at one of the 2-inch or 5-centimeter sides. Repeat steps 2 through 4 to make a second dessert burrito. Ⓒ

5. Generously coat the outside of the burritos with spray on all sides. Set the burritos seam side down in a single layer without touching in the heated machine. Air-fry for 5 minutes, then flip the burritos over with nonstick-safe tongs. Ⓓ

6. Continue air-frying for about 5 more minutes, or until the burritos are well browned and noticeably crisp at the edges. Use those tongs to transfer the burritos to a wire rack. Cool for at least 5 minutes before serving hot. Ⓔ

Mini Lemon Meringue Pies

What could be easier? With purchased lemon curd and mini graham-cracker crusts, you're on your way to pie. Given those two purchased items, we felt free to make a real meringue for this recipe, rather than using Marshmallow Fluff as a substitute.

The trick to a great meringue is twofold: 1) the egg whites must be at room temperature. Get them into the bowl and leave them on the counter for about 20 minutes before you make the meringue. And 2) everything that touches those egg whites must be dry and oil-free: the bowl, the spatula, the beaters. Water can bog down everything as the egg whites begin to capture air and gain loft. After that, it's just a matter of sealing the meringue to the crust all around the mini pies.

---

3 large egg whites, at room temperature

¼ teaspoon table salt

⅛ teaspoon cream of tartar

6 tablespoons or 75 grams granulated white sugar

¾ cup or 270 grams purchased lemon curd

Six 3-inch or 8-centimeter ready-made mini graham cracker pie crusts in aluminum shells

Master the Method

Don't ever be afraid of the machine. Approach it as you do any kitchen tool: well-armed with the knowledge of how it works and what it can do.

RAISE THE BAR

Check out the recipe for microwave lemon curd on our YouTube channel, *Cooking With Bruce & Mark*.

1. With the basket in the machine or the tray set at the center level in a toaster-oven-style model, heat an air fryer to 375°F or 190°C on the air fryer setting.

2. Beat the egg whites, salt, and cream of tartar in a medium bowl with an electric mixer at high speed until foamy. Stop the mixer, scrape down the inside of the bowl with a rubber spatula, and continue beating at high speed until soft peaks form when you dip the turned-off beaters into the mixture. Ⓐ

3. Continue beating at high speed, adding the sugar in about 1-tablespoon or 13-gram increments until the mixture is glossy, thick, and you can form stiff peaks on a dry rubber spatula or the turned-off beaters. Ⓑ

4. Dollop and spread 2 tablespoons or 45 grams of the lemon curd in each of the six pie crust shells. Ⓒ

5. Divide the meringue on top of the pies, using a clean rubber spatula to seal it to the edge of each. Ⓓ

6. Set the pies in a single layer without touching in the heated machine. Work in batches as necessary. Air-fry for 2 to 4 minutes (toaster-oven-style machines will take longer), or until the meringue has begun to brown in spots. Transfer the (hot!) mini pies to a wire rack and cool for at least 30 minutes so the lemon curd resets in the crusts. Serve at room temperature. Ⓔ

A

B

C

D

E

Acknowledgments

This is cookbook thirty-six under our own names, not counting the ones ghost-written for celebrities. How's that possible? With many professional, talented people, of course, who make the book happen far beyond our abilities. People like . . .

- **OUR AGENT**, Susan Ginsburg, and Catherine Bradshaw at **WRITERS HOUSE**;

- **OUR PUBLISHING TEAM AT VORACIOUS AND LITTLE, BROWN:** Michael Szczerban, Bruce Nichols, Thea Diklich-Newell, Fanta Diallo, Juliana Horbachevsky, and Katherine Akey; and the wonderfully efficient and talented design and production team: Laura Palese, Julianna Lee, Nyamekye Waliyaya, Pat Jalbert-Levine, Deri Reed, Suzanne Fass, and Elizabeth Parson;

- **AND OUR BELOVED PHOTOGRAPHER,** Eric Medsker.

Index

Keep Cooking WITH BRUCE AND MARK

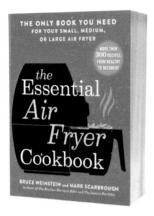

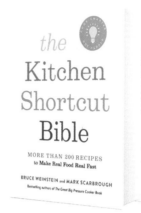

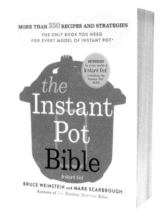

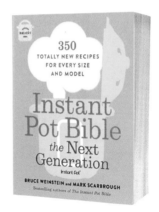

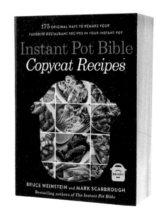

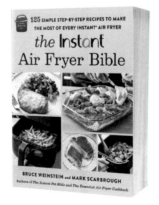